Core Python Programming
A Concise Guide

Contents

Preface

This book, *Core Python Programming: A Concise Guide*, is designed to provide a comprehensive and systematic exploration of Python programming, focusing on core concepts essential for proficiency in the language. It aims to equip readers with the knowledge and skills necessary to build robust and efficient Python programs.

The material covered in this book encompasses key topics including the fundamentals of Python, data types, control flow mechanisms, functions and modules, data structures, file handling, exception handling, object-oriented programming, modules and packages, and leveraging both standard libraries and third-party modules. Each chapter is meticulously structured to ensure a natural progression of learning, allowing readers to build on foundational concepts as they advance through the topics.

This book is targeted towards individuals seeking a solid grounding in Python programming. It is suitable for beginners who are new to programming, as well as experienced programmers looking to deepen their understanding of Python. The content is crafted to be clear and concise, with a focus on practical applications and real-world examples that illustrate the theoretical concepts discussed.

By the end of this book, readers will have a robust understanding of core Python programming principles, equipped to tackle a wide array of programming challenges effectively and efficiently with Python.

Chapter 1

Introduction to Python

This chapter provides an overview of Python, covering its history and philosophy, how to install and run the interpreter, and the essential tools and IDEs used for Python development. It introduces basic syntax, comments, and documentation practices, and demonstrates how to write and execute Python scripts. Guidance on seeking help and understanding different Python implementations is also included, setting a solid foundation for further learning.

1.1   History and Philosophy of Python

Python, an interpreted, high-level, general-purpose programming language, was conceived in the late 1980s and its implementation began in December 1989 by Guido van Rossum at Centrum Wiskunde & Informatica (CWI) in the Netherlands. Van Rossum aimed to create an accessible and readable language that could serve as a successor to the ABC language, itself designed for teaching programming and prototyping.

Python 1.0 was officially released in 1991. This initial release featured core data types like lists, strings, and dictionaries, along with essential functionalities such as error handling and modules. Python's design emphasized code readability with its noticeable use of whitespace indentation and a concise, clear syntax. Van Rossum was inspired by the *Monty Python's Flying Circus* comedy series, which is reflected in the language's name.

Several releases have marked Python's evolution, each contributing significantly to its robustness, functionality, and user base. Notable milestones include:

- **Python 2.0** (2000): Introduced list comprehensions, a full garbage collector, and support for Unicode. This version heralded the beginning of the community's strong involvement in Python's development.

- **Python 3.0** (2008): Also known as "Python 3000" and "Py3k," this release was not backward-compatible with previous versions. It provided cleaner syntax and tackled inherent language design flaws, intending to rectify long-standing issues, particularly with Unicode handling.

- **Python 3.4** (2014): Introduced the `asyncio` module, enhancing the language's ability to handle asynchronous IO operations and paving the way for more efficient, concurrent programming techniques.

- **Python 3.6** (2016): Included formatted string literals (`f-strings`), designed to simplify string formatting mechanisms.

Python's development was influenced deeply by a philosophy which values simplicity and clarity. Python's guiding principles are outlined in PEP 20, *The Zen of Python*, authored by Tim Peters. Key aphorisms from this document include:

- **Readability counts.**

- **Beautiful is better than ugly.**

- **Explicit is better than implicit.**

- **Simple is better than complex.**

- **Sparse is better than dense.**

- **Special cases aren't special enough to break the rules.**

Guido van Rossum set several goals for Python's development, central among them being:

- **Easy and Intuitive Syntax:** Python's clear syntax emphasizes readability and reduces the cost of program maintenance.

- **Interpreted Language:** Unlike compiled languages, Python executes code line by line, meaning developers can write and test small parts of a program interactively.

- **Extensible:** Python can be extended with modules and libraries written in other programming languages such as C or C++.

- **Object-Oriented:** Supports object-oriented programming that encourages code reusability via classes and inheritance.

- **Comprehensive Standard Library:** Python intends to solve real-world problems by providing a large standard library, enabling developers to accomplish a variety of tasks without having to install additional packages.

Since its inception, Python has experienced rapid adoption across various fields including web development, scientific computing, data analysis, artificial intelligence, and more. Its versatility, coupled with a broad and active community, has established Python as one of the most popular programming languages in existence.

Numerous organizations and major tech companies leverage Python for its powerful yet easy-to-understand syntax. The support from educational institutions has also led to Python being prominently used as the first language taught in introductory programming courses.

Python's history and philosophy demonstrate a commitment to creating a language that balances power with approachability, ensuring it remains relevant and essential for developers globally.

1.2 Installing Python

This section provides a comprehensive guide on how to install Python, ensuring you have the appropriate environment to follow all examples and exercises throughout this book.

- Download the Python Installer

- Installation on Windows

- Installation on macOS

- Installation on Linux

- Installing and Verifying `pip`

- Configuring Virtual Environments

Download the Python Installer

1. Open your web browser and go to `https://www.python.org/`.

2. Click on the `Downloads` tab, where the website will suggest the optimal Python version for your operating system.

3. Click on the suggested version or select an alternative by clicking `View the full list of downloads`.

Installation on Windows

1. Double-click the downloaded installer file to run it.

2. On the Python Setup screen, make sure to check the box `Add Python to PATH`. This step allows you to run Python from the command line.

3. Click on `Install Now`.

4. To verify the installation, open Command Prompt and type:

   `python --version`

5. You should see the installed Python version number.

Installation on macOS

1. Open the downloaded installer package by double-clicking it.

2. Follow the installer prompts, Agree to the license and specify the installation location if needed.

3. Upon completion of the installation, open the Terminal and run:

   `python3 --version`

4. The version number shown should correspond to the installed version.

Installation on Linux

Ubuntu and Debian-based Systems

1. Open Terminal.

2. Update the package list by running:

   ```
   sudo apt update
   ```

3. Install Python with the following command:

   ```
   sudo apt install python3
   ```

4. Verify the installation by running:

   ```
   python3 --version
   ```

Fedora and Red Hat-based Systems

1. Open Terminal.

2. Install Python by running:

   ```
   sudo dnf install python3
   ```

3. Check the installation by typing:

   ```
   python3 --version
   ```

Installing and Verifying `pip`

The `pip` tool helps install and manage additional libraries and packages that aren't part of the standard Python library.

- `pip` is installed by default during the Python installation. Verify `pip` by running:

  ```
  pip --version
  ```

- If `pip` is not installed, use the following command to install it:

  ```
  python -m ensurepip --upgrade
  ```

Configuring Virtual Environments

Python virtual environments create isolated environments for projects, ensuring that each project's dependencies are kept separate.

1. Navigate to the project directory and create a virtual environment by typing:

   ```
   python -m venv venv_name
   ```

15

2. Replace venv_name with your desired name for the virtual environment.

3. Activate the virtual environment:

   - On Windows:
     ```
     venv_name\Scripts\activate
     ```
   - On macOS and Linux:
     ```
     source venv_name/bin/activate
     ```

4. The command prompt will change, indicating the active environment.

5. To deactivate the environment, type:
   ```
   deactivate
   ```

By completing these steps, you ensure that your system has a fully configured Python installation suited for development. This setup will allow you to run examples and exercises seamlessly, avoiding environment-related issues.

1.3   Python Interpreter and Interactive Mode

The Python interpreter is a fundamental component of the Python ecosystem, enabling the execution of Python code. This section delves into the various aspects of the Python interpreter and interactive mode, elucidating their significance, usage, and practical applications.

Python Interpreter

The Python interpreter is a program that reads and executes Python code. When a Python script is run, the interpreter parses and converts the high-level, human-readable code into machine-readable format, subsequently executing it. Python interpreters are available for various platforms, including Windows, macOS, and Linux.

To invoke the Python interpreter from the command line, one typically uses the command:

```
python script_name.py
```

The specific command may vary depending on the system configuration and the Python version installed. For instance, on systems with multiple versions of Python, the interpreter may be invoked using:

```
python3 script_name.py
```

Interactive Mode

Interactive mode is a feature of the Python interpreter that allows users to execute Python commands and expressions on-the-fly. This mode is particularly useful for testing code snippets, debugging, and experimenting with the Python language.

To enter the interactive mode, simply type python (or python3, depending on your configuration) in the command line without specifying a script name. On successful entry into the interactive mode, the Python interpreter presents a prompt, denoted by >>>:

```
>>>
```

Within this mode, any valid Python expression or statement can be executed directly. For example:

```
>>> 2 + 2
4
>>> print("Hello, World!")
Hello, World!
```

Output from these commands is displayed immediately, facilitating real-time feedback and iterative development.

Multi-Line Input

While single-line statements are straightforward in interactive mode, multi-line inputs require special handling. Python employs explicit line continuation with a backslash (\) or implicit continuation inside parentheses, brackets, or braces. Entering a compound statement such as a function definition or a loop involves an indented input sequence:

```
>>> def greet(name):
... print(f"Hello, {name}!")
...
>>> greet("Alice")
Hello, Alice!
```

Note the use of the ellipsis (. . .) as the continuation prompt in the interactive mode, indicating the interpreter's expectation of further input.

Editing and History Navigation

Interactive mode provides several conveniences for efficient develop-ment. Up and down arrow keys enable navigation through input his-tory, allowing previously entered commands to be recalled and edited. This feature significantly enhances productivity, reducing the need to retype commands.

Additionally, many interactive environments support tab completion for variable names and keywords, providing a rapid means to enter complex expressions and access documentation.

Enhanced Interactive Environments

Though the default Python interactive mode is useful, several en-hanced environments offer advanced features for an improved devel-opment experience. Notable among these are IPython and Jupyter:

- **IPython**: An interactive shell that extends Python's default REPL (Read-Eval-Print Loop). IPython provides a rich toolkit with features such as syntax highlighting, tab completion, improved tracebacks, and magic commands for extended functionality.

- **Jupyter**: An interactive computing environment that enables the creation and sharing of documents containing live code, equa-tions, visualizations, and narrative text. Jupyter notebooks are particularly popular in data science and academic research for their capability to combine code execution with rich multimedia.

To install IPython, run the following command:

```
pip install ipython
```

To start an IPython session, simply execute:

```
ipython
```

Similarly, Jupyter can be installed with:

```
pip install jupyter
```

To launch a Jupyter notebook:

```
jupyter notebook
```

These tools greatly augment the capabilities of the default interpreter, providing an enriched environment conducive to exploratory programming and interactive analysis.

Applications of Interactive Mode

Interactive mode is particularly advantageous in scenarios requiring rapid prototyping, testing, and debugging. It enables developers and data scientists to:

- **Test Small Code Snippets**: Quickly validate small fragments of code without the need to create and maintain separate script files.

- **Explore Libraries**: Experiment with library functions and modules, facilitating a better understanding of their API and usage.

- **Debug Code**: Identify and resolve issues in code by incrementally testing and debugging individual components.

- **Educational Purposes**: Serve as a teaching tool, allowing learners to interactively engage with Python, experiment with syntax, and immediately see the effects of code execution.

Exiting Interactive Mode

To exit the interactive mode, one can either use the `exit()` function or keyboard shortcuts such as `Ctrl-D` (on Unix-based systems) or `Ctrl-Z` followed by `Enter` (on Windows).

```
>>> exit()
```

Upon exit, the user is returned to the command line, and any unsaved work will be lost. It is prudent to save necessary code before exiting the session.

Understanding the Python interpreter and interactive mode is crucial for effective Python programming. Interactive mode offers a dynamic environment for executing Python code, facilitating testing, debugging, and exploratory development. Enhanced interactive shells, such as IPython and Jupyter, further augment the capabilities provided by the default interpreter, making Python development more efficient and productive.

1.4 Writing and Executing Python Scripts

In Python programming, scripts provide a coherent approach to automate and encapsulate logic within standalone, executable files. This section offers an elaborate guide to writing and executing Python scripts, emphasizing best practices, environment configurations, and vital tools for seamless development.

Creating a Python script involves creating a new file with a `.py` extension using any text editor or integrated development environment (IDE).

Sample Python Script

```python
# hello_world.py

def main():
    print("Hello, World!")

if __name__ == "__main__":
    main()
```

This script defines a simple function, `main()`, which prints "Hello, World!" to the console. The construct `if __name__ == "__main__"` ensures that the `main()` function is invoked only when the script is run directly, not when imported as a module.

Before executing a Python script, confirm that Python is installed and accessible via the command line by running:

```
$ python --version
```

This command should return the installed Python version, indicating successful installation and configuration.

There are multiple methods to execute a Python script:

- **Command Line Interface (CLI):** Navigate to the directory containing the script and run:

  ```
  $ python hello_world.py
  ```
  Output:

  ```
  Hello, World!
  ```

- **Integrated Development Environment (IDE):** Modern IDEs such as PyCharm or VS Code provide features to run scripts directly within the environment. Open the script file in the IDE and use its run feature to execute the script.

- **Interactive Mode:** For quick tests, Python's interactive mode allows line-by-line execution of the code:

```
$ python
>>> def main():
...     print("Hello, World!")
>>> main()
Hello, World!
```

- **Shebang for Unix-like Systems:** On Unix-like systems, add a shebang line at the beginning of the script:

Python Script with Shebang

```
#!/usr/bin/env python

def main():
    print("Hello, World!")

if __name__ == "__main__":
    main()
```

Set execute permission:

```
$ chmod +x hello_world.py
```
Execute directly:

```
$ ./hello_world.py
```

Following best practices enhances script maintainability and robustness:

1. **Modular Design:** Decompose functionality into functions or classes to promote code reuse and testing.

2. **Entry Point Definition:** Use the main entry point idiom (if __name__ == "__main__").

3. **Environment Management:** Employ virtual environments to manage dependencies and avoid conflicts.

4. **Documentation:** Document scripts comprehensively with comments and docstrings.

Incorporate error handling mechanisms to manage unforeseen runtime errors gracefully using try-except blocks:

Error Handling in a Python Script

```
def main():
    try:
        result = 10 / 0
    except ZeroDivisionError:
        print("Error: Division by zero is not allowed.")

if __name__ == "__main__":
    main()
```

Additionally, logging at various severity levels (e.g., DEBUG, INFO, WARNING, ERROR, CRITICAL) aids in debugging and monitoring:

Logging in a Python Script

```
import logging

logging.basicConfig(level=logging.INFO)

def main():
    logging.info("Script execution started.")
    try:
        result = 10 / 0
    except ZeroDivisionError:
        logging.error("Error: Division by zero is not allowed.")
    logging.info("Script execution finished.")

if __name__ == "__main__":
    main()
```

Scripts might require interactions with external systems or advanced execution techniques:

- **Subprocess Module:** Run external commands within a script using the subprocess module.

- **Scheduling:** Use task schedulers like cron on Unix or Task Scheduler on Windows for automated script execution.

Using Subprocess in a Python Script

```
import subprocess

def main():
    result = subprocess.run(['ls', '-l'], capture_output=True, text=True)
    print(result.stdout)

if __name__ == "__main__":
    main()
```

Mastering the creation and execution of Python scripts is crucial for leveraging Python's versatility in various automation and development tasks. Adhering to best practices and using appropriate tools

22

ensures the efficiency, readability, and maintainability of scripts, contributing to the development of robust and scalable solutions.

1.5 Python IDEs and Tools

Python development is significantly enhanced by `Integrated Development Environments (IDEs)` and various tools specifically designed to streamline the coding process. This section elucidates the primary IDEs and tools utilized in Python programming. Each tool's functionalities, strengths, and purposes will be meticulously analyzed to enable developers to make informed choices.

`Integrated Development Environments (IDEs)`

An `Integrated Development Environment (IDE)` amalgamates essential development tools into a unified interface, augmenting productivity and debugging efficiency. The subsequent IDEs are highly regarded in the Python community due to their robust features and developer-friendly environments.

PyCharm

Developed by JetBrains, `PyCharm` is a prominent IDE that offers extensive support for Python. It is available in two editions: Community (free and open source) and Professional (paid). Key features include:

- **Code Completion and Syntax Highlighting:** PyCharm provides intelligent code completion, on-the-fly code analysis, and coding assistance.

- **Debugger and Testing:** Integrated debugger and test runner, aiding in seamless code analysis and testing.

- **Integrated Tools:** Support for web frameworks, SQL, and database tools, as well as integration with version control systems such as Git.

- **Refactoring:** Safe and efficient refactoring capabilities help in maintaining high-quality codebases.

VS Code

Visual Studio Code (VS Code) is an open-source code editor from Microsoft, which, with the aid of extensions, functions as an adept Python IDE. It is lightweight and highly customizable. Key features include:

- **Extensions:** The Python extension for VS Code includes linting, IntelliSense, Jupyter notebooks, and debugging.

- **Built-in Git Integration:** Offers seamless Git operations directly from the IDE.

- **Terminal:** Integrated terminal to execute scripts and manage environments.

- **Customizability:** Users can tailor the IDE with themes, keyboard shortcuts, and additional extensions to fit their workflow.

Spyder

Spyder is an open-source IDE specifically designed for scientific programming in Python. It is part of the Anaconda distribution and caters to data scientists and engineers. Key features include:

- **Scientific Libraries:** Integrated support for popular scientific libraries such as NumPy, SciPy, Pandas, Matplotlib, and SymPy.

- **Variable Explorer:** Allows users to inspect variables, dataframes, and arrays in a user-friendly manner.

- **Integrated IPython Console:** Facilitates interactive testing and debugging.

- **Editor:** Multilanguage editor with code completion and real-time analysis.

Jupyter Notebook

Jupyter Notebook is an open-source web application that enables the creation of documents containing live code, equations, visualizations, and narrative text. It is particularly favored in the data science community. Key features include:

- **Interactive Output:** Interactive output cells allow for immediate visualization of data.

- **Rich Media:** Supports rich media, including HTML, LaTeX, and inline images.

- **Kernel Support:** Supports numerous programming languages through Jupyter kernels, though primarily used with Python.

- **Collaboration:** Facilitates academic and professional collaboration by sharing notebooks.

Tools and Utilities

Apart from IDEs, several tools and utilities augment Python development, providing functionalities that streamline the coding, testing, and deployment processes.

Version Control Systems (VCS)

Version Control Systems (VCS), such as Git, are imperative in maintaining code versions, facilitating collaboration, and managing changes over time.

Basic Git Commands

```
# Initialize a new Git repository
git init

# Add files to staging area
git add .

# Commit changes
git commit -m "Initial commit"

# Add a remote repository
git remote add origin <repository_url>

# Push changes to the remote repository
git push -u origin master
```

Package Management

Package managers like pip and conda simplify the installation and management of Python libraries.

Using pip

```
# Install a package
pip install package_name

# Uninstall a package
pip uninstall package_name

# List installed packages
pip list
```

Using conda

```
# Install a package
conda install package_name

# Update a package
conda update package_name
```

```
# List installed packages
conda list
```

Virtual Environments

Virtual environments are essential for managing project-specific dependencies. Tools such as `virtualenv` and `conda` environments are widely used.

Using virtualenv

```
# Create a virtual environment
virtualenv venv_name

# Activate the virtual environment
source venv_name/bin/activate

# Deactivate the virtual environment
deactivate
```

Using conda environments

```
# Create a conda environment
conda create -n env_name python=3.8

# Activate the conda environment
conda activate env_name

# Deactivate the conda environment
conda deactivate
```

Linters and Formatters

Linters and formatters facilitate maintaining clean and readable code. Popular tools include `pylint`, `flake8`, and `black`.

Using pylint

```
# Run pylint on a Python file
pylint file_name.py
```

Using black

```
# Format a Python file with black
black file_name.py
```

The expansive landscape of Python IDEs and development tools provides developers with a variety of choices tailored to diverse coding styles and project needs. Whether one prefers a fully-featured IDE like PyCharm, a lightweight editor like VS Code, or interactive environments such as Jupyter Notebooks, the available options can significantly elevate productivity and code quality. Coupling these IDEs with robust tools and utilities for version control, package management, and environment isolation creates a conducive ecosystem for efficient and effective Python development.

1.6 Introduction to Python Syntax

Python is renowned for its readable and beginner-friendly syntax, making it an excellent choice for both beginners and experienced developers. This section explores the essential components of Python's syntax, equipping you with a robust understanding of code structure and execution.

Indentation

In Python, indentation is not just a matter of style but a fundamental aspect of the language. Indentation is used to define the scope of loops, functions, classes, and other code blocks.

Example of Indentation

```
if True:
    print("This is indented")
print("This is not indented")
```

In this example, "This is indented" will be executed because it belongs to the `if` statement block. Conversely, "This is not indented" will be executed outside of the `if` block.

Variables and Data Types

Python supports dynamic typing, meaning that you don't need to declare the type of a variable explicitly. The type is inferred at runtime.

Variable Assignment and Data Types

```
x = 5 # Integer
y = 3.14 # Float
name = "John" # String
is_valid = True # Boolean
```

Python's built-in data types include:

- `int`: Integer values (e.g., 5)

- `float`: Floating-point numbers (e.g., 3.14)

- `str`: String literals (e.g., "John")

- `bool`: Boolean values (True/False)

27

Operators

Python provides several types of operators, such as arithmetic, comparison, and logical operators.

Arithmetic Operators

Arithmetic Operations

```
a = 10
b = 3
add = a + b # Addition
sub = a - b # Subtraction
mul = a * b # Multiplication
div = a / b # Division
floor_div = a // b # Floor Division
mod = a % b # Modulus
exp = a ** b # Exponentiation
```

Comparison Operators

Comparison Operations

```
a = 5
b = 2
equal = (a == b) # Equality
not_equal = (a != b) # Inequality
greater = (a > b) # Greater than
less = (a < b) # Less than
greater_equal = (a >= b) # Greater than or equal to
less_equal = (a <= b) # Less than or equal to
```

Logical Operators

Python's logical operators combine conditional statements.

Logical Operations

```
a = True
b = False

logical_and = a and b # Logical AND
logical_or = a or b # Logical OR
logical_not = not a # Logical NOT
```

Control Flow Statements

Python's control flow statements include conditional statements and loops.

Conditional Statements

Conditional Statements

```
x = 10
if x < 0:
    print("x is negative")
elif x == 0:
```

28

```
      print("x is zero")
else:
      print("x is positive")
```

Looping Constructs

For Loop   The `for` loop in Python iterates over a sequence (such as a list or string).

For Loop

```
for i in range(5): # Iterates from 0 to 4
    print(i)
```

While Loop   The `while` loop executes as long as a condition is true.

While Loop

```
count = 0
while count < 5:
    print(count)
    count += 1
```

Functions

Functions in Python are defined using the `def` keyword followed by the function name and parentheses. Functions can accept parameters and return values.

Function Definition and Call

```
def add(a, b):
    return a + b

result = add(3, 4)
print(result) # Outputs: 7
```

Data Structures

Python comes with versatile built-in data structures, such as lists, tuples, sets, and dictionaries.

Lists

Lists are mutable sequences, commonly used to store collections of homogeneous items.

List Operations

```
fruits = ["apple", "banana", "cherry"]
fruits.append("orange") # Add an element
```

29

```
print(fruits[1]) # Access elements
```

Tuples

Tuples are immutable sequences, typically used to store collections of heterogeneous data.

Tuple Operations

```
point = (10, 20)
print(point[0]) # Outputs: 10
```

Sets

Sets are unordered collections of unique elements.

Set Operations

```
unique_numbers = {1, 2, 3, 4}
unique_numbers.add(5)
print(unique_numbers)
```

Dictionaries

Dictionaries are mutable mappings from keys to values.

Dictionary Operations

```
person = {"name": "Alice", "age": 25}
person["age"] = 26
print(person["name"]) # Outputs: Alice
```

Exception Handling

In Python, exception handling is managed using try-except blocks.

Exception Handling

```
try:
    result = 10 / 0
except ZeroDivisionError:
    print("Division by zero error")
```

Armed with this foundational knowledge, you are now equipped to write effective Python code. Building on these fundamentals, subsequent chapters will explore advanced topics and practical applications.

1.7 Comments and Documentation Strings

Comments and documentation strings play a critical role in enhancing the readability and maintainability of Python code. This section explores the syntax and best practices for implementing comments and documentation strings, elucidating their usage and significance in professional Python programming.

Comments

Comments are annotations in the source code intended to clarify the purpose and logic of the code. They are ignored by the Python interpreter during execution, serving solely to aid human readers in understanding the codebase.

Single-Line Comments

A single-line comment begins with a hash symbol #, followed by the comment text. Single-line comments are often utilized to provide brief explanations or to annotate specific lines of code.

```
# This is a single-line comment
x = 42 # Assign the value 42 to variable x
```

Multi-Line Comments

Although Python does not support a dedicated multi-line comment syntax, multiple single-line comments or string literals can be used to achieve this. When using single-line comments, each line must begin with a hash symbol.

```
# This is a multi-line comment
# that spans across several lines
# each beginning with a hash symbol.
```

Alternatively, multi-line comments can be simulated using string literals. Triple-quoted strings (either single or double quotes) can be employed, though they effectively function as multi-line strings and not true comments. These string literals will be ignored if they are not assigned to a variable or used in any function.

```
'''
This is a multi-line string literal
which can be used as a comment
if not assigned to any variable or used otherwise.
'''
```

Best Practices for Comments

31

Effective commenting is succinct and focused. Comments should not restate what the code itself conveys but should provide additional insight into the reasoning behind the code or the algorithms utilized. Adhere to the following best practices when writing comments:

- Use comments to explain the *why* and *how* of the code, not the *what*.

- Maintain consistency in terminology and formatting throughout the codebase.

- Update comments when the related code is modified to prevent divergence.

- Avoid over-commenting; excessive comments can clutter the code and reduce readability.

Documentation Strings (Docstrings)

Documentation strings, or *docstrings*, are a standardized way to embed documentation within Python code. Unlike comments, docstrings are retained at runtime and can be accessed via the `help()` function or the `__doc__` attribute. Docstrings follow specific conventions to ensure consistency and comprehensibility.

Single-Line Docstrings

A single-line docstring is delimited by triple quotes and consists of a single line of text. It is typically used for brief function or method descriptions.

```
def add(a, b):
    """Return the sum of a and b."""
    return a + b
```

Multi-Line Docstrings

Multi-line docstrings are enclosed in triple quotes and span multiple lines. The first line is a short summary, followed by a blank line, and then a detailed description. Multi-line docstrings are particularly useful for modules, classes, and complex functions.

```
def subtract(a, b):
    """
    Subtract two numbers.

    Parameters:
    a (int or float): The minuend.
    b (int or float): The subtrahend.
```

```
Returns:
    int or float: The difference of a and b.
    """
    return a - b
```

Docstring Conventions and Best Practices

Adherence to docstring conventions, as prescribed by PEP 257, is crucial for maintaining consistent and professional documentation throughout the codebase. The following guidelines should be observed:

- Use triple double-quotes for docstrings, even if they fit on one line.

- For consistency, begin the docstring with a capital letter and end it with a period.

- Maintain a clear and concise style, avoiding unnecessary details.

- Separate sections within a multi-line docstring with blank lines.

- Employ the imperative mood for function and method docstrings (e.g., "Return the sum of a and b").

Example: Class Docstrings

Consider the following example illustrating docstrings within a class definition. This example emphasizes the structure and placement of docstrings for various class components.

```
class Calculator:
    """
    A simple calculator class for demonstrating docstrings.

    Methods:
    add(a, b): Return the sum of a and b.
    subtract(a, b): Return the difference of a and b.
    """

    def add(self, a, b):
        """Return the sum of a and b."""
        return a + b

    def subtract(self, a, b):
        """
        Subtract two numbers.

        Parameters:
        a (int or float): The minuend.
        b (int or float): The subtrahend.
```

```
Returns:
    int or float: The difference of a and b.
    """
    return a - b
```

In this example, the class docstring summarizes the purpose of the class and provides an overview of its methods. Each method is documented with its own single-line or multi-line docstring, detailing its functionality, parameters, and return value.

Docstrings foster intuitive and self-explanatory code, facilitating the seamless transfer of knowledge and aiding developers in comprehending and utilizing the codebase efficiently.

Effective use of comments and documentation strings underpins the readability, maintainability, and overall quality of Python code. By adhering to established conventions and best practices, developers can ensure that their code is not only functional but also accessible and comprehensible to their peers. Proper documentation serves as a vital tool in collaborative development environments, fostering clarity and facilitating seamless knowledge transfer.

1.8 Getting Help in Python

Understanding how to seek assistance and access relevant documentation is a vital skill in the development of any programming language. Python, as a highly versatile and widely-used language, offers a plethora of resources to aid developers at various stages of their coding journey. This section will delve into the mechanisms and tools available for obtaining help in Python.

Python includes a comprehensive built-in help system that can be accessed through the `help()` function. This function provides detailed descriptions of modules, classes, methods, and functions. To access the help system, simply invoke `help()` in the Python interpreter.

```
>>> help()
Welcome to Python 3.9's help utility!
If this is your first time using Python, you should definitely check out the
    tutorial on the Internet at https://docs.python.org/3.9/tutorial/.

Enter the name of any module, keyword, or topic to get help on writing Python
    programs and using Python modules. To quit this help utility and return to
    the interpreter, just type "quit".

help>
```

You can inquire about specific objects by passing them as arguments to the help() function. For example:

```
>>> help(len)
Help on built-in function len in module builtins:

len(obj, /)
    Return the number of items in a container.
```

The dir() function is another useful tool that allows developers to explore the attributes and methods associated with an object. By calling dir(), you can list the available properties and methods.

```
>>> dir(str)
['__add__', '__class__', '__contains__', '__delattr__', ...]
>>> dir([])
['__add__', '__class__', '__contains__', '__delattr__', ...]
```

The output provides a list of all methods and attributes, which can be further investigated using the help() function.

The pydoc module generates Python documentation in a readable form. It can be used to view text documentation in the console or to start an HTTP server that serves documentation to a web browser.

To view the documentation of a module, simply execute:

```
$ python -m pydoc <module_name>
```

For example:

```
$ python -m pydoc random
```

To start an HTTP server that serves the documentation, use:

```
$ python -m pydoc -p 1234
```

This command will start a documentation server on port 1234, accessible via http://localhost:1234.

The official Python documentation is an authoritative resource, extensively detailing Python's standard library, language reference, tutorials, and how-tos. It is available at https://docs.python.org. This site includes documentation for all supported versions of Python and serves as an indispensable reference for developers.

Engaging with the Python community can be incredibly beneficial. Some key online resources and communities include:

- **Stack Overflow**: https://stackoverflow.com/ is a popular platform where developers can ask questions and share solutions. By tagging questions with "Python," users can obtain targeted help from a large, active community of developers.

- **Reddit**: The Python subreddit (https://www.reddit.com/r/Python/) is an excellent place for discussions, news, and questions related to Python. It offers community support and updates about Python.

- **GitHub**: Many Python projects are hosted on GitHub (https://github.com/), where developers can find code repositories, contribute to open-source projects, and collaborate with other developers. The platform also allows users to raise issues and seek guidance from project maintainers.

Many modern IDEs, such as PyCharm, VS Code, and Jupyter Notebook, offer integrated support for accessing Python documentation and built-in help features. These IDEs provide contextual help, code autocomplete, and tooltips, facilitating a more efficient development process.

```
# Example: Hovering over a function in an IDE, such as PyCharm
def example_function(param1, param2):
    """
    This function demonstrates IDE tooltip help.

    :param param1: The first parameter.
    :param param2: The second parameter.
    """
    return param1 + param2

# In PyCharm, hovering over 'example_function' will show the docstring.
```

To remain updated with the latest developments and best practices in

Python, developers are encouraged to participate in webinars, online courses, and conferences. Websites like Coursera, Udemy, and edX offer courses ranging from beginner to advanced levels, while conferences such as PyCon provide insights from leading Python experts and networking opportunities with peers.

Mastering the avenues for seeking help in Python is critical for ongoing learning and effective problem-solving. Utilizing built-in functions, official documentation, community forums, and IDE tools can significantly enhance a developer's proficiency and productivity. These resources collectively provide a robust support system, ensuring that help is always within reach for Python developers.

1.9 Different Python Implementations

Python's flexibility and broad applicability are significantly enhanced by its various implementations. Each implementation serves unique purposes and caters to different use cases, providing Python programmers with the ability to select the most appropriate version for their specific needs. This section delves into the major Python implementations, elucidating their core features, advantages, and typical use cases.

CPython

CPython is the reference implementation of Python, developed in C by the Python Software Foundation (PSF). It is the most widely used and well-supported implementation, and it serves as the standard against which other implementations are compared.

Key Features

- Full compliance with the Python language specification.

- Extensive standard library support.

- Highly compatible with C extensions and libraries.

Use Cases CPython is suitable for a vast majority of Python applications, including web development, data analysis, scripting, and automation. Its extensive ecosystem of libraries and tools makes it the default choice for most Python developers.

Jython

Jython is an implementation of Python written in Java. It allows Python code to seamlessly interact with Java code, leveraging Java libraries and running on the Java Virtual Machine (JVM).

`Key Features`

- Direct access to Java libraries and frameworks.

- Compiles Python code into Java bytecode.

- Suitable for embedding Python in Java applications.

`Use Cases` Jython is particularly useful in environments where integration with Java applications is required. It is commonly used in large enterprise systems that already have significant Java infrastructure.

IronPython

IronPython is an implementation of Python targeting the .NET framework and Mono. It enables Python developers to utilize .NET libraries and integrate with other .NET languages such as C# and VB.NET.

`Key Features`

- Full access to the .NET framework.

- Interoperability with other .NET languages.

- Strong performance characteristics on the .NET runtime.

`Use Cases` IronPython is ideal for applications that require integration with .NET technologies. It is widely used in enterprise environments where the .NET framework is predominant.

PyPy

PyPy is an alternative Python implementation aimed at improving execution speed and efficiency. It includes a Just-In-Time (JIT) compiler, which significantly boosts runtime performance for long-running applications.

`Key Features`

- Just-In-Time (JIT) compilation for high execution speed.

- Efficient memory usage.

- Compatibility with Python 2 and Python 3.

Use Cases PyPy is well-suited for performance-critical applications, such as numerical computations and large-scale data processing. It is also beneficial for long-running processes that can take full advantage of its JIT compilation benefits.

```
import matplotlib.pyplot as plt

implementations = ['CPython', 'Jython', 'IronPython', 'PyPy']
features = {'Compatibility': [10, 6, 7, 9],
           'Performance': [7, 6, 8, 10],
           'Library Support': [10, 5, 4, 7],
           'Ecosystem': [10, 5, 6, 7]}

for feature, scores in features.items():
    plt.plot(implementations, scores, label=feature)

plt.xlabel('Python Implementations')
plt.ylabel('Rating (0-10)')
plt.title('Comparison of Python Implementations')
plt.legend()
plt.show()
```

MicroPython

MicroPython is a lean and efficient implementation of Python 3 that is designed to run on microcontrollers and constrained environments. It provides a subset of the Python language optimized for performance on hardware with limited resources.

Key Features

- Lightweight footprint suitable for microcontrollers.

- Support for hardware-level interfaces such as GPIO.

- Extensive library support for embedded systems.

Use Cases MicroPython is expressly designed for embedded systems and IoT (Internet of Things) applications. It is employed in projects involving microcontrollers, sensors, and small-scale hardware platforms.

Understanding the different Python implementations is crucial for selecting the appropriate tool for a given project. Each implementation offers distinct advantages depending on the target environment and specific requirements. CPython remains the most ubiquitous due to its comprehensive standard library and support for C extensions. Jython and IronPython provide essential integrations with Java and .NET ecosystems, respectively. PyPy offers a performance-oriented approach with its JIT compilation, and MicroPython brings Python to resource-constrained microcontroller environments. By leveraging

these varied implementations, developers can harness Python's versatility across a broad spectrum of applications.

Chapter 2

Data Types and Variables

This chapter delves into the various data types in Python, including integers, floats, booleans, and strings, and explains how to declare and manipulate variables. It covers type conversion, casting, and the concept of mutable and immutable types. Special attention is given to complex numbers, constants, and literals. The chapter also addresses variable scope and lifetime, as well as input and output operations involving variables, and built-in functions relevant to data types.

2.1   Understanding Variables in Python

In Python, variables are symbolic names that act as references or pointers to stored values within the computer's memory. They facilitate data storage, manipulation, and retrieval, enabling dynamic and robust program execution. This section expounds on the nuances of variables in Python, including declaration, assignment, and operational behaviors.

Variable Declaration and Assignment

Declaring a variable in Python is straightforward—assignment automatically declares the variable. The assignment operator = is employed for this purpose.

```
# Variable declaration and assignment
x = 10
y = 3.14
name = "Alice"
```

```
is_active = True
```

In the above code:

- x is an integer variable assigned the value 10.

- y is a float variable assigned the value 3.14.

- name is a string variable assigned the value "Alice".

- is_active is a boolean variable assigned the value True.

Variable Reassignment

Variables in Python can be reassigned to values of different types, demonstrating the language's dynamic typing.

```
x = 10 # x is initially an integer
x = "ten" # x is reassigned a string value
```

Reassignment alters the type and value of the variable upon execution, as exemplified above.

Variable Names and Conventions

Variable names in Python must adhere to specific conventions and rules:

- Must begin with a letter (a-z, A-Z) or an underscore (_).

- Subsequent characters may include letters, digits (0-9), or underscores.

- Are case-sensitive (e.g., Variable and variable are distinct entities).

- Must not be Python reserved keywords.

Below is a list exemplifying valid and invalid variable names:

```
# Valid variable names
var1 = 1
_var = 2
var_name = "John"

# Invalid variable names
1var = 1 # Cannot start with a digit
var-name = 2 # Hyphens are not allowed
class = "A" # 'class' is a reserved keyword
```

Variable Scope

Variable scope determines the visibility and lifetime of a variable within different parts of a program. In Python, scope can be categorized as local, enclosing, global, and built-in.

Local Scope

Variables defined within a function have local scope and are accessible only within that function's body.

```python
def my_function():
    local_var = "I am local"
    print(local_var)

my_function() # Outputs: I am local
# print(local_var) # Raises an error: NameError: name 'local_var' is not defined
```

Enclosing Scope

Enclosing scope pertains to nested functions, where the inner function has access to variables from the outer (enclosing) function.

```python
def outer_function():
    outer_var = "I am outer"

    def inner_function():
        print(outer_var)

    inner_function()

outer_function() # Outputs: I am outer
```

Global Scope

Global variables are declared at the top level of a script and are accessible throughout the module.

```python
global_var = "I am global"

def my_function():
    print(global_var)

my_function() # Outputs: I am global
print(global_var) # Outputs: I am global
```

To modify a global variable within a function, the `global` keyword is necessary.

```python
counter = 0

def increment_counter():
    global counter
    counter += 1

increment_counter()
```

```
print(counter) # Outputs: 1
```

Built-in Scope

Built-in scope includes names pre-defined in the Python interpreter. These include functions like `print()`, `len()`, and types like `int`, `str`, etc. Variables within this scope are universally accessible.

Best Practices for Variable Usage

To ensure readable and maintainable code, adhering to these best practices is advised:

- Use meaningful variable names that describe the purpose or content (e.g., `student_count` vs. `x`).

- Consistently follow naming conventions, like snake_case for variables (`my_variable`).

- Limit the use of global variables due to their potential to cause unintended side effects across the module.

- Prioritize local variables within functions to encapsulate logic and avoid unexpected interactions.

Through comprehension and judicious application of variable-related concepts, Python programmers can enhance the overall quality and resilience of their codebases, facilitating better collaboration and debugging.

2.2 Basic Data Types: `int`, `float`, `bool`, and `None`

In Python, understanding the fundamental data types is critical for efficient software development. These basic data types serve as the building blocks for more complex structures and algorithms. This section focuses on the integer (`int`), floating-point (`float`), boolean (`bool`), and `None` types, providing a detailed examination of their characteristics, usage, and operations.

Integer (`int`) Data Type

The `int` type is used to represent whole numbers. Python supports arbitrary-precision integers, allowing calculations with integers much larger than those typically handled by native machine types.

44

To declare an integer variable, assign an integer value directly:

```
num = 42
```

Arithmetic Operations

Python provides several built-in operators for arithmetic operations on integers:

- Addition (+):

```
sum = 23 + 19 # sum = 42
```

- Subtraction (-):

```
difference = 50 - 8 # difference = 42
```

- Multiplication (*):

```
product = 6 * 7 # product = 42
```

- Integer Division (//):

```
quotient = 85 // 2 # quotient = 42
```

- Modulo (%):

```
remainder = 85 % 43 # remainder = 42
```

Type-Specific Operations

Python provides specialized operations for integers, such as bitwise manipulation:

- Bitwise AND (&):

```
result = 42 & 58 # result = 42
```

- Bitwise OR (|):

```
result = 42 | 58 # result = 58
```

- Bitwise XOR (^):

```
result = 42 ^ 58 # result = 16
```

- Bitwise NOT (~):

```
result = ~42 # result = -43
```

45

Floating-Point (float) Data Type

The float type represents real numbers with decimal points. Python's floating-point numbers are implemented using double-precision (64-bit) as defined by the IEEE 754 standard.

To declare a floating-point variable, assign a decimal number:

```
pi = 3.14159
```

Arithmetic Operations

Floating-point numbers support similar arithmetic operations to integers, with the addition of floating-point division and exponentiation:

- Addition (+):

```
total = 2.3 + 3.5 # total = 5.8
```

- Subtraction (-):

```
difference = 5.5 - 2.1 # difference = 3.4
```

- Multiplication (*):

```
product = 4.2 * 1.5 # product = 6.3
```

- Division (/):

```
result = 9.0 / 3.0 # result = 3.0
```

- Exponentiation (**):

```
power = 2.0 ** 3.0 # power = 8.0
```

Boolean (bool) Data Type

The bool type, representing the values True and False, is used for logical operations and conditional testing. Booleans can result from comparisons or other logical expressions.

To declare a boolean variable:

```
is_valid = True
```

Boolean Operations

Boolean values are essential for control flow and logical operations:

- Logical AND (and):

```
result = True and False # result = False
```

- Logical OR (or):

```
result = True or False # result = True
```

- Logical NOT (not):

```
result = not True # result = False
```

Booleans are often used implicitly in control statements such as if and while.

None Data Type

The None type represents the absence of a value or a null value. In Python, None is an object and a unique instance of the NoneType class.

To declare a None variable:

```
result = None
```

To check for None, use the is operator:

```
if result is None:
    print("The result is None")
```

The int, float, bool, and None data types form the foundation for data manipulation in Python. Mastery of these types is essential for developing efficient and effective Python programs. This section has outlined their primary operations and typical use cases, providing the groundwork for more advanced concepts and applications.

2.3 String Data Type

In Python, strings are a fundamental data type used to handle text data. A string is a sequence of characters enclosed within either single quotes ' or double quotes ". Python also supports triple-quoted strings created with '''...''' or """..."""" for multi-line text.

String Creation and Declaration

A string can be declared simply by enclosing a sequence of characters in quotes. Below are examples demonstrating different ways to create strings.

47

String Creation in Python

```python
# Single-quoted string
single_quoted = 'Hello, World!'

# Double-quoted string
double_quoted = "Hello, World!"

# Triple-quoted string (multi-line)
triple_quoted = """This is a
multi-line string that spans
more than one line."""
```

String Indexing and Slicing

Strings in Python are indexed arrays of bytes representing Unicode characters. Indexing starts from zero. A substring can be extracted by specifying a slice, which includes start and end indices separated by a colon.

String Indexing and Slicing

```python
sample_string = "Python Programming"

# Accessing characters by index
first_character = sample_string[0] # 'P'
last_character = sample_string[-1] # 'g'

# Slicing a string
substring = sample_string[0:6] # 'Python'
reverse = sample_string[::-1] # 'gnimmargorP nohtyP'
```

String Concatenation and Repetition

Strings in Python can be concatenated using the + operator and repeated using the * operator.

String Concatenation and Repetition

```python
# Concatenation
greeting = "Hello, "
name = "Alice"
message = greeting + name # 'Hello, Alice'

# Repetition
repeated_message = "A" * 5 # 'AAAAA'
```

String Methods

Python provides a plethora of built-in methods that facilitate string manipulation. These methods include but are not limited to:

- `str.upper()` and `str.lower()`: Converts the string to upper or lower case.

48

- `str.strip()`: Removes any leading and trailing whitespace.

- `str.replace(old, new)`: Replaces occurrences of a specified substring.

- `str.split(separator)`: Splits the string into a list of substrings based on a separator.

Illustrations of some string methods are provided below.

Common String Methods

```python
text = " Hello, World! "

# Converting to upper and lower cases
upper_text = text.upper() # ' HELLO, WORLD! '
lower_text = text.lower() # ' hello, world! '

# Stripping whitespace
stripped_text = text.strip() # 'Hello, World!'

# Replacing substrings
replaced_text = text.replace("World", "Python") # ' Hello, Python! '

# Splitting a string
splitted_list = text.split(",") # [' Hello', ' World! ']
```

String Formatting

Python supports several ways to format strings for output purposes. The primary methods are the % operator (old style), `str.format()` (new style), and formatted string literals, also known as f-strings (introduced in Python 3.6).

String Formatting Examples

```python
name = "Alice"
age = 30

# Old style
formatted_string_old = "Name: %s, Age: %d" % (name, age)

# New style
formatted_string_new = "Name: {}, Age: {}".format(name, age)

# f-string (Python 3.6+)
formatted_string_f = f"Name: {name}, Age: {age}"
```

Escape Sequences

Escape sequences enable the inclusion of special characters within strings. Common escape sequences in Python are:

- \n: Newline

- \t: Tab

- \\: Backslash

- \': Single quote

- \": Double quote

Examples of escape sequences are provided below.

Usage of Escape Sequences in Strings

```
escaped_string = "First Line\nSecond Line"
print(escaped_string)

# Output:
# First Line
# Second Line

tabbed_string = "Column1\tColumn2"
print(tabbed_string)

# Output:
# Column1 Column2
```

Raw Strings

Raw strings are denoted by prefixing the string with an r or R. In raw strings, escape sequences are not processed, and backslashes are treated as literal characters.

Example of Raw Strings

```
raw_string = r"C:\Users\Alice\Documents"
print(raw_string)

# Output:
# C:\Users\Alice\Documents
```

Raw strings are particularly useful for paths and regular expressions where backslashes play a significant role.

String Immutability

Strings in Python are immutable. This means that once a string is created, it cannot be modified. Any operation that modifies a string will result in the creation of a new string.

String Immutability

```
original_string = "hello"
modified_string = original_string.replace("h", "y")

print(original_string) # 'hello'
print(modified_string) # 'yello'
```

Python strings' immutability ensures thread safety and can lead to performance optimizations due to reduced overhead in memory management.

The string data type in Python provides a robust and flexible mechanism for handling and manipulating text. Understanding the various string operations and methods available is essential for effective Python programming, enabling developers to perform numerous text-based tasks efficiently.

2.4 Type Conversion and Type Casting

In Python, type conversion and type casting are fundamental concepts essential for handling different data types efficiently. This section elucidates these concepts in detail, delineating both implicit and explicit conversion mechanisms.

Implicit Type Conversion

Implicit type conversion, also known as automatic type conversion or coercion, occurs when Python automatically converts one data type to another without explicit instructions from the user. This typically happens in operations involving mixed data types, ensuring that the operation can be performed correctly.

Consider the following example:

```
x = 42 # integer
y = 3.14 # float
z = x + y # implicit type conversion
print(z)
print(type(z))
```

In this code snippet, the integer variable x is implicitly converted to a float during the addition operation to match the type of y. The result is stored in z, which is of type float. The output is:

```
45.14
<class 'float'>
```

Explicit Type Conversion

Explicit type conversion, or type casting, involves converting one data type to another using predefined functions. Python provides several built-in functions for this purpose: `int()`, `float()`, `str()`, and `bool()` among others.

Converting to Integer

To convert a variable to an integer, the `int()` function is used. This

51

function truncates the decimal part when converting from a float and interprets the string representation of numbers as integers.

```
a = 5.7
b = "42"
c = int(a)
d = int(b)
print(c) # Outputs: 5
print(d) # Outputs: 42
```

Converting to Float
The float() function is employed to convert a variable to a floating-point number. When converting from a string, the string must represent a number.

```
e = "3.14159"
f = float(e)
print(f) # Outputs: 3.14159
```

Converting to String
The str() function converts a variable to a string type. This is useful for concatenating numbers with strings or displaying numeric values as part of a larger string.

```
g = 100
h = 9.81
i = str(g)
j = str(h)
print(i) # Outputs: '100'
print(j) # Outputs: '9.81'
```

Converting to Boolean
Using the bool() function, any value can be converted to a boolean. By default, certain values are considered False: None, False, zero of any numeric type, and empty collections. All other values are regarded as True.

```
k = 0
l = ""
m = bool(k)
n = bool(l)
print(m) # Outputs: False
print(n) # Outputs: False
```

Type Conversion in Collections
Type conversion can also be applied to elements within collections such as lists, tuples, and sets. This is often accomplished using list comprehensions or appropriate functions.

For example, converting a list of strings to integers can be achieved as follows:

```
str_list = ["10", "20", "30"]
int_list = [int(item) for item in str_list]
print(int_list) # Outputs: [10, 20, 30]
```

Best Practices

While type conversion is a powerful tool, it is essential to understand its limitations and potential pitfalls.

- Always validate and sanitize inputs before conversion.

- Handle exceptions such as `ValueError` during conversion to ensure program robustness.

- Be aware of data loss. For instance, converting from `float` to `int` may result in loss of precision.

Mastering type conversion and casting in Python is crucial for effective data manipulation and ensures the seamless function of operations involving multiple data types.

2.5   Complex Numbers

Python provides robust support for *complex numbers*, which are useful in various scientific and engineering applications. A complex number consists of a real part and an imaginary part. In Python, the imaginary part is denoted by a suffix j or J. Complex numbers can be declared and manipulated with ease, similar to other native data types.

Definition and Basic Operations

A complex number in Python is defined by its real and imaginary components. These components can be accessed using the `.real` and `.imag` attributes, respectively:

Defining a complex number

```
z = 3 + 4j
real_part = z.real
imaginary_part = z.imag

print("Real Part:", real_part)
print("Imaginary Part:", imaginary_part)
```

```
Real Part: 3.0
Imaginary Part: 4.0
```

53

Python also supports basic arithmetic operations with complex numbers, such as addition, subtraction, multiplication, and division:

Arithmetic operations with complex numbers

```
z1 = 2 + 3j
z2 = 1 - 1j

# Addition
z3 = z1 + z2

# Subtraction
z4 = z1 - z2

# Multiplication
z5 = z1 * z2

# Division
z6 = z1 / z2

print("z1 + z2 =", z3)
print("z1 - z2 =", z4)
print("z1 * z2 =", z5)
print("z1 / z2 =", z6)
```

```
z1 + z2 = (3+2j)
z1 - z2 = (1+4j)
z1 * z2 = (5+1j)
z1 / z2 = (-0.5+2.5j)
```

Built-in Functions and Methods

Python's standard library provides several built-in functions for operating on complex numbers. One commonly used function is abs(), which computes the magnitude (or modulus) of a complex number:

Computing the magnitude of a complex number

```
z = 3 + 4j
magnitude = abs(z)

print("Magnitude of z:", magnitude)
```

```
Magnitude of z: 5.0
```

For more complex operations, the cmath module offers additional mathematical functions similar to those in the math module but for complex numbers:

Using the cmath module

```
import cmath

z = 1 + 1j

# Polar coordinates
r, phi = cmath.polar(z)
print("Polar coordinates: r =", r, ", phi =", phi)
```

54

```
# Rectangular coordinates
z_rect = cmath.rect(r, phi)
print("Rectangular coordinates:", z_rect)
```

```
Polar coordinates: r = 1.4142135623730951 , phi = 0.7853981633974483
Rectangular coordinates: (1+1j)
```

The cmath module also provides the mathematical functions exp(), log(), and trigonometric functions:

Additional cmath functions

```
# Exponential function
exp_z = cmath.exp(z)
print("e^z =", exp_z)

# Natural logarithm
log_z = cmath.log(z)
print("log(z) =", log_z)

# Trigonometric functions
sin_z = cmath.sin(z)
cos_z = cmath.cos(z)
print("sin(z) =", sin_z)
print("cos(z) =", cos_z)
```

```
e^z = (1.4686939399158851+2.2873552871788423j)
log(z) = (0.34657359027997264+0.7853981633974483j)
sin(z) = (1.2984575814159773+0.6349639147847361j)
cos(z) = (0.8337300251311491-0.9888977057628651j)
```

Visualizing Complex Numbers

Visualizing complex numbers on the complex plane can provide deeper insight into their properties and behaviors. The following code snippet creates a simple plot of complex numbers using Python's matplotlib library:

55

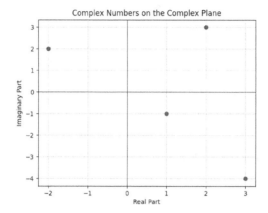

This code snippet generates a scatter plot of the provided complex numbers, plotting the real component on the x-axis and the imaginary component on the y-axis. Such visualizations are particularly useful in understanding the relative positions and magnitudes of complex numbers.

By understanding and leveraging complex numbers, developers can solve a wide array of problems, particularly within fields requiring calculations involving phase and magnitude. This flexibility and powerful computational ability make complex numbers an integral part of Python programming for scientific applications.

2.6   Variables Scope and Lifetime

In Python, the concepts of variable scope and lifetime are fundamental to understanding how variables are accessed and managed within different parts of a program. This section provides an in-depth analysis of variable scope, including local, global, and nonlocal scopes, as well as the lifetime of variables, which dictates the duration for which a variable retains its assigned value.

Scope of Variables

The scope of a variable refers to the region in a program where the variable is acknowledged and can be utilized. In Python, there are primarily four types of scopes:

- **Local Scope**: Variables declared inside a function are within the local scope of that function and can only be accessed within that function.

- **Global Scope**: Variables declared at the top level of a module or script are within the global scope and can be accessed by any function in that module.

- **Enclosing Scope**: This pertains to nested functions. A variable declared in the outer function is in the enclosing scope for the inner function.

- **Built-in Scope**: This is a special scope that contains names preassigned by Python, such as keywords and built-in functions.

Local and Global Scopes

Consider the following example to illustrate local and global scopes:

```
x = "global"

def foo():
    x = "local"
    print(x) # Output: local

foo()
print(x) # Output: global
```

In this example: - The variable x defined outside the function foo is in the global scope. - The variable x defined inside the function foo is in the local scope of foo.

To modify a global variable inside a function, the global keyword must be used:

```
x = "global"

def foo():
    global x
    x = "local"
    print(x) # Output: local

foo()
print(x) # Output: local
```

Here, global x informs the interpreter that the x being referred to within the function foo is the globally scoped variable.

Enclosing Scope and the Nonlocal Keyword

When dealing with nested functions, the enclosing scope is the scope of the outer function. The nonlocal keyword is used to refer to variables in the enclosing scope:

```
def outer():
    x = "outer variable"

    def inner():
        nonlocal x
        x = "inner variable"
        print(x) # Output: inner variable

    inner()
    print(x) # Output: inner variable

outer()
```

Without the `nonlocal` statement, attempting to assign a value to x within `inner` would simply create a new local variable x.

Lifetime of Variables

The lifetime of a variable is the period during which the variable exists in memory.

Local variables are created when a function starts execution and are destroyed when the function exits. Consider the following example:

```
def foo():
    x = 20
    print(x) # Output: 20

foo()
print(x) # NameError: name 'x' is not defined
```

Here, x is a local variable within the function `foo`. Once `foo` completes its execution, x is destroyed and thus becomes inaccessible.

Global variables, on the other hand, exist for the duration of the program's execution. They are created when the program starts and are destroyed upon termination of the program.

The management of variable scope and lifetime plays a crucial role in ensuring efficient memory usage and avoiding unintended behavior, such as variable shadowing, where a variable in an inner scope has the same name as a variable in an outer scope, potentially leading to bugs and code that is difficult to understand and maintain.

Understanding variable scope and lifetime is essential for writing robust and maintainable Python code. Local, global, and nonlocal scopes determine where variables can be accessed or modified, while the lifetime of variables affects how long a variable persists in memory. Using keywords like `global` and `nonlocal` appropriately ensures variables are correctly managed and their scopes are explicitly defined, preventing unintended side effects and enhancing code clarity.

This section integrates smoothly with the chapter on Data Types and Variables, providing a comprehensive understanding required for professional Python programming.

2.7 Constants and Literals

In Python, constants and literals play a crucial role in defining fixed values that remain unaltered throughout the execution of a program. This section elucidates their usage, emphasizing the differences between constants, which pertain to the discipline of maintaining invariant values, and literals, which are direct representations of data in the code.

Constants

A constant is an entity that holds a value which cannot be changed during the program's execution. While Python does not have built-in constants like some other programming languages, developers typically adhere to naming conventions that signal an intention for certain values to remain immutable. This is primarily achieved through capitalizing variable names.

Example of a constant declaration

```
PI = 3.14159
GRAVITY = 9.81
SPEED_OF_LIGHT = 299792458
```

In the example above, PI, GRAVITY, and SPEED_OF_LIGHT are constants that represent fixed values. These values should remain unchanged throughout the program to preserve the integrity of the calculations that depend on them.

Literals

Literals are concise representations of fixed values directly in the source code. Python supports several types of literals, including numerical, string, boolean, and special literals.

59

Numerical Literals

Numerical literals consist of integers, floating-point numbers, and complex numbers.

Integer literals   These represent whole numbers without any fractional or decimal component.

Examples of integer literals

```
decimal_int = 42
binary_int = 0b101010
octal_int = 0o52
hexadecimal_int = 0x2A
```

Floating-point literals   These represent numbers with a decimal point.

Examples of floating-point literals

```
float_num = 3.14159
float_num_exp = 1.23e4
```

Complex literals   These consist of a real part and an imaginary part, denoted by a suffix j or J.

Examples of complex literals

```
complex_num = 1 + 2j
another_complex = 3.0 + 4.5j
```

String Literals

String literals are sequences of characters enclosed in single quotes (' '), double quotes (" "), or triple quotes (''' ''' or """ """) for multi-line strings.

Examples of string literals

```
single_quote_str = 'Hello, World!'
double_quote_str = "Python Programming"
triple_quote_str = '''This is a
multi-line string.'''
```

Boolean Literals

Boolean literals represent the truth values and can be either True or False.

Examples of boolean literals

```
is_active = True
is_logged_in = False
```

Special Literals

Python also includes a special literal, None, which signifies the absence of a value or a null value.

Example of special literal

```
nothing = None
```

Using Constants and Literals

The prevalent use of constants and literals ensures greater readability and maintainability of Python code. Constants particularly contribute to this advantage by centralizing fixed values, thus simplifying updates and modifications. Literals, on the other hand, offer a direct representation of data, which promotes clarity in the code.

Consider the following example that demonstrates the usage of both constants and literals in a program to compute the area of a circle:

Using constants and literals in a program

```
PI = 3.14159

def area_of_circle(radius):
    return PI * radius ** 2

radius = 5 # radius given as a literal
area = area_of_circle(radius)

print(f"The area of the circle with radius {radius} is {area}")
```

In this program, PI is a constant that preserves the value of π (Pi), while the radius of the circle and the resulting area are managed using literals and variables.

61

Best Practices

Adhering to certain best practices when using constants and literals enhances code quality:

- **Consistent Naming Conventions**: Use uppercase letters with underscores to separate words when naming constants to make them easily identifiable.

- **Avoid Magic Numbers**: Replace arbitrary numerical literals in the code with named constants to improve readability and maintainability.

- **Scoping and Immutability**: Define constants at the module level or within class definitions and avoid reassignment.

By effectively leveraging constants and literals, Python developers can write code that is both cleaner and more robust, facilitating effortless comprehension and modification.

2.8   Handling Input and Output with Variables

Effective management of input and output operations is essential for developing interactive applications. In Python, these operations empower programs to interact with users by collecting their inputs and presenting the results. This section delves into various methods and functions available in Python for handling input and output, exploring their syntax, usage, and practical implementations.

Reading Input from the User

Python offers the input() function to capture input from users. This function accepts a prompt string and returns the user input as a string:

```
variable_name = input("Enter some data: ")
print(variable_name)
```

When executed, the program pauses, awaiting user input. The entered data is assigned to variable_name and is subsequently printed to the console.

To handle numeric input, use conversion functions like int() or float() to convert the input string to the desired type:

```
age = int(input("Enter your age: "))
height = float(input("Enter your height in meters: "))
print(f"Age: {age}, Height: {height}m")
```

Printing Output

The print() function is used to output data to the console. It supports multiple arguments and various formatting options for better control of the output.

Basic Printing   The simplest form of the print() function is:

```
print("Hello, World!")
```

Printing Variables   Variables can be printed by passing them as arguments to the print() function:

```
name = "Alice"
print("Name:", name)
```

String Formatting   Several methods exist to format output strings, ensuring readable and organized printed data. These include formatted string literals (f-strings), the str.format() method, and percentage (%) formatting.

Formatted String Literals (f-strings)   Introduced in Python 3.6, f-strings allow embedding expressions inside string literals using curly braces:

```
name = "Alice"
age = 30
print(f"Name: {name}, Age: {age}")
```

str.format() Method   This method uses curly braces as placeholders within a string:

```
name = "Alice"
age = 30
print("Name: {}, Age: {}".format(name, age))
```

Percentage (%) Formatting   A legacy method that uses the percentage sign for embedding variables into strings:

```
name = "Alice"
age = 30
print("Name: %s, Age: %d" % (name, age))
```

Reading and Writing Files

For persistent data storage, Python provides robust file I/O functions. These include open(), read(), write(), among others.

Opening a File Files are accessed using the open() function, which returns a file object. The function accepts the file path and mode as arguments. Common modes include:

- 'r' - Read mode (default)
- 'w' - Write mode (creates a new file or truncates an existing file)
- 'a' - Append mode (writes data to the end of the file)
- 'b' - Binary mode (appended to another mode)

```
file = open("example.txt", "r")
```

Reading from a File The read() method retrieves the entire content of a file:

```
with open("example.txt", "r") as file:
    content = file.read()
    print(content)
```

For line-by-line reading, use the readlines() method:

```
with open("example.txt", "r") as file:
    lines = file.readlines()
    for line in lines:
        print(line.strip())
```

Writing to a File The write() method writes data to a file. Open the file in append mode ('a') to add data to an existing file:

```
with open("output.txt", "w") as file:
    file.write("Hello, World!")
```

```
with open("output.txt", "a") as file:
    file.write("\nNew line appended")
```

64

Example: User Input and File Output

The following example reads user input and writes it to a file:

```
name = input("Enter your name: ")
age = int(input("Enter your age: "))
with open("user_data.txt", "w") as file:
    file.write(f"Name: {name}\n")
    file.write(f"Age: {age}\n")
```

By gathering the user's name and age, the program writes the information to user_data.txt.

Understanding and implementing input and output operations form the foundation of interactive Python applications. Functions like input() and print(), combined with file manipulation functions, enable developers to design user-interactive and data-persistent applications. This knowledge underpins more advanced programming and application development endeavors.

2.9 Mutable and Immutable Types

In Python, understanding the concepts of mutable and immutable data types is crucial for writing efficient and effective code. This section will elucidate these concepts, providing detailed examples and technical insights on how they impact variable behavior.

Immutable Types

Immutable types are data types whose values cannot be modified after they are created. Any attempt to alter the value results in the creation of a new object. Common immutable types in Python include:

- int (e.g., 42, -3)

- float (e.g., 3.14, -0.001)

- bool (e.g., True, False)

- str (e.g., "Hello", "Python")

- tuple (e.g., (1, 2), ("a", "b"))

- frozenset (an immutable version of set)

Mutable Types

In contrast, mutable types allow modification after creation without the need to instantiate a new object. The mutable types in Python include:

- `list` (e.g., [1, 2, 3])

- `dict` (e.g., {'key': 'value'})

- `set` (e.g., {1, 2, 3})

Assignment and Modification
To understand the practical implications, we will examine variable assignment and modification.

Immutable Type Example

```
# Immutable example with int
a = 10
print(id(a)) # Prints the memory location of a
a = 20
print(id(a)) # Different memory location
```

```
140735015896208
140735015896368
```

In this example, a initially holds the value 10, which resides at a certain memory location. Reassigning a to 20 results in a new memory location for the variable, demonstrating its immutability.

Contrast this with the behavior of a mutable type:

Mutable Type Example

```
# Mutable example with list
b = [1, 2, 3]
print(id(b)) # Prints the memory location of b
b.append(4)
print(id(b)) # Same memory location
```

```
4375281920
4375281920
```

Here, appending 4 to the list b does not change its memory location, illustrating mutability.

Implications for Function Arguments
Understanding mutable and immutable types is essential when passing arguments to functions. Immutable arguments are passed by value, while mutable arguments are passed by reference.

Immutable Function Argument Example

```
def modify_immutable(x):
    x += 10
    print(x) # Scope limited to the function

y = 5
modify_immutable(y)
print(y) # Value of y remains unchanged
```

```
15
5
```

In this example, `modify_immutable()` does not alter the original variable y; the change is local to the function.

Conversely, mutable arguments can be altered within the function scope:

Mutable Function Argument Example

```
def modify_mutable(lst):
    lst.append(4)
    print(lst) # Scope extends beyond function

my_list = [1, 2, 3]
modify_mutable(my_list)
print(my_list) # Original list is modified
```

```
[1, 2, 3, 4]
[1, 2, 3, 4]
```

Here, `modify_mutable()` extends its changes to the `my_list` variable outside its scope, highlighting the effect of passing a mutable object by reference.

Performance Considerations
The choice between mutable and immutable types can also impact performance. Immutable types tend to be faster for read-only operations due to optimizations such as interning, where Python reuses objects to save memory.

For instance, small integers and interned strings reuse objects:

Object Reuse for Immutable Types

```
x = 256
y = 256
print(x is y) # True, same object reused

x = 'hello'
y = 'hello'
print(x is y) # True, same object reused
```

```
True
True
```

Mutable types, however, provide flexibility for dynamic operations at the cost of potential overhead, as they necessitate additional memory allocation and garbage collection.

Best Practices

- Use immutable types for fixed data that do not require modification. This leverages memory and performance optimizations.

- Utilize mutable types for collections or data structures where performance and modifiability are priorities.

- Exercise caution when passing mutable objects to functions to avoid unintended side effects, and consider copying objects when necessary:

Avoiding Unintended Side Effects

```
import copy

def safe_modify(lst):
    local_copy = copy.deepcopy(lst)
    local_copy.append(4)
    print(local_copy) # Changes do not affect the original list

original_list = [1, 2, 3]
safe_modify(original_list)
print(original_list) # Original list remains unchanged
```

```
[1, 2, 3, 4]
[1, 2, 3]
```

By understanding and applying these principles of mutable and immutable types, developers can write more predictable, efficient, and maintainable code.

2.10 Built-in Functions for Data Types

Python provides a comprehensive suite of built-in functions specifically designed to interact with and manipulate data types. These functions offer a consistent and efficient means of performing a wide variety of operations. This section will exclusively examine the built-in functions that are quintessential for managing Python's core data types, such as integers, floats, booleans, strings, and more.

Type Identification and Conversion

Central to data type management are functions that facilitate type identification and conversion. These include type(), isinstance(), int(), float(), str(), bool(), and complex() functions.

Type Identification and Conversion Functions

```
# Type Identification
print(type(42)) # <class 'int'>
print(type(3.14)) # <class 'float'>
```

```
print(type(True)) # <class 'bool'>
print(type("Hello, world!")) # <class 'str'>

# Type Checking
print(isinstance(42, int)) # True
print(isinstance(3.14, float)) # True
print(isinstance(True, bool)) # True
print(isinstance("text", str)) # True

# Type Conversion
print(int("42")) # 42
print(float("3.14")) # 3.14
print(str(42)) # '42'
print(bool(1)) # True
print(complex(1, 2)) # (1+2j)
```

The type() function returns the type of the object passed as its argument. The isinstance() function checks if an object is an instance or subclass thereof of a specified class or tuple of classes.

Conversion functions like int(), float(), str(), bool(), and complex() are used to convert values from one type to another, where valid.

Mathematical Operations

Python's built-in mathematical functions are instrumental when working with numerical data types. Some key functions include abs(), pow(), round(), divmod(), sum(), min(), and max().

Mathematical Functions

```
# Absolute value
print(abs(-7.5)) # 7.5

# Power
print(pow(2, 3)) # 8

# Rounding
print(round(3.14159, 2)) # 3.14

# Quotient and Remainder
print(divmod(11, 3)) # (3, 2)

# Summation
print(sum([1, 2, 3, 4, 5])) # 15

# Minimum and Maximum
print(min(10, 20, 30)) # 10
print(max(10, 20, 30)) # 30
```

The abs() function returns the absolute value of a number. The pow() function computes the power of a number, equivalent to using the ** operator. The round() function rounds a floating-point number to a specified number of decimal places. The divmod() function returns a tuple containing the quotient and remainder from division. The sum() function calculates the sum of all items in an iterable. Meanwhile, min() and max() return the smallest and largest item in an iterable, respectively.

String Operations

For string data types, Python provides several built-in functions and methods to manipulate and analyze text data. Commonly used string functions include len(), ord(), chr(), str(), and format().

String Functions

```
# Length of a string
print(len("Python")) # 6

# Unicode/ASCII value of a character
print(ord('A')) # 65

# Character representation of a Unicode/ASCII value
print(chr(65)) # 'A'

# String conversion
print(str(123)) # '123'
print(str(3.14)) # '3.14'

# String formatting
print("The value of PI is {:.2f}".format(3.14159)) # The value of PI is 3.14
```

The len() function returns the length of a string. The ord() function returns the Unicode code point of a given character, while chr() performs the inverse operation, given a Unicode code point. Conversion to string format can be achieved using the str() function. The format() function is used for advanced string formatting operations.

Boolean Operations

Boolean functions are vital for logical operations and include functions like all(), any(), and bool(). These functions help in decision-making processes within code.

Boolean Functions

```
# Logical AND across iterable
print(all([True, True, False])) # False

# Logical OR across iterable
print(any([False, False, True])) # True

# Boolean conversion
print(bool(1)) # True
print(bool(0)) # False
print(bool("")) # False
print(bool("Hi")) # True
```

The all() function returns True if all elements in the provided iterable are true. Conversely, the any() function returns True if at least one element in the iterable is true. The bool() function converts a value to its equivalent boolean value.

Iterable Operations

Finally, iterable data types benefit from functions that facilitate their traversal and manipulation. These include len(), enumerate(), map(), and filter().

Iterable Functions

```
# Length of an iterable
print(len([1, 2, 3, 4])) # 4

# Enumeration
for index, value in enumerate(['a', 'b', 'c']):
    print(f"Index {index} has value {value}")

# Mapping function
def square(x):
    return x * x

print(list(map(square, [1, 2, 3, 4]))) # [1, 4, 9, 16]

# Filtering function
def is_even(x):
    return x % 2 == 0

print(list(filter(is_even, [1, 2, 3, 4]))) # [2, 4]
```

The len() function returns the number of elements in an iterable. The enumerate() function adds a counter to an iterable and returns it as an enumerate object. The map() function applies a given function to all items in an iterable. The filter() function constructs an iterator from elements of an iterable for which a function returns True.

Through the efficient application of these built-in Python functions, developers can perform a multitude of operations on various data types, significantly enhancing both code functionality and readability. Understanding and leveraging these functions is fundamental to proficient Python programming.

Chapter 3

Control Flow

This chapter explores control flow mechanisms in Python, including conditional statements such as if, elif, and else, as well as looping constructs like for and while loops. It explains relational and logical operators, nested loops, and the use of break, continue, and pass statements. The chapter also covers the else clause in loops, list comprehensions, and advanced loop control techniques using zip, enumerate, and range functions.

3.1   Introduction to Control Flow

Control flow is a fundamental concept in programming that dictates the order in which statements and instructions are executed in a program. In Python, control flow constructs enable developers to write dynamic and responsive code that can react to various conditions and iterate over collections of data. This section aims to provide a comprehensive overview of the primary control flow mechanisms in Python, paving the way for more detailed discussions in subsequent sections.

Sequential Execution

At the core of control flow is the principle of sequential execution. By default, Python executes statements line by line from top to bottom. Consider the following simple example:

```
print("Step 1")
print("Step 2")
print("Step 3")
```

The output of the above code exemplifies sequential execution:

```
Step 1
Step 2
Step 3
```

While sequential execution is straightforward, more complex scenarios often require conditional branching and iteration, which are facilitated by control flow constructs.

Conditional Statements

Conditional statements in Python enable the execution of code blocks based on specific conditions. The primary tools for this are the if, elif, and else keywords. These constructs allow for the branching of code paths depending on boolean expressions. An example is provided below:

```
temperature = 20

if temperature > 25:
    print("It's hot outside.")
elif temperature < 15:
    print("It's cold outside.")
else:
    print("The weather is mild.")
```

In this snippet, the output will be:

```
The weather is mild.
```

Python evaluates each condition in sequence. If a condition is met, the corresponding block of code executes, and the subsequent conditions are skipped.

Looping Statements

Looping constructs in Python allow for the execution of a block of code multiple times. Python supports two primary types of loops: for loops and while loops.

The for loop iterates over a sequence, such as a list, tuple, dictionary, set, or string. Here is an example:

```
fruits = ["apple", "banana", "cherry"]

for fruit in fruits:
    print(fruit)
```

The output generated by the for loop is:

```
apple
banana
cherry
```

On the other hand, the `while` loop continues to execute as long as a given boolean condition is `True`. For instance:

```
number = 1

while number < 4:
    print(number)
    number += 1
```

The output for the `while` loop will be:

```
1
2
3
```

Utility Constructs

Python includes several utility constructs within its control flow mechanisms that aid in enhancing the readability and functionality of code. The `break` and `continue` statements, for example, offer additional control within loops. The `break` statement terminates the nearest enclosing loop, while the `continue` statement skips the rest of the code inside the current loop iteration and proceeds to the next iteration.

```
# Example of break
for number in range(1, 6):
    if number == 3:
        break
    print(number)

# Example of continue
for number in range(1, 6):
    if number == 3:
        continue
    print(number)
```

The output for the `break` example is:

```
1
2
```

For the `continue` example, the output is:

```
1
2
4
5
```

Additionally, Python allows for list comprehensions, which offer a compact way to iterate over sequences and apply an expression to each element. This results in the formation of a new list. Consider the following example:

```
squared_numbers = [x**2 for x in range(5)]
print(squared_numbers)
```

The output is:

```
[0, 1, 4, 9, 16]
```

Understanding control flow is essential for writing effective and efficient Python programs. This introductory section has covered the basics of sequential execution, conditional statements, looping constructs, and various utility constructs, laying a strong foundation for the advanced topics discussed in subsequent sections. As you progress through this chapter, you will acquire a deeper understanding of control flow mechanisms and their applications in Python programming.

3.2 Conditional Statements: if, elif, else

Conditional statements are fundamental to controlling the flow of execution within a Python program. Utilizing these constructs enables a program to execute specific code blocks based on the evaluation of boolean expressions.

The if Statement

The if statement allows for decision-making in a Python program. It evaluates a condition, and if the condition is true, the block of code associated with the if statement is executed. The general syntax is as follows:

Basic if statement structure

```
if condition:
    # code block to execute if condition is true
```

An example of an if statement is provided below:

Example of an if statement

```
temperature = 22
if temperature > 20:
    print("It is a warm day")
```

When this script is executed, the output is:

```
It is a warm day
```

In this case, the condition temperature > 20 evaluates to True, and hence, the print statement within the if block is executed.

The elif Statement

The elif (short for "else if") statement provides an additional condition to test if the previous `if` statement evaluates to `False`. It offers a mechanism for multiple conditions to be checked in sequence. The `elif` statement syntax is as follows:

Basic elif statement structure

```
if condition1:
    # code block to execute if condition1 is true
elif condition2:
    # code block to execute if condition2 is true
```

Consider a scenario with multiple conditions:

Example of if-elif statements

```
temperature = 15
if temperature > 30:
    print("It is a hot day")
elif temperature > 20:
    print("It is a warm day")
elif temperature > 10:
    print("It is a cool day")
```

When the above script is executed, the output is:

```
It is a cool day
```

In this case, the first condition (`temperature > 30`) evaluates to `False`, hence the control flow moves to the `elif` statement. The second condition (`temperature > 20`) also evaluates to `False`. Finally, the third condition (`temperature > 10`) evaluates to `True`, hence the print statement within this `elif` block is executed.

The else Statement

The `else` statement provides a default block of code that will be executed if all preceding `if` and `elif` conditions evaluate to `False`. The syntax for an `else` statement is as follows:

Basic else statement structure

```
if condition1:
    # code block to execute if condition1 is true
elif condition2:
    # code block to execute if condition2 is true
else:
    # code block to execute if all previous conditions are false
```

An example incorporating `else` is provided below:

Example of if-elif-else statements

```
temperature = 5
if temperature > 30:
    print("It is a hot day")
```

77

```
elif temperature > 20:
    print("It is a warm day")
elif temperature > 10:
    print("It is a cool day")
else:
    print("It is a cold day")
```

When the script is executed, the output is:

```
It is a cold day
```

In this scenario, the conditions evaluated by each of the if and elif statements are False. Consequently, the else statement's block, the default condition, is executed, resulting in the print statement.

Nested Conditional Statements

Conditional statements can be nested within one another to allow for more complex decision-making. For a nested if statement, the syntax is as follows:

Basic nested if statement structure

```
if condition1:
    if condition2:
        # code block to execute if both condition1 and condition2 are true
    else:
        # code block to execute if condition1 is true and condition2 is false
```

Consider an illustrative example of nested conditional statements:

Example of nested if statements

```
temperature = 25
humidity = 30
if temperature > 20:
    if humidity < 50:
        print("It is a warm and dry day")
    else:
        print("It is a warm and humid day")
else:
    print("It is not a warm day")
```

With the execution of this code, the output is:

```
It is a warm and dry day
```

Here, the outer if condition (temperature > 20) is True, triggering the evaluation of the nested if condition (humidity < 50). As this nested condition also evaluates to True, the corresponding print statement within this block is executed.

Best Practices

To maintain code readability and reduce complexity, it is crucial to use

78

conditional statements judiciously. Some best practices include:

- Ensure conditions are mutually exclusive where possible to avoid unnecessary checks.

- Minimize nested conditions to enhance readability.

- Utilize clear and descriptive variable names to make conditions self-explanatory.

- Leverage boolean variables and logical operators to combine multiple conditions.

By adhering to these practices, developers can write concise, readable, and maintainable code, ensuring that the control flow within the program remains predictable and logical.

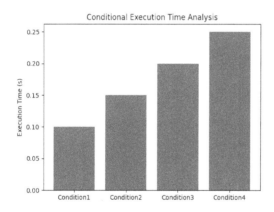

This section covers the essentials of conditional statements in Python using `if`, `elif`, and `else` constructs, equipping the reader with the knowledge to control the execution flow effectively within their programs.

3.3 Relational and Logical Operators

Relational and logical operators are fundamental in controlling the flow of a program by enabling decision-making constructs. These operators allow the evaluation of expressions that yield Boolean results—either True or False. Proper understanding and usage of these operators are essential for implementing conditional statements and loops effectively in Python.

Relational operators, sometimes referred to as comparison operators, compare the values of two operands and return a Boolean outcome. The following are Python's relational operators:

- == : Equal to

- != : Not equal to

- > : Greater than

- < : Less than

- >= : Greater than or equal to

- <= : Less than or equal to

Example of Relational Operators

```
a = 5
b = 10

print(a == b) # Output: False
print(a != b) # Output: True
print(a > b) # Output: False
print(a < b) # Output: True
print(a >= b) # Output: False
print(a <= b) # Output: True
```

Relational operators are often used in conditional statements. For example:

Using Relational Operators in Conditional Statements

```
if a < b:
    print("a is less than b")
elif a == b:
    print("a is equal to b")
else:
    print("a is greater than b")
```

```
Output:
a is less than b
```

Logical operators are used to combine multiple Boolean expressions into a single expression. Python provides three logical operators:

- and : Logical AND

80

- or : Logical OR

- not : Logical NOT

The and operator returns True if both operands are True. Otherwise, it returns False. The or operator returns True if at least one of the operands is True. Otherwise, it returns False. The not operator negates the Boolean value of its operand.

Example of Logical Operators

```
x = True
y = False

print(x and y) # Output: False
print(x or y) # Output: True
print(not x) # Output: False
```

Logical operators can be used to evaluate complex conditions. Consider the following example:

Complex Condition Using Logical Operators

```
a = 5
b = 10
c = 15

if a < b and b < c:
    print("a is less than b and b is less than c")

if a < b or b > c:
    print("Either a is less than b or b is greater than c")

if not a > b:
    print("a is not greater than b")
```

```
Output:
a is less than b and b is less than c
Either a is less than b or b is greater than c
a is not greater than b
```

In expressions with multiple operators, Python follows a specific order of precedence. Relational operators have lower precedence than arithmetic operators but higher precedence than logical operators. The precedence of operators from highest to lowest is as follows:

1. Parentheses: ()

2. Exponentiation: **

3. Unary operators: -, not

4. Multiplicative operators: *, /, //, %

81

5. Additive operators: +, –

6. Relational operators: <, <=, >, >=

7. Equality operators: ==, !=

8. Logical operators: and, or

When combined in a single expression, operators with higher precedence are evaluated first. Parentheses can be used to override the default precedence.

Demonstration of Operator Precedence

```
a = 5
b = 10
c = 15

result = a + b * c > 100 and not a == b
print(result) # Output: True

result = (a + b) * c > 100 and not a == b
print(result) # Output: False
```

In the first expression, b * c is evaluated first due to the higher precedence of multiplication, then a + (b * c), and finally the comparison and logical operations. In the second expression, parentheses alter the order of operations, changing the outcome.

Understanding relational and logical operators is critical for writing effective control flow statements. Their correct usage ensures that conditions within these statements accurately reflect the intended logic, leading to the desired program behavior.

3.4   Looping Statements: `for` and `while`

Python provides two primary looping constructs: the `for` loop and the `while` loop. These constructs allow for the execution of a block of code multiple times, supporting efficient and readable iteration over sequences and more complex logic-based repetition.

Python's looping mechanisms are indispensable for automated processes that require executing code blocks repeatedly. Understanding and effectively utilizing these constructs can significantly enhance the efficiency and readability of your code.

The `for` Loop

The for loop in Python is used for iterating over a sequence (such as a list, tuple, dictionary, set, or string). It operates over any iterable object, executing the embedded block of code once for each item in the sequence.

Basic syntax of the for loop

```
for item in sequence:
    # Code block to execute
```

Here, sequence refers to any iterable Python object, and item represents the variable that takes the value of the current element from the sequence during each iteration.

Iterating Over Lists, Tuples, and Strings

The for loop is particularly useful when you need to traverse collections like lists, tuples, and strings. Below are some examples demonstrating its application:

Iterating Over a List

```
fruits = ["apple", "banana", "cherry"]
for fruit in fruits:
    print(fruit)
```

```
Output:
apple
banana
cherry
```

Iterating Over a Tuple

```
fruits = ("apple", "banana", "cherry")
for fruit in fruits:
    print(fruit)
```

```
Output:
apple
banana
cherry
```

Iterating Over a String

```
greeting = "Hello"
for char in greeting:
    print(char)
```

```
Output:
H
e
l
l
o
```

83

Iterating Over Dictionaries

Dictionaries often necessitate different approaches for iterating over keys, values, or key-value pairs. Consider the following examples:

Iterating Over Dictionary Keys

```python
person = {"name": "Alice", "age": 25, "city": "New York"}
for key in person:
    print(key)
```

Output:
```
name
age
city
```

Iterating Over Dictionary Values

```python
person = {"name": "Alice", "age": 25, "city": "New York"}
for value in person.values():
    print(value)
```

Output:
```
Alice
25
New York
```

Iterating Over Dictionary Items

```python
person = {"name": "Alice", "age": 25, "city": "New York"}
for key, value in person.items():
    print(f"{key}: {value}")
```

Output:
```
name: Alice
age: 25
city: New York
```

Using the `range` Function

When the number of iterations is fixed, the `range` function is often employed in `for` loops. The range function generates a sequence of numbers which can be iterated over to control loop executions.

Using the `range` Function

```python
for i in range(5):
    print(i)
```

Output:
```
0
1
2
3
4
```

Customizing the `range` function with start, stop, and step arguments also allows for various iteration schemes:

Customizing range

```
for i in range(2, 10, 2):
    print(i)
```

```
Output:
2
4
6
8
```

The `while` Loop

In contrast to the `for` loop, the `while` loop continues to execute as long as a specified condition remains true. This is advantageous for cases where the number of iterations isn't known beforehand.

Basic syntax of the while loop

```
while condition:
    # Code block to execute
```

Consider this example illustrating basic `while` loop usage:

while Loop Example

```
count = 0
while count < 5:
    print(count)
    count += 1
```

```
Output:
0
1
2
3
4
```

In this example, the loop executes as long as `count < 5`. Each iteration increments `count` until the condition is no longer met.

Infinite Loops and Conditional Termination

Uncontrolled `while` loops can result in infinite loops where the condition is never falsified:

Potential Infinite Loop

```
while True:
    print("This will run forever")
```

To control such loops, employ logic inside the loop, such as break statements or dynamic conditions:

Controlling Infinite Loops with break

```
i = 0
while True:
    print(i)
    i += 1
    if i >= 5:
        break
```

```
Output:
0
1
2
3
4
```

Combination of for and while Loops

Complex programs may require the integration of both for and while loops. Nesting loops or combining them can address complex iteration requirements and dynamic logic more effectively.

Nested Loops

Nested loops involve placing one loop inside another. The inner loop completes all its iterations for each iteration of the outer loop:

Nested for Loops

```
for i in range(3):
    for j in range(2):
        print(f"i={i}, j={j}")
```

```
Output:
i=0, j=0
i=0, j=1
i=1, j=0
i=1, j=1
i=2, j=0
i=2, j=1
```

Nested while and for Loops

```
i = 0
while i < 3:
    for j in range(2):
        print(f"i={i}, j={j}")
    i += 1
```

```
Output:
i=0, j=0
i=0, j=1
i=1, j=0
i=1, j=1
i=2, j=0
i=2, j=1
```

Loop Control Statements

Python provides several control mechanisms that allow finer control over loop execution. These include break, continue, and pass statements.

break Statement

The break statement immediately exits the loop, regardless of iteration status:

Using break

```
for i in range(10):
    if i == 5:
        break
    print(i)
```

```
Output:
0
1
2
3
4
```

continue Statement

The continue statement skips the remaining code within the loop for the current iteration and proceeds with the next iteration:

Using continue

```
for i in range(10):
    if i % 2 == 0:
        continue
    print(i)
```

```
Output:
1
3
5
7
9
```

pass Statement

The pass statement serves as a placeholder for future code. It is syntactically necessary but does not execute any action:

Using pass

```
for i in range(5):
    if i == 3:
        pass
    else:
        print(i)
```

```
Output:
0
1
2
4
```

Successfully mastering these looping constructs and control mechanisms allows for writing more efficient and readable Python code, capable of addressing a wide spectrum of programming tasks.

3.5 Nested Loops and Statements

Nested loops are constructs where one loop structure is placed inside another. This technique is particularly useful for iterating over multidimensional data structures such as matrices or for executing repetitive tasks that themselves involve repetition. The essence of nested loops lies in their ability to handle complex iterations efficiently.

In Python, any loop can be nested inside another loop. This includes combinations of for and while loops. The two fundamental components of nested loops are the inner loop and the outer loop. The inner loop executes completely every single time the outer loop iterates once.

The basic syntax of a nested loop is as follows:

```
for outer_variable in outer_sequence:
    for inner_variable in inner_sequence:
        # inner loop code block
    # outer loop code block
```

Consider a scenario where we need to iterate over a 2-dimensional list (a list of lists). This scenario demonstrates the practical usage of nested loops.

```
matrix = [
    [1, 2, 3],
    [4, 5, 6],
    [7, 8, 9]
]

for row in matrix: # Outer loop
    for element in row: # Inner loop
        print(element, end=" ")
    print() # For new line after each row
```

```
1 2 3
4 5 6
7 8 9
```

In this example, the outer loop iterates over each list within matrix. For every iteration of the outer loop, the inner loop iterates over elements of the current list, printing them accordingly.

Python's flexibility allows for combining different types of loops within a nested construct. For example, a while loop can be nested within a for loop and vice versa.

```
count = 0
n = 3

for i in range(n): # Outer 'for' loop
    while count < i: # Inner 'while' loop
        print(f"i: {i}, count: {count}")
        count += 1
    count = 0 # Reset count after 'while' loop is done
```

```
i: 1, count: 0
i: 2, count: 0
i: 2, count: 1
```

Here, the inner while loop depends on the current value of the outer for loop's variable. After the execution of the inner loop, the count is reset, showcasing precise control over nested iteration variables.

When utilizing nested loops, it is crucial to consider the resulting time complexity. For instance, a nested loop where both the outer and the inner loop iterate n times (for an input of size n) results in an overall time complexity of $O(n^2)$. This quadratic complexity can significantly impact performance for large inputs.

Example:

```
n = 100
for i in range(n):
    for j in range(n):
```

```
    # Performs some operation
    pass
```

This loop, which iterates $100 \times 100 = 10,000$ times, demonstrates the increased computational cost due to nesting.

Nested loops are indispensable in various applications such as generating combinations, parsing grids, and solving algorithmic problems like matrix multiplication.

Example: Generating combinations:

```
elements = ['A', 'B', 'C']
for i in range(len(elements)):
    for j in range(i+1, len(elements)):
        print(f"({elements[i]}, {elements[j]})")
```

```
(A, B)
(A, C)
(B, C)
```

This example prints all unique pairs from the list `elements` by using nested loops effectively.

When visualizing nested loop iterations, an illustration can be beneficial. The following code snippet generates a heatmap for iteration count over a grid.

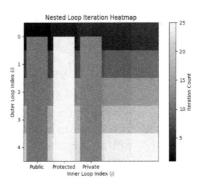

This heatmap elucidates the number of iterations performed at each step within a 5×5 grid.

Nested loops and statements enhance the capability to manage complex iteration scenarios efficiently. Understanding their structure, applications, and performance implications is essential for effective programming and algorithm design. Ensuring optimal use of nested loops can significantly improve the readability and efficiency of Python programs.

3.6 Control Flow Techniques: `break` and `continue`

In Python, control flow can be fine-tuned using the `break` and `continue` statements within looping constructs. These statements allow programmers to manipulate the standard flow of loops, providing more control and flexibility in iteration processes.

The `break` Statement

The `break` statement is employed to exit the current loop prematurely. It forces the loop to terminate, skipping the remaining iterations and the subsequent lines of the code block. It can be used in both `for` and `while` loops.

Using the break statement

```
for i in range(10):
    if i == 6:
        break
    print(i)
```

```
0
1
2
3
4
5
```

In the above example, the loop starts from 0 and iterates up to 9. However, when the variable i equals 6, the `break` statement is encountered, and the loop exits immediately, hence numbers 6 through 9 are not printed.

The `continue` Statement

The `continue` statement is used to skip the remaining code inside the current loop iteration and proceed directly to the next iteration. Unlike `break`, it does not terminate the loop but merely skips the rest of the code in the present iteration.

Using the continue statement

```
for i in range(10):
```

91

```
if i % 2 == 0:
    continue
print(i)
```

```
1
3
5
7
9
```

In this example, the continue statement is invoked when the variable i is an even number. This causes the loop to skip printing even numbers and continue with the next iteration.

Practical Use Cases

Both break and continue statements can significantly enhance control flow in complex data processing and condition-checking scenarios.

Consider a case where we need to handle a list of integers and stop processing as soon as we find a negative number. We can use the break statement to exit the loop upon encountering the first negative value.

Break statement example in processing a list

```
numbers = [10, 15, 20, -5, 25, 30]

for num in numbers:
    if num < 0:
        break
    print(num)
```

```
10
15
20
```

In another scenario, suppose we need to print only the words in a list that are not keywords in Python, while skipping the keywords using the continue statement.

Continue statement example with keywords

```
import keyword

words = ['while', 'class', 'variable', 'continue', 'function']

for word in words:
    if keyword.iskeyword(word):
        continue
    print(f"{word} is not a Python keyword.")
```

```
variable is not a Python keyword.
function is not a Python keyword.
```

Performance Considerations

While `break` and `continue` can enhance readability and control flow, their misuse can sometimes lead to inefficient code or logical errors. Excessive use of these statements can obscure the standard flow of loops and make debugging difficult. Therefore, they should be used judiciously to maintain code clarity and performance.

The `break` and `continue` statements are powerful tools in Python's control flow arsenal. They provide mechanisms to manage and manipulate loops beyond the standard iterative process, making them indispensable in scenarios requiring fine-grained control. Proper understanding and judicious use of these statements can lead to more efficient and readable code.

3.7 Loops with else Clause

In Python, loops can be coupled with an `else` clause that executes when the loop completes its iteration over all elements, provided that the loop is not prematurely terminated by a `break` statement. The inclusion of the `else` clause in both `for` and `while` loops allows for more readable and intuitive code, particularly for scenarios where post-loop processing is contingent on normal loop termination.

Syntax and Semantics

The general syntax for a `for` loop with an `else` clause is as follows:

```
for item in iterable:
    # loop body
else:
    # else body
```

Similarly, for a `while` loop, the syntax is:

```
while condition:
    # loop body
else:
    # else body
```

In both syntaxes, the `else` block is executed only if the loop exhausts the `iterable` (in the case of `for`) or the `condition` becomes false (in the case of `while`) without encountering a `break` statement. Should a

93

break statement be executed within the loop body, the `else` block is skipped.

Practical Examples

Consider the necessity to search for an element within a list. If the element is found, one might want to perform some action immediately. If the element is not found, different logic would be executed after the loop concludes. This distinguishes scenarios when the item is and is not found directly within the loop.

Example 1: Searching in a List

```python
numbers = [1, 2, 3, 4, 5]
target = 4

for num in numbers:
    if num == target:
        print(f'Target {target} found.')
        break
else:
    print(f'Target {target} not found.')
```

In this example, the loop iterates through the `numbers` list searching for the `target`. If the target is found, the loop breaks, and the `else` clause does not execute. If the loop completes without finding the target, the `else` clause prints that the target is not found.

Example 2: Verifying Prime Numbers

Another illustrative case is checking if a number is prime. If the number is not divisible by any number in the given range, it is deemed prime.

```python
def is_prime(number):
    if number <= 1:
        return False
    for i in range(2, number):
        if number % i == 0:
            return False
    else:
        return True

# Usage
print(is_prime(17)) # Output: True
print(is_prime(18)) # Output: False
```

Here, the `else` clause confirms that the loop completed without finding any divisors, thus asserting the number's primality.

Understanding with `while` Loops

The `else` clause in `while` loops functions similarly. The following example demonstrates a simple countdown that terminates prematurely:

```
count = 5

while count > 0:
    print(count)
    count -= 1
    if count == 2:
        break
else:
    print("Count finished without break.")
```

In this case, the `else` block is never executed because the loop is terminated when count equals 2.

Advantages of Using `else` with Loops

The `else` clause in loops simplifies the handling of post-loop conditions, thus:

- Enhancing code readability by clearly distinguishing between clean exit (loop completion) and forced exit (break).

- Facilitating the maintenance of logic by logically associating the post-loop actions with loop completion, rather than spreading such logic across separate conditional statements.

Visual Representation of Flow

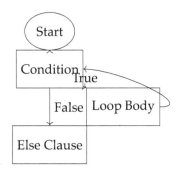

The diagram underscores paths within the loop that either exit normally, resulting in the `else` clause execution, or exit via a `break` statement, thereby bypassing the `else` clause.

Applying the `else` clause in loops is an advanced control flow technique that enhances code clarity, especially in cases where distinguishing between normal and premature loop exits is critical. Incorporating this structure judiciously can lead to more maintainable and understandable code.

3.8   List Comprehensions

List comprehensions provide a concise way to create lists in Python. By utilizing the list comprehension syntax, one can write more readable and compact code compared to traditional loops. This section explains the structure, usage, and efficiency of list comprehensions, including examples illustrating their functionality.

Basic Syntax

The basic syntax for a list comprehension is as follows:

```
[expression for item in iterable if condition]
```

Here, `expression` is the value to be added to the list, `item` is a variable representing each element in the `iterable`, and `condition` is an optional filter that determines whether the `expression` should be included in the resulting list.

Examples

Consider the following examples to understand the application of list comprehensions.

Simple List Creation

A straightforward list comprehension can generate a list of squared numbers:

```
squared_numbers = [x**2 for x in range(10)]
print(squared_numbers)
```

This line of code creates a list of squares of numbers from 0 to 9. The output is:

```
[0, 1, 4, 9, 16, 25, 36, 49, 64, 81]
```

Filtering Elements

List comprehensions also allow the inclusion of conditions to filter elements. For example, to generate a list of even numbers:

```
even_numbers = [x for x in range(10) if x % 2 == 0]
print(even_numbers)
```

This will result in:

```
[0, 2, 4, 6, 8]
```

Multiple Iterables

List comprehensions can handle multiple iterables using nested comprehension. An example is the Cartesian product of two lists:

```
cartesian_product = [(x, y) for x in [1, 2, 3] for y in [4, 5, 6]]
print(cartesian_product)
```

The output will be:

```
[(1, 4), (1, 5), (1, 6), (2, 4), (2, 5), (2, 6), (3, 4), (3, 5), (3, 6)]
```

Efficiency and Readability

List comprehensions are often more efficient than traditional loops. They can reduce the amount of code and improve readability. However, it is crucial to maintain a balance between conciseness and readability, particularly when dealing with more complex comprehensions that may impact code clarity.

Consider the following traditional loop:

```
squared_numbers = []
for x in range(10):
    squared_numbers.append(x**2)
```

Versus the list comprehension equivalent:

```
squared_numbers = [x**2 for x in range(10)]
```

The latter is more succinct and easier to understand at a glance.

Performance Considerations

While list comprehensions can be more memory efficient than creating lists with loops, it is essential to be mindful of the potential impact when working with large datasets. Using generator expressions can mitigate memory consumption issues:

```
squared_numbers_gen = (x**2 for x in range(10))
```

This creates a generator instead of a list, which yields items one at a time and can be iterated over without occupying the memory that a list would. This is particularly useful when dealing with large sequences.

Visualization Example

To further illustrate the application of list comprehensions, consider plotting the list of squared numbers:

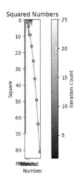

The accompanying plot provides a visual representation of the squared numbers, useful for data analysis and presentation.

List comprehensions are a powerful feature in Python that simplifies list creation and enhances code readability. They are particularly useful for generating filtered and transformed lists efficiently. However, developers must strike a balance between conciseness and clarity, especially when complex comprehensions may reduce code readability. Opting for generator expressions can also be advantageous when dealing with large data sets, achieving memory efficiency without compromising on performance.

3.9 Iterators and Generators

In Python, iterators and generators provide powerful constructs for managing sequences of data in a memory-efficient manner. This section delineates the concepts, implementation, and practical usage of iterators and generators, which facilitate the creation and manipulation of iterable objects.

Iterators

An iterator in Python is an object that implements the iterator protocol, which consists of the methods __iter__() and __next__(). It is used to traverse a container (e.g., lists, tuples) and access its elements incrementally.

Creating an Iterator

To create an iterator, one must define a class that includes the __iter__() and __next__() methods. The __iter__() method returns the iterator object itself, and the __next__() method returns the next value from the container. If there are no more items to return, __next__() raises the StopIteration exception.

Simple Iterator Example

```python
class MyIterator:
    def __init__(self, data):
        self.data = data
        self.index = 0

    def __iter__(self):
        return self

    def __next__(self):
        if self.index < len(self.data):
            result = self.data[self.index]
            self.index += 1
            return result
        else:
            raise StopIteration

# Usage
my_list = [1, 2, 3, 4]
iterator = MyIterator(my_list)
for element in iterator:
```

```
    print(element)
```

Generators

Generators in Python offer a simpler way to create iterators. A generator is a function that uses the `yield` statement to produce a sequence of values. Each time the generator's `__next__()` method is called, execution resumes from where it last left off until it encounters another `yield` statement or raises `StopIteration`.

Creating a Generator Function

Generator functions are defined like regular functions but use `yield` instead of `return` to return data.

Simple Generator Function

```python
def simple_generator():
    yield 1
    yield 2
    yield 3

# Usage
gen = simple_generator()
for value in gen:
    print(value)
```

Generator Expressions

Generator expressions provide a concise syntax for creating generators. They are similar to list comprehensions but use parentheses () instead of square brackets [].

Generator Expression

```python
gen_expr = (x * x for x in range(5))

# Usage
for value in gen_expr:
    print(value)
```

Practical Examples

Fibonacci Sequence

The Fibonacci sequence is a canonical example of using a generator to produce an infinite series efficiently.

Fibonacci Sequence Generator

```python
def fibonacci():
    a, b = 0, 1
    while True:
        yield a
        a, b = b, a + b

# Usage
fib_gen = fibonacci()
for _ in range(10):
    print(next(fib_gen))
```

File Reading

Generators can be used for efficient reading of large files, yielding one line at a time to avoid memory overload.

File Line Generator

```python
def read_file_line_by_line(file_path):
    with open(file_path, 'r') as file:
        for line in file:
            yield line

# Usage
for line in read_file_line_by_line('large_file.txt'):
    print(line)
```

Comparison with Other Constructs

Generators are similar to iterators but offer a more compact and readable way to create iterable sequences. They are particularly useful for operations where the generation of values is computationally intensive or when working with large data sets.

Memory Efficiency

Since generators yield items one at a time, they are more memory-efficient compared to lists that pre-store all items. This is clear in the following code snippet:

Memory Efficiency of Generators

```
gen = (x * x for x in range(1000000)) # Generator Expression
lst = [x * x for x in range(1000000)] # List Comprehension

print(type(gen))
print(type(lst))
```

```
<class 'generator'>
<class 'list'>
```

The generator gen computes values as needed, saving memory compared to the list lst.

Advanced Generator Features

Generators also support combining with other generators, sending values back into the generator, and using the close() method to terminate the generator early.

Combining Generators

Multiple generators can be chained together using generator comprehensions or leveraging functionalities from the itertools library.

Sending Values

By using the send(value) method, one can inject values into the generator, allowing coroutines to be implemented, enhancing the flexibility of generators.

Using send() with Generators

```
def accumulator():
    total = 0
    while True:
        x = yield total
        if x is None:
            break
        total += x

# Usage
gen = accumulator()
next(gen) # Initialize the generator
print(gen.send(10)) # Output: 10
print(gen.send(20)) # Output: 30
gen.close()
```

Understanding and utilizing iterators and generators effectively allows one to write cleaner, more efficient Python code. These constructs are indispensable tools for handling large datasets and implementing complex iteration logic with minimal memory overhead. They form a critical part of the Python programmer's toolkit.

3.10 Using the pass Statement

The pass statement in Python serves as a syntactic placeholder that achieves programmatic continuity without any operational effect. Its primary purpose is to fill blocks of code that are syntactically required but which currently have no implementation. This allows developers to outline the structure of their programs during the initial stages of code development without causing syntax errors.

Consider the following example:

```
def my_function():
    pass
```

Here, my_function is syntactically complete and can be invoked without any immediate side effects, allowing other components of the program to reference it safely.

The pass statement is particularly useful in several scenarios, as detailed below:

- **Function and Class Stubs**: During development, it is often necessary to outline the functions and classes that will be implemented at a later stage. The pass statement facilitates this by providing a no-operation placeholder.

- **Handling Conditionals**: When constructing conditional logic, developers might face situations where specific branches do not require any immediate action. The pass statement ensures that the conditional structure remains intact.

- **Loop Structures**: During the development phase, loop constructs often require placeholders to maintain the syntactic and logical structure.

Function and Class Stubs

103

```
class MyClass:
    def method_a(self):
        pass

    def method_b(self):
        pass
```

This code defines a class `MyClass` with two methods, `method_a` and `method_b`, which currently do nothing. Such stubs ensure that the class skeleton is in place, and future code can safely instantiate `MyClass` and call its methods without encountering `NotImplementedError`.

Handling Conditionals

```
if condition1:
    # Code for condition1
    pass
elif condition2:
    # Code for condition2
    pass
else:
    # Code for else
    pass
```

In this example, placeholders for each conditional branch are specified, ensuring that the program runs syntactically without implementing the actual logic.

Loop Structures

```
for item in iterable:
    pass
```

The pass statement allows developers to focus on other aspects of the code while the loop construct remains syntactically correct.

Practical Considerations

Although pass is useful for maintaining code structure during development, it is crucial to eventually replace all instances of pass with meaningful code. Failure to do so can lead to incomplete implementations and potential logical errors.

Moreover, pass should not be confused with other control statements such as `continue` and `break`, which respectively control the flow by skipping the current iteration and exiting the loop entirely.

In addition, pass does not produce any bytecode, making it an efficient placeholder. Utilizing pass during large-scale codebases planning ensures that code is both syntactically correct and maintainable without incurring extraneous computation or memory overhead.

Below is an illustrative example, combining function stubs, conditionals, and loop structures:

```
class DataProcessor:
    def __init__(self, data):
        self.data = data

    def clean_data(self):
        pass

    def process_data(self):
        if not self.data:
            pass
        else:
            for item in self.data:
                pass

    def display_data(self):
        pass
```

```
Creating an instance of DataProcessor:
processor = DataProcessor([1, 2, 3])

Invoking methods (currently they perform no actions):
processor.clean_data()
processor.process_data()
processor.display_data()
```

This example demonstrates a class `DataProcessor` with methods `clean_data`, `process_data`, and `display_data`, each currently using pass. This approach ensures the overall program structure can be incrementally refined without causing interruptions.

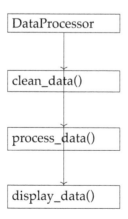

The pass statement serves as an invaluable tool for developers, providing a clear and concise means to maintain program structure during various development stages. It enables the creation of robust code outlines by serving as a placeholder in functions, classes, conditionals, and loop constructs. Its use should be temporary, with an eventual replacement by substantive logic as development progresses.

3.11 Advanced Loop Control with `zip`, `enumerate`, and `range`

In Python, the built-in functions `zip`, `enumerate`, and `range` provide enhanced control and functionality for loop constructs. This section delves into their applications and offers a comprehensive analysis of their utility in advanced loop management.

The `zip` Function

The `zip` function is used to aggregate elements from two or more iterables (e.g., lists, tuples), producing tuples containing elements from each iterable at the corresponding positions. This is particularly useful when iterating over multiple sequences simultaneously.

```python
# Example of zip function
list1 = [1, 2, 3]
list2 = ['a', 'b', 'c']

for num, char in zip(list1, list2):
    print(num, char)
```

```
1 a
2 b
3 c
```

By zipping `list1` and `list2`, we create pairs of elements to iterate over in tandem, significantly simplifying code where simultaneous iteration over multiple collections is required.

The `enumerate` Function

The `enumerate` function adds a counter to an iterable and returns it as an enumerate object. This is often used in conjunction with the `for` loop to access both the index and the value of each item in the iterable.

```python
# Example of enumerate function
words = ['apple', 'banana', 'cherry']
```

106

```
for index, word in enumerate(words):
    print(index, word)
```

```
0 apple
1 banana
2 cherry
```

Using enumerate elegantly circumvents the need to manually manage an index variable, leading to more readable and maintainable code.

The range Function

The range function generates a sequence of numbers, which is particularly useful for controlling loop iterations. range can take one, two, or three arguments to specify the start, stop, and step of the sequence.

```
# Example of range function
for i in range(5): # Generates numbers 0 to 4
    print(i)

for i in range(1, 10, 2): # Generates numbers 1, 3, 5, 7, 9
    print(i)
```

```
0
1
2
3
4
1
3
5
7
9
```

The range function supports complex iteration patterns without requiring explicit initialization and incrementation, enhancing both brevity and clarity.

Combined Usage of zip, enumerate, and range

Combining zip, enumerate, and range within loops can lead to powerful and succinct solutions to complex iteration problems.

```
# Combined usage example
ids = [101, 102, 103]
names = ['Alice', 'Bob', 'Charlie']
scores = [88, 92, 80]

# Loop with zip, enumerate, and range
for i, (id, name, score) in enumerate(zip(ids, names, scores), start=1):
    print(f"{i}: ID={id}, Name={name}, Score={score}")
```

107

```
1: ID=101, Name=Alice, Score=88
2: ID=102, Name=Bob, Score=92
3: ID=103, Name=Charlie, Score=80
```

In this example, zip aggregates ids, names, and scores, enumerate provides an index starting at 1, and all elements are printed neatly. Such combinations underscore the flexibility and power of Python's advanced loop control mechanisms.

Incorporating these functions systematically enhances code readability and efficiency, reduces the potential for errors, and aligns with Python's design philosophy of clarity and simplicity. Employing zip, enumerate, and range in loop constructs is a hallmark of proficient Python programming.

Chapter 4

Functions and Modules

This chapter covers the definition and usage of functions in Python, including function arguments, return values, and scope of variables. It explains default and keyword arguments, variable-length arguments using *args and **kwargs, and recursive functions. Additionally, the chapter introduces lambda functions, decorators, and the concept of modules for code organization. Techniques for importing modules, creating custom modules, and utilizing built-in modules from the Python Standard Library are also discussed.

4.1 Introduction to Functions

A function in Python constitutes a block of organized, reusable code that performs a single, related action. Functions provide a higher degree of modularity and code reuse, enhancing the clarity and maintainability of the code. In this section, we will examine the fundamental concepts of defining and invoking functions in Python.

Function Definition and Syntax

A function is defined using the `def` keyword, followed by the function name and a set of parentheses delineating the function's parameters. The body of the function is indented and includes the code to be executed when the function is called.

Simple Function Definition

```
def greet():
    print("Hello, world!")
```

In the above example, the function greet is defined without any parameters and prints a greeting message when invoked.

Invoking Functions

A defined function can be called by its name followed by parentheses. If the function requires parameters, argument values must be supplied.

Function Call Example

```
greet()
```

When greet() is executed, it outputs:

```
Hello, world!
```

Parameters and Arguments

Functions can accept parameters, allowing for the dynamic input of data when the function is invoked. Parameters are specified within the parentheses in the function definition.

Function with Parameters

```
def greet_person(name):
    print(f"Hello, {name}!")
```

The greet_person function accepts a single parameter name. When the function is called, the argument value is passed to this parameter:

Calling a Function with an Argument

```
greet_person("Alice")
```

This will output:

```
Hello, Alice!
```

Return Statement

Functions can return values using the return statement. The return value can then be assigned to a variable or used directly.

Function with Return Value

```
def add(a, b):
    return a + b
```

110

In this example, the add function computes the sum of its two parameters and returns the result.

Using Return Value

```
result = add(3, 4)
print(result)
```

This code will output:

7

Multiple Return Values

A function can return multiple values by returning a tuple.

Function Returning Multiple Values

```
def arithmetic_operations(a, b):
    return a + b, a - b, a * b, a / b if b != 0 else None
```

When called, this function returns a tuple containing the results of the basic arithmetic operations: addition, subtraction, multiplication, and division.

Receiving Multiple Return Values

```
sum, difference, product, quotient = arithmetic_operations(10, 5)
print(sum, difference, product, quotient)
```

This invocation will output:

15 5 50 2.0

The ability to define and call functions is a foundational aspect of Python programming. As we progress through this chapter, we will explore more advanced features of functions, including arguments, variable scopes, lambda expressions, decorators, recursion, and modules, to build a robust understanding of function utilization and management in Python.

4.2 Defining and Calling Functions

In Python, functions are fundamental building blocks for creating modular, reusable code. This section elucidates the syntax and semantics

111

of defining and calling functions in Python, ensuring a comprehensive understanding of these essential constructs.

Function Definition Syntax

A function in Python is defined using the def keyword, followed by the function name, a pair of parentheses that may enclose parameters, and a colon. The function body contains the statements that constitute the function, indented under the function definition line. The general syntax is presented below:

Function Definition Syntax

```
def function_name(parameters):
    """Docstring describing the function."""
    # Function body statements
    return return_value
```

Docstrings

A docstring is a triple-quoted string that describes the function's purpose and usage. It is a good practice to include a docstring in every function definition to promote code readability and maintainability.

Function Definition with Docstring

```
def greet(name):
    """Function to greet a person with their name."""
    print(f"Hello, {name}!")
```

Calling Functions

To execute a function, it must be invoked or called. This is done by writing the function name followed by parentheses enclosing any required arguments.

Function Call

```
greet("Alice")
```

```
Hello, Alice!
```

112

Arguments and Parameters

When defining functions, the terms 'parameters' and 'arguments' are frequently used:

- **Parameters** are the names listed in the function definition.

- **Arguments** are the values passed to the function when it is called.

Consider the following example:

Function with Multiple Parameters

```
def add(a, b):
    """Function to add two numbers."""
    return a + b
```

When calling the function, the arguments a and b are assigned the values provided:

Function Call with Arguments

```
result = add(5, 7)
print(result)
```

12

Positional and Keyword Arguments

Python supports positional and keyword arguments. Positional arguments must be provided in the order in which the parameters appear in the function definition:

Positional Arguments

```
def power(base, exponent):
    """Function to raise a number to a power."""
    return base ** exponent

print(power(2, 3)) # Positional arguments
```

8

Keyword arguments specify argument values by their parameter names, allowing for flexible order:

Keyword Arguments

```
print(power(exponent=3, base=2)) # Keyword arguments
```

113

8

Mixing Positional and Keyword Arguments

It is possible to mix positional and keyword arguments in function calls. However, positional arguments must precede keyword arguments. The following example demonstrates this:

Mixing Positional and Keyword Arguments

```
print(power(2, exponent=3)) # Valid
# print(power(base=2, 3)) # Invalid: SyntaxError
```

8

Function with Default Parameter Values

Function definitions can include default parameter values, allowing the caller to omit those arguments:

Function with Default Parameter Values

```
def connect_to_server(host='localhost', port=8080):
    """Function to connect to a server with default values for host and port."""
    print(f"Connecting to {host} on port {port}")

connect_to_server() # Calls with default values: 'localhost', 8080
connect_to_server('example.com') # Calls with default host, port 8080
connect_to_server('example.com', 9090) # Calls with both specified
```

```
Connecting to localhost on port 8080
Connecting to example.com on port 8080
Connecting to example.com on port 9090
```

Important Considerations for Default Values

Default values are evaluated only once at function definition time. This detail is crucial when using mutable objects (e.g., lists or dictionaries) as default values:

Mutable Default Parameter Pitfall

```
def append_to_list(value, my_list=[]):
    """Function appending a value to a list with a mutable default parameter."""
    my_list.append(value)
    return my_list

print(append_to_list(1)) # [1]
print(append_to_list(2)) # [1, 2]
```

114

```
[1]
[1, 2]
```

To avoid this, use None as the default value:

Avoiding Mutable Default Parameter Pitfall

```
def append_to_list(value, my_list=None):
    """Function avoiding mutable default parameter pitfall."""
    if my_list is None:
        my_list = []
    my_list.append(value)
    return my_list

print(append_to_list(1)) # [1]
print(append_to_list(2)) # [2]
```

```
[1]
[2]
```

Defining and calling functions in Python involves a clear understanding of function syntax, including parameters and arguments, as well as positional and keyword arguments. Additionally, careful consideration of default parameter values ensures correct function behavior, especially when dealing with mutable objects. The ensuing sections will build upon this foundation, exploring advanced function constructs and practices.

4.3   Function Arguments and Parameters

Function arguments and parameters are fundamental aspects of defining and utilizing functions in Python. Understanding the distinction between these two concepts is crucial for writing modular, reusable, and maintainable code.

Parameters vs. Arguments

Parameters are the variables listed inside the parentheses in the function definition. They serve as placeholders for the values that will be passed to the function when it is called. Arguments, on the other hand, are the actual values provided to the function during a function call.

Example of Parameters and Arguments

```
def add(a, b): # 'a' and 'b' are parameters
    return a + b

result = add(3, 5) # 3 and 5 are arguments
print(result) # Output: 8
```

In the above code, a and b are parameters in the function definition of

115

add. The values 3 and 5 are arguments provided to the function during the call.

Positional Arguments

Positional arguments are the most common form of arguments. They are assigned to parameters based on their position in the function call.

Using Positional Arguments

```
def greet(first_name, last_name):
    print(f"Hello, {first_name} {last_name}!")

greet("John", "Doe")
```

In this example, the string "John" is assigned to the parameter first_name, and "Doe" is assigned to last_name based on their positions.

Keyword Arguments

Keyword arguments allow you to specify the value of a parameter by name, making the function calls more explicit and readable. They also allow you to provide arguments in any order.

Using Keyword Arguments

```
def greet(first_name, last_name):
    print(f"Hello, {first_name} {last_name}!")

greet(last_name="Doe", first_name="John")
```

Here, the name of the parameter is explicitly stated in the function call, making it clear which value is being assigned to which parameter.

Mixing Positional and Keyword Arguments

You can mix positional and keyword arguments in a function call. However, positional arguments must precede keyword arguments.

Mixing Positional and Keyword Arguments

```
def greet(first_name, last_name):
    print(f"Hello, {first_name} {last_name}!")

greet("John", last_name="Doe")
```

Combining the two types can enhance readability and flexibility, as shown above.

Default Arguments

Default arguments allow you to define default values for parameters.

If no argument is provided for a parameter with a default value, the default value is used.

Default Arguments

```
def greet(first_name, last_name="Smith"):
    print(f"Hello, {first_name} {last_name}!")

greet("John")
greet("Jane", "Doe")
```

In this example, the function greet is called twice. The first call uses the default value for last_name, while the second call provides a specific value.

Variable-Length Arguments: *args and **kwargs

Python allows you to define functions that accept a variable number of arguments using *args and **kwargs.

Using *args

The *args syntax allows a function to accept any number of positional arguments. Inside the function, args is a tuple containing the positional arguments.

Variable-Length Positional Arguments with *args

```
def print_numbers(*args):
    for number in args:
        print(number)

print_numbers(1, 2, 3, 4, 5)
```

This function can handle an arbitrary number of positional arguments.

Using **kwargs

The **kwargs syntax allows a function to accept any number of keyword arguments. Inside the function, kwargs is a dictionary containing the keyword arguments.

Variable-Length Keyword Arguments with **kwargs

```
def print_key_value_pairs(**kwargs):
    for key, value in kwargs.items():
        print(f"{key}: {value}")

print_key_value_pairs(name="Alice", age=30, city="New York")
```

This function can handle an arbitrary number of keyword arguments.

Combining *args and **kwargs

117

You can combine *args and **kwargs to create functions that can accept both variable-length positional and keyword arguments.

Combining *args and **kwargs

```
def flexible_function(*args, **kwargs):
    print("Positional arguments:", args)
    print("Keyword arguments:", kwargs)

flexible_function(1, 2, 3, name="Alice", age=30)
```

This combination offers maximum flexibility in terms of the number and type of arguments that can be passed to a function.

In this section, we explored various ways to define and use function arguments and parameters in Python. The distinction between parameters and arguments was clarified, followed by detailed explanations and code examples of positional arguments, keyword arguments, default arguments, and variable-length arguments using *args and **kwargs. Mastery of these concepts is essential for crafting versatile and reusable functions, a foundational skill in Python programming.

4.4 Default and Keyword Arguments

In Python, functions offer a flexible means of dealing with different input scenarios by supporting default and keyword arguments. These features enhance code readability and provide defaults for function parameters, thereby simplifying function calls under varying conditions.

Default arguments allow specifying default values for one or more function parameters. If the caller does not provide values for these parameters, the default values are used. Default arguments must be specified at the end of the parameter list.

Example of Default Arguments

```
def greet(name, msg="Hello"):
    print(f"{msg}, {name}!")

# Function call with both arguments
greet("Alice", "Hi")

# Function call with only the mandatory argument
greet("Bob")
```

The above example demonstrates a function greet that has a mandatory parameter name and an optional parameter msg with a default value of "Hello".

118

```
Hi, Alice!
Hello, Bob!
```

If the caller provides only the name argument, the default value for msg is used, thus simplifying code when default behavior is acceptable.

It is important to note that default argument values are evaluated only once at the time of function definition. This can lead to unexpected behavior when mutable objects (e.g., lists or dictionaries) are used as default values.

Default Argument with Mutable Object

```
def append_to_list(value, my_list=[]):
    my_list.append(value)
    return my_list

# Initial call
result1 = append_to_list(1)
print(result1)

# Subsequent call
result2 = append_to_list(2)
print(result2)
```

```
[1]
[1, 2]
```

As seen, using a mutable object such as a list as a default argument can yield cumulative effects across function calls.

Keyword arguments are another powerful feature that allows calling functions by explicitly stating the parameter names within the call. This promotes readability and helps avoid errors, especially when dealing with functions that have multiple parameters.

Example of Keyword Arguments

```
def describe_pet(animal_type, pet_name):
    print(f"I have a {animal_type}.")
    print(f"My {animal_type}'s name is {pet_name}.")

# Calling function with keyword arguments
describe_pet(animal_type="hamster", pet_name="Harry")

# Reordering keyword arguments
describe_pet(pet_name="Tom", animal_type="cat")
```

```
I have a hamster.
My hamster's name is Harry.
I have a cat.
My cat's name is Tom.
```

When using keyword arguments, the order in which arguments are specified does not matter as long as they are correctly mapped to the corresponding parameter names.

Keyword arguments can be particularly useful in functions with numerous parameters, as they eliminate the need to remember the exact order of parameters.

Default and keyword arguments can be combined to create highly flexible and user-friendly function signatures. When defining such functions, it is imperative to follow specific ordering rules: mandatory positional arguments first, followed by default arguments, and lastly, variable-length arguments such as *args and **kwargs.

Combining Default and Keyword Arguments

```
def build_profile(first, last, age=30, city="unknown", **user_info):
    profile = {
        "first_name": first,
        "last_name": last,
        "age": age,
        "city": city
    }
    profile.update(user_info)
    return profile

# Function call with both positional and keyword arguments
user_profile = build_profile("John", "Doe", city="New York", hobby="reading")
print(user_profile)
```

```
{'first_name': 'John', 'last_name': 'Doe', 'age': 30, 'city': 'New York', 'hobby': 'reading'}
```

In the above example, the build_profile function utilizes a mix of mandatory positional arguments (first, last), default arguments (age, city), and a variable number of keyword arguments (**user_info). This combination provides a versatile way to handle various input configurations.

Default and keyword arguments are vital tools for enhancing function flexibility and readability in Python. Default arguments allow specifying fallback values, while keyword arguments permit explicit naming of parameters in function calls. The strategic combination of these features can lead to more maintainable and user-friendly code.

4.5 Variable-length Arguments: *args and **kwargs

In Python, functions can accept a varying number of arguments using the special syntax of *args and **kwargs. These constructs provide flexibility, allowing functions to operate on different numbers and types of input parameters. This section delves deeply into these mechanisms, explaining their usage, implications, and best practices.

Using *args

The *args syntax allows a function to accept any number of positional arguments. These arguments are captured as a tuple. This is particularly useful when the number of input arguments is not fixed.

Using *args to accept variable-length positional arguments

```
def example_function(*args):
    for arg in args:
        print(arg)

example_function(1, 2, 3)
example_function('a', 'b', 'c', 'd')
```

In the above example, `example_function` can handle different numbers of positional arguments seamlessly. The *args variable collects additional arguments into a tuple, enabling iteration and further processing within the function.

```
1
2
3
a
b
c
d
```

Using **kwargs

The **kwargs syntax allows a function to accept any number of keyword arguments. These keyword arguments are captured as a dictionary. This approach is beneficial when dealing with a dynamic set of keyword-value pairs.

Using **kwargs to accept variable-length keyword arguments

```
def example_function(**kwargs):
    for key, value in kwargs.items():
        print(f"{key} = {value}")

example_function(first_name="John", last_name="Doe")
example_function(a=1, b=2, c=3)
```

In the above example, `example_function` can process any number of keyword arguments, facilitating flexible function calls.

```
first_name = John
last_name = Doe
a = 1
b = 2
c = 3
```

Combining *args and **kwargs

It is possible to use both *args and **kwargs in a single function definition. However, the order in the function signature must be followed: *args should precede **kwargs.

Combining *args and **kwargs in a function

```
def example_function(arg1, *args, **kwargs):
    print(f"arg1 = {arg1}")
    print("args:", args)
    print("kwargs:", kwargs)

example_function(10, 20, 30, first_name="John", last_name="Doe")
```

In this function, arg1 captures the first positional argument, *args captures any additional positional arguments, and **kwargs captures keyword arguments.

```
arg1 = 10
args: (20, 30)
kwargs: {'first_name': 'John', 'last_name': 'Doe'}
```

Usage Scenarios

*args and **kwargs are particularly useful in scenarios where a function might need to handle a variable number of parameters, such as in:

- **Logging Functions**: Capturing variable amounts of log information.

- **Event Handlers**: Handling diverse events with different parameters.

- **Utility Functions**: Implementing generalized functions that apply to a wide range of inputs.

Best Practices

When using *args and **kwargs, consider adopting the following best practices:

122

- **Explicit is Better**: Clearly document the expected arguments and their types.

- **Validation**: Validate and handle arguments inside the function to ensure correctness and robustness.

- **Readability**: Use meaningful names for parameters, such as *values or **options, to enhance code readability.

Understanding and utilizing *args and **kwargs is essential for writing flexible and maintainable Python code. These constructs empower developers to create functions that can handle varying inputs gracefully, contributing to more reusable and robust software designs.

4.6 Return Statement and Returning Multiple Values

The return statement is a fundamental concept in Python that enables functions to output values back to the caller. This section delves into the operational mechanics of the return statement, detailing how it is used to return single and multiple values effectively.

A function's execution culminates upon encountering a return statement. This directive terminates the function, optionally sending an expression's value back to the caller. If no expression follows return, or if return is entirely omitted, the function returns None by default.

Basic usage of the return statement

```
def add(a, b):
    return a + b

result = add(5, 3)
print(result) # Output: 8
```

In the example above, the return statement concludes the add function and returns the sum of a and b.

Python's functions support multiple return values utilizing tuples. This feature allows functions to return multiple pieces of data simultaneously in a structured manner.

Returning multiple values using tuples

```
def get_name_and_age():
    name = "Alice"
```

123

```
    age = 30
    return name, age

name, age = get_name_and_age()
print(name) # Output: Alice
print(age) # Output: 30
```

Here, get_name_and_age returns two values: name and age. These values are automatically packed into a tuple and can subsequently be unpacked by the caller.

To return multiple values, Python implicitly packs them into a tuple, as demonstrated earlier. On the caller side, this tuple can be unpacked into individual variables.

Tuple packing and unpacking

```
def get_coordinates():
    x = 10
    y = 20
    return x, y

coordinates = get_coordinates()
print(coordinates) # Output: (10, 20)

x, y = get_coordinates()
print(x) # Output: 10
print(y) # Output: 20
```

In this example, a tuple is packed with the x and y values from get_coordinates. This tuple is then either directly accessed or unpacked into separate variables, x and y.

For more readability, especially when returning multiple values, Python offers named tuples through the collections.namedtuple module. Named tuples provide descriptive fields, enhancing code clarity.

Using named tuples for returning multiple values

```
from collections import namedtuple

Person = namedtuple('Person', ['name', 'age'])

def get_person():
    return Person(name="Bob", age=25)

person = get_person()
print(person) # Output: Person(name='Bob', age=25)
print(person.name) # Output: Bob
print(person.age) # Output: 25
```

By returning a named tuple, get_person allows access to its elements by names, improving both readability and maintainability of the code.

124

When designing functions that return multiple values, consider the following best practices:

- Use single return values whenever possible for simplicity.

- When returning multiple values, ensure they are logically related.

- Employ named tuples for improved readability and context.

- Document the returned values clearly to aid maintainability.

These practices help maintain code clarity and enhance functionality, making the return statements more predictable and intuitive.

Proper use of the `return` statement is critical for controlling the flow of Python functions and managing output values. The capability to return multiple values through tuples, especially named tuples, adds flexibility and clarity. By adhering to best practices, developers can create more maintainable and readable code that efficiently communicates a function's purpose and output.

4.7 Scope and Lifetime of Variables in Functions

Understanding the scope and lifetime of variables in functions is crucial for effective Python programming. This section delves into how variables interact with function calls, including local and global scopes, the LEGB rule, and the implications of variable lifetimes.

The concept of variable scope determines where in the code a variable can be accessed. In Python, variable scope is categorized into four distinct types, following the LEGB rule:

- **Local scope**: Variables created inside a function belong to the local scope of that function, which means they can only be used within that function.

- **Enclosing scope**: Variables in the local scope of enclosing functions (non-global) can be accessed in nested functions.

- **Global scope**: Variables declared at the top level of a script or module, or explicitly declared as global using the `global` keyword.

- **Built-in scope**: Variables that are predefined in the Python interpreter, such as `len` or `range`.

Variables declared inside a function are local to that function. Local variables are created when a function starts executing and are destroyed when the function exits.

Example of local scope

```
def local_scope_example():
    local_var = 10
    print(local_var)

local_scope_example()
# Output: 10
print(local_var)
# Output: NameError: name 'local_var' is not defined
```

In the example above, `local_var` is not accessible outside `local_scope_example()`. Attempting to access it outside the function results in a `NameError`.

Variables defined outside of functions are in the global scope and can be accessed from anywhere in the module. To modify a global variable inside a function, the `global` keyword must be used.

Example of global scope

```
global_var = 20

def global_scope_example():
    global global_var
    global_var = 30
    print(global_var)

global_scope_example()
# Output: 30
print(global_var)
# Output: 30
```

Without the `global` keyword, attempts to modify the global variable inside the function would create a new local variable instead.

Functions defined inside other functions have a special scope known as the enclosing or nonlocal scope. Enclosing scopes are neither local to the nested function nor global, but they can be accessed and modified using the `nonlocal` keyword.

Example of enclosing scope

```
def outer_function():
    enclosing_var = 40

    def inner_function():
```

126

```
        nonlocal enclosing_var
        enclosing_var = 50
        print(enclosing_var)

    inner_function()
    print(enclosing_var)

outer_function()
# Output: 50
# Output: 50
```

The nonlocal keyword allows inner_function() to modify enclosing_var from the outer_function() scope.

The built-in scope contains Python's predefined functions and exceptions. Built-in names can be accessed from any scope within a Python program.

Example of built-in scope

```
def built_in_scope_example():
    print(len([1, 2, 3]))

built_in_scope_example()
# Output: 3
```

Here, len is a built-in function that is accessible within the local scope of built_in_scope_example().

The lifetime of a variable refers to the duration for which it exists in memory. Local variables are created when a function is called and destroyed when the function exits. Global variables, on the other hand, persist for the duration of the program's execution.

Consider the function below to demonstrate this concept:

Lifetime demonstration of local variables

```
def lifetime_example():
    local_var = 'I exist only within this function'
    print(local_var)

lifetime_example()
# Output: I exist only within this function
print(local_var)
# Output: NameError: name 'local_var' is not defined
```

In the preceding example, local_var is created, utilized, and destroyed all within the call to lifetime_example(). Attempting to access local_var outside the function results in a NameError.

Understanding the scope and lifetime of variables in Python functions is fundamental for writing effective and bug-free code. Proper man-

127

agement of local, nonlocal/enclosing, global, and built-in scopes can significantly influence the behavior and readability of your programs.

4.8 Lambda Functions and Anonymous Functions

Lambda functions, also known as anonymous functions, are a compact way to define simple functions in Python. They are particularly useful in scenarios where a small function is required for a short duration or for functional programming constructs like map, filter, and reduce.

A lambda function is defined using the lambda keyword, followed by a list of parameters, a colon, and an expression. The syntax is as follows:

```
lambda arguments: expression
```

The lambda keyword is used to create a new function object, and the created function is an anonymous function because it does not have a name:

```
# Example of a lambda function
square = lambda x: x * x
print(square(4)) # Outputs: 16
```

In the example above, square is a lambda function that takes one argument x and returns x squared.

Lambda functions are often used within higher-order functions, which are functions that take other functions as arguments. Common higher-order functions used with lambda functions include map(), filter(), and reduce().

The map() function applies a given function to all items in an input list:

```
# Apply a lambda function to square each item in a list
numbers = [1, 2, 3, 4]
squared_numbers = list(map(lambda x: x * x, numbers))
print(squared_numbers) # Outputs: [1, 4, 9, 16]
```

The filter() function constructs an iterator from elements of an iterable for which a function returns True:

```
# Filter out the even numbers from a list
numbers = [1, 2, 3, 4]
even_numbers = list(filter(lambda x: x % 2 == 0, numbers))
print(even_numbers) # Outputs: [2, 4]
```

The reduce() function, which is part of the functools module, applies a rolling computation to sequential pairs of values in a list:

```
from functools import reduce

# Use a lambda function to sum the numbers in a list
numbers = [1, 2, 3, 4]
sum_of_numbers = reduce(lambda x, y: x + y, numbers)
print(sum_of_numbers) # Outputs: 10
```

While lambda functions provide a concise way to define functions, they have limitations compared to regular functions defined with the def keyword. Lambda functions are restricted to a single expression and cannot contain statements or annotations. This makes them less versatile than regular functions but very useful for short-lived, simple functions.

Regular function definition:

```
# Define a regular function
def add(x, y):
    return x + y

print(add(3, 4)) # Outputs: 7
```

Equivalent lambda function:

```
# Define a lambda function equivalent to the add() function
add = lambda x, y: x + y
print(add(3, 4)) # Outputs: 7
```

While lambda functions are powerful for writing concise code, it's essential to use them judiciously. Overuse of lambda functions, especially for complex operations, can lead to code that is difficult to read and maintain. Lambda functions are best suited for simple operations and should be avoided for more complex logic where regular functions provide better readability and maintainability.

When using lambda functions, ensure that:

- They perform simple operations that are easily understandable.

- They are used within higher-order functions like map(), filter(), and reduce() when appropriate.

- Code readability is not sacrificed for conciseness.

By maintaining these practices, you can leverage the power of lambda functions effectively while ensuring your code remains clean and comprehensible.

4.9 Decorators

Decorators are a powerful and elegant feature in Python that enable the modification of the behavior of functions or methods. They are especially useful for code reuse and for the augmentation of function capabilities in a clean and readable manner. Decorators are themselves functions that return wrapped functions, thereby allowing additional functionality to be added to existing code seamlessly.

A decorator is essentially a higher-order function that takes another function as input and returns a new function that adds or alters the behavior of the original function. Decorators are often used to log function calls, validate parameters, modify outputs, and add pre- or post-processing steps.

Basic Decorator Example

```python
def my_decorator(func):
    def wrapper():
        print("Something before the function executes.")
        func()
        print("Something after the function executes.")
    return wrapper

@my_decorator
def say_hello():
    print("Hello!")

say_hello()
```

In this example, the my_decorator function is applied to the say_hello function by using the @my_decorator syntax. When say_hello is called, the output will be:

```
Something before the function executes.
Hello!
Something after the function executes.
```

Function decorators are the most common type of decorators and can accept and return any type of callable (functions, methods, lambda functions). The following example demonstrates a simple decorator for measuring the execution time of a function:

Execution Time Decorator

```python
import time

def timer_decorator(func):
    def wrapper(*args, **kwargs):
        start_time = time.time()
        result = func(*args, **kwargs)
        end_time = time.time()
        print(f"Function {func.__name__} took {end_time - start_time} seconds to
```

```
              complete.")
        return result
    return wrapper

@timer_decorator
def perform_task(seconds):
    time.sleep(seconds)
    return "Task Completed"

print(perform_task(2))
```

When perform_task(2) is called, the output will display the execution time of the function, providing insights into performance characteristics.

Decorators can also be defined to accept arguments by introducing another layer of function encapsulation. This is useful when you need to parameterize your decorator. Below is an example of a decorator that can log function calls with a customizable message.

Decorator with Arguments

```
def log_message(message):
    def decorator(func):
        def wrapper(*args, **kwargs):
            print(f"{message} - Function {func.__name__} is called.")
            return func(*args, **kwargs)
        return wrapper
    return decorator

@log_message("INFO")
def process_data(data):
    return f"Processing {data}"

print(process_data("Sample Data"))
```

The output will include the customizable log message:

```
INFO - Function process_data is called.
Processing Sample Data
```

Decorators can also be applied to classes. Such decorators usually perform tasks like modifying class attributes or methods. The following example demonstrates a class decorator that adds a timestamp to an instance when it is created.

Class Decorator Example

```
import datetime

def timestamp_decorator(cls):
    class Wrapped(cls):
        def __init__(self, *args, **kwargs):
            super().__init__(*args, **kwargs)
            self.timestamp = datetime.datetime.now()
    return Wrapped
```

131

```
@timestamp_decorator
class DataModel:
    def __init__(self, data):
        self.data = data

model = DataModel("Sample Data")
print(f"Data: {model.data}, Timestamp: {model.timestamp}")
```

The output will show the instance data along with the creation timestamp:

```
Data: Sample Data, Timestamp: 2023-01-01 12:00:00
```

Python provides several built-in decorators, such as @staticmethod, @classmethod, and @property. These decorators are used to define methods that are not tied to instance creation, methods that are bound to class instead of instance, and properties that act like attributes but provide getter and setter methods respectively.

Built-in Decorator Example

```
class ExampleClass:
    @staticmethod
    def static_method():
        return "This is a static method"

    @classmethod
    def class_method(cls):
        return f"This is a class method from {cls}"

    @property
    def example_property(self):
        return "This is a property"

example = ExampleClass()
print(ExampleClass.static_method())
print(ExampleClass.class_method())
print(example.example_property)
```

The outputs are as shown below:

```
This is a static method
This is a class method from <class '__main__.ExampleClass'>
This is a property
```

Decorators offer a robust mechanism for extending and modifying the behavior of functions and classes in Python. They promote the principles of code reuse and separation of concerns by isolating secondary aspects like logging, timing, and validation from the core logic. Mastery of decorators is essential for advanced Python programming, enabling the creation of cleaner, more maintainable, and scalable software systems.

4.10   Recursive Functions

Recursive functions are a powerful technique for solving problems that can be broken down into smaller, simpler subproblems. A recursive function calls itself within its own definition, allowing it to operate on smaller instances of the same problem until a base case is reached.

Defining Recursive Functions

To create a recursive function, one must identify the base case that will terminate the recursive calls and the recursive step that reduces the complexity of the problem. The base case is essential to prevent infinite recursion and eventual stack overflow errors.

Example of a Recursive Function: Factorial Calculation

```
def factorial(n):
    if n == 0:
        return 1 # Base case
    else:
        return n * factorial(n-1) # Recursive step

print(factorial(5)) # Output: 120
```

In the example above, the factorial function calculates the factorial of a non-negative integer n. The base case is when $n = 0$, wherein the function returns 1. Otherwise, the function calls itself with $n - 1$ and multiplies the result by n.

Understanding the Call Stack

Recursive functions utilize the call stack to keep track of the different states of each function call. Each call to a recursive function places a new frame on the call stack until the base case is reached. After reaching the base case, the function returns and the call stack unwinds.

Consider the trace of the call stack for factorial(3):

```
factorial(3) --> 3 * factorial(2)
factorial(2) --> 2 * factorial(1)
factorial(1) --> 1 * factorial(0)
factorial(0) --> 1
```

When the base case is reached with factorial(0), it returns 1, and each previous call on the stack completes in reverse order.

Common Problems Solved Using Recursion

Many classic computer science problems are naturally suited for recursive solutions. Some of these include:

133

- **Fibonacci Sequence**: Each number in the sequence is the sum of the two preceding ones.

- **Tree Traversals**: Traversing binary trees and other hierarchical structures.

- **Backtracking Algorithms**: Solving puzzles and combinatorial problems, such as the N-Queens problem.

Example of Recursive Fibonacci Sequence

```python
def fibonacci(n):
    if n == 0:
        return 0 # Base case
    elif n == 1:
        return 1 # Base case
    else:
        return fibonacci(n-1) + fibonacci(n-2) # Recursive step

print(fibonacci(6)) # Output: 8
```

In the fibonacci function, there are two base cases: when $n = 0$ and $n = 1$. For all other values, the function calls itself with $n - 1$ and $n - 2$, summing their results.

Optimizing Recursive Functions

Recursive algorithms can sometimes be inefficient due to repeated calculations. Memoization is a technique to optimize recursive functions by storing the results of expensive function calls and reusing them when the same inputs occur again.

Memoized Fibonacci Function

```python
def fibonacci_memo(n, memo={}):
    if n in memo:
        return memo[n]
    if n == 0:
        return 0
    elif n == 1:
        return 1
    else:
        result = fibonacci_memo(n-1, memo) + fibonacci_memo(n-2, memo)
        memo[n] = result
        return result

print(fibonacci_memo(6)) # Output: 8
```

In the fibonacci_memo function, a dictionary memo is used to store the results of previously computed Fibonacci numbers, significantly reducing the time complexity from exponential to linear.

Recursion Versus Iteration

134

While recursion provides an elegant approach for problems that exhibit self-similarity, it can sometimes be more resource-intensive than iterative solutions, especially in languages or environments with limited stack depth. It is important to analyze the nature of the problem and choose the most appropriate method accordingly.

Iterative Fibonacci Function

```python
def fibonacci_iterative(n):
    if n == 0:
        return 0
    elif n == 1:
        return 1
    a, b = 0, 1
    for _ in range(2, n+1):
        a, b = b, a + b
    return b

print(fibonacci_iterative(6)) # Output: 8
```

The `fibonacci_iterative` function provides the same result as its recursive counterpart but uses an iterative approach, which avoids the overhead associated with recursive calls.

Recursive functions are a versatile and powerful tool in a programmer's toolkit, especially for problems that can be naturally divided into simpler subproblems. However, careful consideration is needed to ensure that the base case is well-defined and that performance impacts are managed, either through optimization techniques like memoization or by employing iterative solutions where appropriate.

4.11 Introduction to Modules

In Python, a module is a file containing Python code, which can include functions, classes, and variables. Modules are used to logically organize code by grouping related functionalities into a single file or namespace. This organization promotes code reuse, maintainability, and readability, making complex applications easier to manage.

The Python Standard Library provides a rich set of built-in modules offering various functionalities ready for use. This section covers the basics of modules, including creating, importing, and utilizing them effectively.

- Creating a Module
- Importing a Module

- Understanding Module Search Path

- Using __name__ and __main__

- Reloading a Module

- Module Packages

Creating a Module

A Python module is simply a file with a .py extension that contains Python code. A module can include definitions of functions, classes, and variables, as well as executable statements.

Sample module `mymodule.py`

```python
# mymodule.py

def add(a, b):
    return a + b

def subtract(a, b):
    return a - b

class Calculator:
    def multiply(self, a, b):
        return a * b

    def divide(self, a, b):
        if b == 0:
            raise ValueError("Cannot divide by zero")
        return a / b

PI = 3.14159
```

In this example, `mymodule.py` contains two function definitions, a class definition with methods, and a variable.

Importing a Module

To use the code from a module, it needs to be imported into your script or interactive session. Python offers several ways to import modules.

- Basic Import

- Import Specific Items

- Renaming Modules

- Import All Names

Basic Import:

The simplest form of import uses the `import` statement.

Importing `mymodule`

```
import mymodule

result = mymodule.add(10, 5)
print(result) # Output: 15
```

In this example, the entire `mymodule` is imported, and its `add` function is called using the dot notation.

Import Specific Items:

You can import specific attributes from a module using the `from` clause.

Importing specific functions from `mymodule`

```
from mymodule import add, subtract

result = add(7, 3)
print(result) # Output: 10

difference = subtract(7, 3)
print(difference) # Output: 4
```

This approach makes the imported functions directly accessible by their names without the module prefix.

Renaming Modules:

For convenience or to avoid name conflicts, you can rename a module during import using the as keyword.

Renaming `mymodule`

```
import mymodule as mm

result = mm.add(5, 5)
print(result) # Output: 10
```

Here, `mymodule` is imported as `mm`, which can be used as a shorter alias.

Import All Names:

You can import all names from a module using the * symbol. However, this is generally discouraged as it can lead to namespace pollution.

Importing all names from `mymodule`

```
from mymodule import *

print(add(8, 2)) # Output: 10
print(subtract(8, 2)) # Output: 6
```

This imports all public attributes from `mymodule` into the current namespace, making them accessible without prefix.

Understanding Module Search Path

When a module is imported, Python searches for the module in specific locations. These locations are defined by the sys.path list, which includes the directory containing the input script (or the current directory), followed by directories listed in the PYTHONPATH (an environment variable), and finally the installation-dependent default directories.

Printing sys.path

```
import sys
print(sys.path)
```

```
['', '/usr/local/lib/python3.9', '/usr/lib/python3.9', ...]
```

By modifying sys.path, you can control where Python looks for modules.

Using __name__ and __main__

Modules can be executed as standalone scripts or imported by other modules. The __name__ special variable determines the module's execution context. When a module is run directly, __name__ is set to __main__. This allows conditional execution of code blocks.

Using __name__ and __main__

```
# mymodule.py

def main():
    print("This is a script running directly")

if __name__ == "__main__":
    main()
```

When mymodule.py is executed directly, the main function will be called.

Reloading a Module

During development, you may need to reload a module after modifying it. This can be accomplished using the reload function from the importlib module.

Reloading a module

```
import importlib
import mymodule

importlib.reload(mymodule)
```

This can be useful in interactive sessions where the same module is repeatedly modified and tested.

Module Packages

A package is a way of organizing related modules hierarchically using a directory structure. Each package is represented by a directory containing a special __init__.py file, indicating that the directory is a package.

Directory structure for `mypackage`

```
mypackage/
    __init__.py
    module1.py
    module2.py
```

`__init__.py` can be empty or execute the package initialization code. Modules within the package can be imported as follows:

Importing from a package

```
from mypackage import module1, module2

module1.some_function()
module2.another_function()
```

Modules are fundamental units for organizing Python code into manageable, reusable components. By leveraging modules, developers can create clean, modular, and maintainable code. Understanding the various import techniques, the module search path, and the concept of packages is essential for effective Python programming.

4.12 Importing Modules and Packages

Modules and packages are fundamental to organizing, maintaining, and navigating large codebases in Python. By compartmentalizing code into smaller, reusable components, developers can enhance both code readability and modularity. This section delves into the syntax and mechanisms for importing modules and packages, and elaborates on strategies to leverage these imports effectively.

Basic Import Syntax

Importing a module in Python is achieved using the `import` statement. Consider the following example where we import the `math` module:

```
import math
```

Once imported, module functions and constants are accessed using dot notation:

```
result = math.sqrt(16)
print(result) # Output: 4.0
```

Selective Importing with `from ... import`

To minimize namespace clutter and enhance readability, Python allows selective importing of specific attributes or functions from a module using the `from ... import` construct. For instance:

```
from math import sqrt
result = sqrt(16)
print(result) # Output: 4.0
```

Importing All Attributes with `from ... import *`

In situations where a large number of attributes are needed from a module, importing everything using the wildcard `*` is an option. This approach, however, should be used cautiously due to potential namespace pollution:

```
from math import *
result = sqrt(16)
print(result) # Output: 4.0
```

Alias Importing with `as`

For convenience, especially with modules having lengthy names, Python supports aliasing via the as keyword:

```
import numpy as np
array = np.array([1, 2, 3])
print(array)
```

Importing Packages

Packages are directories containing a collection of modules and an `__init__.py` file. Importing packages follows the same principles as modules. Given a package directory structure as:

```
mypackage/
    __init__.py
    module1.py
    module2.py
```

Different import scenarios include:

```
# Import the entire package
import mypackage

# Import a single module from the package
from mypackage import module1

# Import a specific function from a module in the package
```

```
from mypackage.module1 import my_function
```

Relative Imports in Packages

Within a package, modules may import each other using relative imports:

```
# In module2.py, importing module1 using a relative import
from . import module1

# Importing a specific attribute from module1
from .module1 import some_function
```

Relative imports use dot notation to indicate the current and parent directories.

Ensuring Efficient Imports

Efficient imports are vital for optimizing performance and memory usage in Python applications.

- **Minimize redundancy:** Avoid re-importing modules within the same file.

- **Lazy imports:** Import a module only when it is needed rather than at the start of the file.

- **Optimize search paths:** Manipulate the sys.path if necessary to ensure relevant modules are located efficiently.

Practical Example: Building a Package

Consider the following scenario of building a practical package:

```
mypackage/
    __init__.py
    arithmetic.py
    geometry.py
```

arithmetic.py:

```
def add(a, b):
    return a + b

def subtract(a, b):
    return a - b
```

geometry.py:

```
import math

def area_of_circle(radius):
    return math.pi * (radius ** 2)
```

141

Clients can use the package as follows:

```python
# Importing the entire package
import mypackage

# Using functions from individual modules
from mypackage.arithmetic import add, subtract
from mypackage.geometry import area_of_circle

print(add(5, 3)) # Output: 8
print(subtract(5, 3)) # Output: 2
print(area_of_circle(3)) # Output: 28.274333882308138
```

This concise example illustrates how modular code organization facilitates ease of use and efficient development practices.

Mastering module and package imports is paramount for scalable and maintainable Python applications. The mechanisms for importing—ranging from basic imports to more advanced techniques such as selective, alias, and relative imports—enable developers to maintain clean and efficient namespaces. Leveraging these import strategies permits streamlined and organized code, fostering both collaborative and solo development efforts. The principles and examples provided herein should serve as a foundational guide, empowering you with the knowledge to structure your Python projects with increased clarity and efficiency.

4.13   Creating and Using Custom Modules

In Python, organizing code into modules is a fundamental practice that facilitates maintainability and reuse. A module is simply a file containing Python definitions and statements. The module's name is the same as the file name, excluding the .py extension. This section will delve into the creation of custom modules and their utilization within Python programs.

Creating a Custom Module

To create a custom module, follow these steps:

1. Create a new Python file with a .py extension.

2. Define functions, classes, and variables as needed within this file.

Consider the following example. We will create a module named mymath.py that contains a set of mathematical functions:

File: mymath.py

```
def add(a, b):
    """Return the sum of a and b."""
    return a + b

def subtract(a, b):
    """Return the difference of a and b."""
    return a - b

def multiply(a, b):
    """Return the product of a and b."""
    return a * b

def divide(a, b):
    """Return the division of a by b. Raise an error if b is zero."""
    if b == 0:
        raise ValueError("Cannot divide by zero")
    return a / b
```

Importing Custom Modules

To use the mymath module in another Python program, we import it using Python's import statement. This can be done in several ways:

Standard Import

A standard import statement allows access to all the module's functions and classes:

Standard Import Example

```
import mymath

result = mymath.add(10, 5)
print(f"Addition: {result}")
```

Import Specific Functions

To import specific functions from the module, use the from ... import ... syntax:

Import Specific Functions Example

```
from mymath import add, divide

addition_result = add(10, 5)
```

```
division_result = divide(10, 2)
print(f"Addition: {addition_result}, Division: {division_result}")
```

Import with Alias

Sometimes module names may be lengthy or conflict with other names in your code. In such cases, you can assign an alias to the module using the as keyword:

Import with Alias Example

```
import mymath as mm

result = mm.multiply(7, 6)
print(f"Multiplication: {result}")
```

Module Search Path

Python looks for modules in specific directories. The search path is stored in the sys.path list, which includes the directory containing the input script (or current directory), PYTHONPATH (if set), and the installation-dependent default path.

View Module Search Path

```
import sys

print(sys.path)
```

You can modify sys.path to include additional directories where your modules might be located:

Modify Module Search Path

```
import sys

# Add a specific directory to the module search path
sys.path.append('/path/to/your/modules')

import mymath

# Now you can use mymath as usual
result = mymath.add(3, 4)
print(f"Addition: {result}")
```

Module Initialization Code

Modules can execute initialization code at the import time. This is helpful for setting up necessary configurations or initializing state.

Initialization Code in Module

```
# File: mymodule.py
print("Initializing mymodule...")

initialized = True
```

When this module is imported, the initialization code is executed:

Using Module with Initialization Code

```
import mymodule
# Output: Initializing mymodule...
```

Organizing Code with Packages

A package is a collection of modules organized in directories that include a special __init__.py file. This file can be empty or contain initialization code for the package. Below is an example of a package structure:

```
mypackage/

    __init__.py
    module1.py
    module2.py
```

File: mypackage/module1.py

```
# module1.py

def func1():
    print("Function 1 in module 1")
```

File: mypackage/module2.py

```
# module2.py

def func2():
    print("Function 2 in module 2")
```

To use the functions within these modules:

Importing from a Package

```
from mypackage import module1, module2

module1.func1()
```

```
module2.func2()
```

Packages allow for a hierarchical structuring of the module namespace, making it easier to manage large codebases.

Best Practices for Modules

When creating and using custom modules, adhere to the following best practices:

- Keep the module's purpose clear and focused. Each module should serve a specific, coherent purpose.

- Avoid circular imports. These occur when two modules depend on each other. Refactor the code to minimize such dependencies.

- Document your modules with docstrings, detailing the functionality of functions, classes, and modules.

- Use descriptive names for modules to clarify their purpose and avoid naming conflicts.

Following these guidelines ensures that your modules are reusable, maintainable, and easy to understand.

4.14 Built-in Modules and Standard Library

The Python programming language is renowned for its extensive standard library, which equips developers with a rich set of modules and packages that cater to various applications, thereby simplifying the software development process. This section explores the concept of built-in modules within Python's standard library, discussing their utility and presenting examples of some commonly used modules.

Overview of the Standard Library

Python's standard library comprises a vast collection of modules bundled with the Python installation. These modules span numerous domains like file I/O, system calls, sockets, data serialization, and more, enabling developers to address a wide range of programming tasks without the need for third-party libraries. The standard library embodies Python's core design philosophy of simplifying common programming tasks and enhancing developer productivity.

Commonly Used Standard Library Modules

Here, we present some of the most frequently utilized modules from the Python standard library:

sys

The sys module grants access to variables used or maintained by the Python interpreter and includes functions to interact with the interpreter.

Example usage of the sys module

```
import sys

# Get the list of command line arguments
print(sys.argv)

# Exit the program
sys.exit()
```

os

The os module provides a way to interact with the operating system in a platform-independent manner.

Example usage of the os module

```
import os

# Get the current working directory
cwd = os.getcwd()
print("Current Working Directory:", cwd)

# List the contents of a directory
contents = os.listdir(cwd)
print("Directory Contents:", contents)
```

datetime

The datetime module supplies classes for manipulating dates and times.

Example usage of the datetime module

```python
from datetime import datetime

# Get the current date and time
now = datetime.now()
print("Current Date and Time:", now)

# Format the current date and time
formatted_date = now.strftime("%Y-%m-%d %H:%M:%S")
print("Formatted Date:", formatted_date)
```

math

The math module provides access to mathematical functions and constants defined by the C standard.

Example usage of the math module

```python
import math

# Calculate the square root
sqrt_value = math.sqrt(16)
print("Square Root of 16:", sqrt_value)

# Calculate the sine of a value
sine_value = math.sin(math.pi / 2)
print("Sine of /2:", sine_value)
```

json

The json module offers methods to encode and decode JSON (JavaScript Object Notation) data.

Example usage of the json module

```python
import json

# Convert a Python dictionary to a JSON string
data = {'name': 'Alice', 'age': 30, 'city': 'New York'}
json_string = json.dumps(data)
print("JSON String:", json_string)

# Convert a JSON string to a Python dictionary
python_dict = json.loads(json_string)
print("Python Dictionary:", python_dict)
```

148

Locating and Understanding Standard Library Modules

To explore more modules within the standard library, Python provides comprehensive documentation accessible online or via the local machine. The pydoc utility is a valuable tool for viewing detailed documentation about standard library modules and functions directly from the command line.

Using pydoc to browse the standard library documentation

```
pydoc sys
pydoc os
```

Additionally, the official Python documentation website offers an exhaustive list of all available modules in the standard library, complete with examples and usage guidelines. This resource is indispensable for developers looking to leverage the full potential of Python's built-in capabilities.

Advantages of Built-in Modules

The built-in modules of the Python standard library provide several key advantages:

- **Reduced Development Time**: Ready-to-use modules eliminate the need to write common functionalities from scratch.

- **Consistency and Reliability**: Being part of the core distribution, these modules undergo thorough testing and are maintained by the Python core development team.

- **Portability**: Code written using standard library modules is generally more portable across different systems and Python installations.

By exploring the significance and utility of Python's built-in modules and the standard library, it is evident that these modules furnish a robust set of tools for various programming tasks, streamlining the development process and enhancing code reliability and portability. The examples and guidelines provided should equip developers to effectively utilize the ample resources available in the standard library, thus augmenting productivity and contributing to the creation of efficient and maintainable Python programs.

Chapter 5

Data Structures

This chapter provides an in-depth look at Python's built-in data structures, including lists, tuples, sets, and dictionaries. It covers the creation, access, modification, and common operations for each data structure, along with specialized techniques like list comprehensions and nested data structures. The chapter also introduces advanced data structures such as stacks, queues, and linked lists, emphasizing their practical applications and implementation in Python.

5.1 Introduction to Data Structures

In this section, we delineate the concept of data structures, focusing on their significance, classification, and practical applications within the context of Python programming. Data structures are a foundational aspect of computer science, providing a systematic way to manage and organize data to enable efficient access and modification.

\pagebreak

Definition and Importance

A data structure is a particular way of organizing data in a computer so that it can be used efficiently. Different data structures are suited for different kinds of applications, and some are highly specialized to certain tasks.

The importance of data structures is underscored by their ability to:

- Optimize resource use, such as CPU time and memory.

- Enable efficient data retrieval and update.

- Facilitate data storage in a manner that best suits the problem at hand.

- Provide a framework for creating more complex structures, contributing to better software design.

Classification of Data Structures

Data structures can broadly be categorized into two types: primitive and non-primitive.

Primitive Data Structures

Primitive data structures are basic structures that hold single values. Examples include:

- **Integer**
- **Float**
- **Character**
- **Boolean**

Non-Primitive Data Structures

Non-primitive data structures are more complex and can be further classified into linear and non-linear structures.

Linear Data Structures   In linear data structures, data elements are arranged in a sequential manner. Examples include:

- **Arrays**
- **Linked Lists**
- **Stacks**
- **Queues**

152

Non-Linear Data Structures   Non-linear data structures, on the other hand, involve hierarchical relationships among data elements. Examples include:

- **Trees**
- **Graphs**

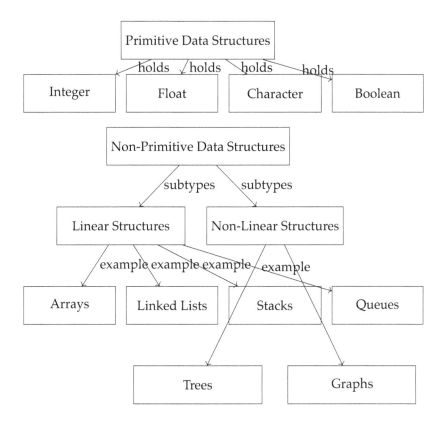

Data Structures in Python

Python provides robust and versatile built-in data structures, which can be directly employed to solve complex computational problems. This chapter will specifically focus on the following data structures:

- **Lists** - Ordered and mutable sequences.

153

- **Tuples** - Ordered and immutable sequences.

- **Sets** - Unordered collections of unique elements.

- **Dictionaries** - Collections of key-value pairs.

- **Stacks** - LIFO (Last In, First Out) structures.

- **Queues** - FIFO (First In, First Out) structures.

- **Linked Lists** - Linear data structures consisting of nodes.

List Initialization in Python

```
# Initializing various data structures
my_list = [1, 2, 3, 4, 5]
my_tuple = (1, 2, 3, 4, 5)
my_set = {1, 2, 3, 4, 5}
my_dict = {"one": 1, "two": 2, "three": 3}

print("List: ", my_list)
print("Tuple: ", my_tuple)
print("Set: ", my_set)
print("Dictionary: ", my_dict)
```

```
Output:
List:  [1, 2, 3, 4, 5]
Tuple:  (1, 2, 3, 4, 5)
Set:  {1, 2, 3, 4, 5}
Dictionary:  {'one': 1, 'two': 2, 'three': 3}
```

Common Operations on Data Structures

Data structures support an array of operations, which facilitate efficient data manipulation and retrieval. Some of these common operations include:

- **Insertion** - Adding an element to the data structure.

- **Deletion** - Removing an element from the data structure.

- **Traversal** - Accessing each element exactly once to process it.

- **Searching** - Finding the location of an element within the data structure.

- **Sorting** - Arranging elements in a particular order.

In Python, these operations can often be carried out using built-in methods associated with each data structure, enhancing simplicity and readability of the code.

154

Algorithmic Complexity

Understanding the performance implications of different operations on data structures is crucial. Algorithmic complexity, commonly expressed using Big O notation, provides a way to describe the efficiency of these operations in terms of time and space. For example:

- Accessing an element in a list by index: $O(1)$

- Inserting or deleting an element in a list: $O(n)$

- Looking up a value in a dictionary: $O(1)$ on average.

- Inserting or deleting a node in a linked list: $O(1)$

Practical Applications

The choice of an appropriate data structure can significantly impact the performance and complexity of an application. Some practical examples include:

- Utilizing a stack for expression evaluation and syntax parsing.

- Employing a queue for task scheduling algorithms.

- Using dictionaries to implement associative arrays or hash maps for quick lookups.

- Leveraging trees and graphs for hierarchical data representation and navigation.

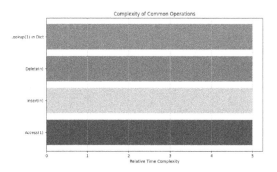

Data structures are integral to efficient software development and computational problem-solving. Mastering them is essential for writing optimal and maintainable code. The subsequent sections of this chapter will delve into each of Python's built-in data structures, providing insights into their creation, manipulation, and practical applications.

5.2   Lists: Creation, Access, and Modification

Creation of Lists

Lists in Python are dynamic arrays capable of holding elements of various data types, including integers, floats, strings, and even other lists. They are created using square brackets [] or the built-in list() function.

```python
# Example of list creation using square brackets
numbers = [1, 2, 3, 4, 5]

# Creating a list with mixed data types
mixed_list = [1, "string", 3.14, True]

# List of lists
nested_list = [[1, 2], [3, 4], [5, 6]]

# Using the list() function
empty_list = list()
```

Accessing List Elements

Python lists support indexing, slicing, and nested indexing for accessing their elements. Indexing starts at 0 for the first element.

```python
# Accessing elements by index
first_element = numbers[0] # returns 1
last_element = numbers[-1] # returns 5

# Accessing a sublist using slicing
sublist = numbers[1:4] # returns [2, 3, 4]

# Accessing elements in a nested list
nested_element = nested_list[0][1] # returns 2
```

Modifying Lists

Lists are mutable, meaning elements can be added, removed, or changed. Various methods are available for these operations, including `append()`, `insert()`, `extend()`, `remove()`, and `pop()`.

Adding Elements

To add elements, we can use `append()` to add to the end, `insert()` to add at a specific position, or `extend()` to concatenate another list.

```
# Append an element to the end
numbers.append(6) # numbers becomes [1, 2, 3, 4, 5, 6]

# Insert an element at a specific position
numbers.insert(2, 7) # numbers becomes [1, 2, 7, 3, 4, 5, 6]

# Extend the list by another list
numbers.extend([8, 9]) # numbers becomes [1, 2, 7, 3, 4, 5, 6, 8, 9]
```

Removing Elements

Elements can be removed using `remove()` to delete the first occurrence, `pop()` to remove by index, or `clear()` to remove all elements.

```
# Remove the first occurrence of a value
numbers.remove(7) # numbers becomes [1, 2, 3, 4, 5, 6, 8, 9]

# Remove an element by index, default is last element
removed_element = numbers.pop(3) # numbers becomes [1, 2, 3, 5, 6, 8, 9]

# Remove all elements from the list
numbers.clear() # numbers becomes []
```

Replacing Elements

Elements can be replaced by assigning new values to specific indices or slices.

```
# Reassign a single element
numbers[1] = 10 # numbers becomes [1, 10, 3, 4, 5]

# Reassign multiple elements using slicing
numbers[1:3] = [20, 30] # numbers becomes [1, 20, 30, 4, 5]
```

numbers: | 1 | 20 | 30 | 4 | 5 |

157

Understanding the basics of list creation, access, and modification is fundamental for handling data effectively in Python. These core operations provide a foundation for more advanced data manipulation techniques, crucial for proficient algorithm implementation and efficient problem solving in the language.

5.3   List Comprehensions

List comprehensions provide a concise way to create lists in Python. They are an elegant and efficient tool commonly used for generating new lists by applying an expression to each element in an existing iterable. The syntax is more compact and readable, making it an essential feature for Python developers.

Basic Syntax

The basic syntax for a list comprehension in Python is as follows:

```
[<expression> for <item> in <iterable>]
```

Where:

- `<expression>` can be any valid Python expression that operates on the elements of the iterable.

- `<item>` is the variable that takes the value of the element from the iterable.

- `<iterable>` is any Python iterable, such as a list, tuple, set, or range.

For example, to create a list of squares from 0 to 9:

```
squares = [x**2 for x in range(10)]
print(squares)
```

```
[0, 1, 4, 9, 16, 25, 36, 49, 64, 81]
```

Conditional List Comprehensions

List comprehensions can also include conditional statements, allowing the inclusion or exclusion of elements based on specific criteria. The syntax for a list comprehension with a conditional statement is:

```
[<expression> for <item> in <iterable> if <condition>]
```

Here, `<condition>` is an optional part of the comprehension that filters elements.

For instance, to create a list of even numbers from 0 to 9:

```
even_numbers = [x for x in range(10) if x % 2 == 0]
print(even_numbers)
```

```
[0, 2, 4, 6, 8]
```

Nested List Comprehensions

A list comprehension can include multiple `for` clauses, allowing iteration over nested iterables. This feature is particularly useful for creating lists from multi-dimensional data structures.

For example, to create a list of coordinate pairs where x and y are both in the range from 0 to 2:

```
coordinates = [(x, y) for x in range(3) for y in range(3)]
print(coordinates)
```

```
[(0, 0), (0, 1), (0, 2), (1, 0), (1, 1), (1, 2), (2, 0), (2, 1), (2, 2)]
```

Conditional statements can also be applied within nested comprehensions. To filter the coordinates for those pairs where the sum of x and y is even:

```
filtered_coords = [(x, y) for x in range(3) for y in range(3) if (x + y) % 2 == 0]
print(filtered_coords)
```

```
[(0, 0), (0, 2), (1, 1), (2, 0), (2, 2)]
```

List Comprehension with Functions

Expressions within a list comprehension can call functions, facilitating more complex operations. Consider a function to convert temperatures from Celsius to Fahrenheit:

```
def celsius_to_fahrenheit(celsius):
    return (celsius * 9/5) + 32

sample_temps_c = [0, 10, 20, 30]

fahrenheit_temps = [celsius_to_fahrenheit(c) for c in sample_temps_c]
print(fahrenheit_temps)
```

```
[32.0, 50.0, 68.0, 86.0]
```

List Comprehension vs. Lambda Functions

While both list comprehensions and lambda functions serve to simplify code, their use cases differ. Lambda functions are typically used within higher-order functions like map, `filter`, and `reduce`. In contrast, list comprehensions are often preferred for their readable and expressive syntax, especially when transforming or filtering lists.

For instance, using list comprehension to multiply elements by 2:

```
doubles = [x * 2 for x in range(5)]
print(doubles)
```

```
[0, 2, 4, 6, 8]
```

Using a lambda function with map to achieve the same result:

```
doubles = list(map(lambda x: x * 2, range(5)))
print(doubles)
```

```
[0, 2, 4, 6, 8]
```

List comprehensions are a powerful and essential feature in Python, offering a compact and readable way to create and manipulate lists. By understanding their syntax and applications, developers can write more concise, efficient, and Pythonic code. The versatility and expressiveness of list comprehensions make them invaluable for a wide range of use cases, from simple iterations to complex nested operations.

List comprehensions enable cleaner code that is easier to maintain and understand, aligning with Python's philosophy of simplicity and readability. As they eliminate the need for boilerplate code associated with traditional loops and conditionals, mastering list comprehensions is crucial for any Python developer aiming to write code that is both effective and elegant.

5.4 Tuples: Immutable Sequences

Tuples in Python are ordered collections of elements, similar to lists, but with a key distinction: tuples are immutable. Once a tuple is created, its contents cannot be altered. This immutability provides certain advantages, particularly in contexts where a constant set of values is required, thus ensuring the integrity and reliability of the data throughout its lifecycle. This section explores the creation, access, and practical applications of tuples.

Creating Tuples

Tuples can be created using parentheses () or the `tuple()` constructor. Elements within the tuple are separated by commas.

```
# Creating a tuple using parentheses
my_tuple = (1, 2, 3, 4, 5)

# Creating a tuple using the tuple() constructor
another_tuple = tuple([10, 20, 30])
```

Note that a single value within parentheses does not constitute a tuple unless followed by a comma:

```
# Not a tuple
single_value = (5)

# Correctly defining a tuple with one element
single_value_tuple = (5,)
```

Accessing Tuple Elements

Tuples support indexing, allowing access to individual elements using zero-based indices. Slicing operations are also permissible, returning subsequent elements within the specified range.

```
# Accessing elements in a tuple
third_element = my_tuple[2] # Returns 3

# Slicing a tuple
sub_tuple = my_tuple[1:4] # Returns (2, 3, 4)
```

Tuple Unpacking

Tuple unpacking is a feature where tuple elements are assigned to a sequence of variables in a single statement. This can be particularly useful for functions that return multiple values.

```
# Tuple unpacking
a, b, c = (1, 2, 3)

# Unpacking a function return value
def get_coordinates():
    return (50.123, -0.123)

latitude, longitude = get_coordinates()
```

Immutability of Tuples

The immutability of tuples implies that any attempt to modify the tuple results in an error. For example, trying to change an element directly will raise a TypeError.

```
# Attempting to modify a tuple
immutable_tuple = (1, 2, 3)
# immutable_tuple[0] = 10 # This will raise a TypeError
```

However, tuples can contain mutable objects, such as lists, which can be altered without changing the tuple's structure.

```
# Tuple containing a mutable object
mutable_inside_tuple = (1, [2, 3], 4)
mutable_inside_tuple[1][0] = 999 # This is allowed
print(mutable_inside_tuple) # Output: (1, [999, 3], 4)
```

Use Cases for Tuples

Tuples are widely used in scenarios where a constant sequence of values is required. Common use cases include:

- Function Return Values: Functions returning multiple values can do so efficiently using tuples. This is particularly advantageous for ensuring that the returned set of values remains intact and unmodified.

- Dictionary Keys: Due to their immutability, tuples can be used as keys in dictionaries (unlike lists). This enables the use of composite keys, where each key is a tuple consisting of multiple elements.

```
# Using tuples as dictionary keys
location_data = {
    ("New York", "USA"): {"population": 8_336_817},
    ("Tokyo", "Japan"): {"population": 37_833_000}
}
```

- Immutable Records: For data consistency, tuples are ideal for representing fixed records, such as database entries or constant configurations, thereby ensuring that the core data remains unaffected by inadvertent modifications.

Operations on Tuples

Several operations can be performed on tuples for analysis and manipulation purposes:

Concatenation

Tuples can be concatenated using the plus operator (+), producing a new tuple comprised of elements from the operands.

```
# Concatenating tuples
tuple1 = (1, 2)
tuple2 = (3, 4)
combined_tuple = tuple1 + tuple2 # Returns (1, 2, 3, 4)
```

Repetition

The repetition operator (*) repeats the elements of a tuple a specified number of times, returning a larger tuple.

```
# Repeating a tuple
repeated_tuple = (1, 2) * 3 # Returns (1, 2, 1, 2, 1, 2)
```

Membership Testing

Tuples support membership testing using the in keyword to check for the presence of an element.

```
# Membership testing
is_present = 3 in (1, 2, 3) # Returns True
is_absent = 4 in (1, 2, 3) # Returns False
```

Built-in Tuple Functions

Python provides a number of built-in functions that operate on tuples, including:

- len(): Returns the number of elements in a tuple.

- max(): Returns the maximum element.

- min(): Returns the minimum element.

- sum(): Returns the sum of elements (for numeric tuples).

```
sample_tuple = (5, 1, 3, 9)
length = len(sample_tuple) # Returns 4
maximum = max(sample_tuple) # Returns 9
minimum = min(sample_tuple) # Returns 1
total = sum(sample_tuple) # Returns 18
```

Iterating over Tuples

Similar to other sequences, tuples can be iterated over using for loops. This is particularly useful when coupled with tuple unpacking inside the loop for enhanced readability.

```
# Iterating over a tuple
for element in sample_tuple:
    print(element)

# Tuple unpacking in iterations
pairs = [(1, 'one'), (2, 'two'), (3, 'three')]
for number, name in pairs:
    print(f"Number: {number}, Name: {name}")
```

Understanding tuples and their immutability provides a foundation for leveraging their strengths in scenarios where constant data sets are required. By utilizing effective tuple operations and methodologies, developers can ensure data integrity and enhance their application's robustness.

5.5   Sets: Unordered Collections

A set in Python is an unordered collection data type that is iterable, mutable, and has no duplicate elements. Sets are instrumental for membership testing, eliminating duplicate entries, and executing mathematical operations such as union, intersection, difference, and symmetric difference.

Sets can be created using the set() constructor or by enclosing a comma-separated sequence of elements within curly braces {}.

```
# Creating an empty set
empty_set = set()

# Creating a set with initial elements
num_set = {1, 2, 3, 4}

# Creating a set from a list
list_set = set([1, 2, 2, 3, 4]) # Result: {1, 2, 3, 4}
```

It is important to remember that sets do not permit mutable elements, such as lists or dictionaries, as members.

Python sets support various standard operations. Below are some fundamental methods:

```
num_set = {1, 2, 3, 4}

# Adding an element to a set
num_set.add(5) # Result: {1, 2, 3, 4, 5}

# Removing an element from the set
num_set.remove(3) # Result: {1, 2, 4, 5}

# Discarding an element not present in the set
num_set.discard(6) # Result: {1, 2, 4, 5}

# Popping an element
popped_element = num_set.pop() # Result: Set with one arbitrary element removed
```

Note that pop() removes an arbitrary element because sets are unordered. For safe removal without error if the element is absent, use discard().

Sets are optimized for membership tests using the in and not in operators.

```
num_set = {1, 2, 3, 4}

# Check membership
is_member = 3 in num_set # True
is_not_member = 5 not in num_set # True
```

Python sets provide built-in functionality for common mathematical operations such as union, intersection, difference, and symmetric difference.

```
A = {1, 2, 3}
B = {3, 4, 5}

# Union: Elements in A or B
union_set = A.union(B) # Result: {1, 2, 3, 4, 5}

# Intersection: Elements in both A and B
intersection_set = A.intersection(B) # Result: {3}

# Difference: Elements in A but not in B
difference_set = A.difference(B) # Result: {1, 2}

# Symmetric Difference: Elements in either A or B, but not both
symmetric_difference_set = A.symmetric_difference(B) # Result: {1, 2, 4, 5}
```

These operations can also be performed using corresponding operators: |, &, -, and ^ for union, intersection, difference, and symmetric difference, respectively.

Checking for subset and superset relationships is straightforward with sets.

```
A = {1, 2, 3}
B = {1, 2, 3, 4, 5}

# Subset: Check if A is a subset of B
is_subset = A.issubset(B) # True

# Superset: Check if B is a superset of A
is_superset = B.issuperset(A) # True
```

These relationships can also be evaluated using comparison operators: <= for subset, and >= for superset.

Understanding how to create and manipulate sets is crucial for effectively managing collections of unique elements in Python. Sets provide a powerful and efficient way to handle unique data and perform essential operations on it. Exploring and mastering the use of sets will enhance your ability to write efficient and clean Python code.

5.6   Operations on Sets

Sets in Python provide a high-level abstraction for mathematical sets, supporting operations like union, intersection, difference, and symmetric difference. These operations are essential for performing complex data manipulation tasks and form the cornerstone of handling collections in various applications. This section will delve into each of these operations, illustrating their usage through code snippets and explanations.

- **Union of Sets**

  The union of two sets A and B includes all elements that are in A, in B, or in both. In Python, the union operation can be performed using the | operator or the union() method.

  ```
  # Using the | operator
  A = {1, 2, 3}
  B = {3, 4, 5}
  union_set = A | B
  print(union_set)
  ```

  Output:
  {1, 2, 3, 4, 5}

  ```
  # Using the union() method
  A = {1, 2, 3}
  B = {3, 4, 5}
  union_set = A.union(B)
  print(union_set)
  ```

  Output:
  {1, 2, 3, 4, 5}

- **Intersection of Sets**

  The intersection of two sets A and B includes only the elements that are present in both A and B. This can be represented using the & operator or the intersection() method.

  ```
  # Using the & operator
  A = {1, 2, 3}
  B = {3, 4, 5}
  intersection_set = A & B
  print(intersection_set)
  ```

  Output:
  {3}

  ```
  # Using the intersection() method
  A = {1, 2, 3}
  B = {3, 4, 5}
  intersection_set = A.intersection(B)
  ```

166

```
print(intersection_set)
```

Output:
{3}

- **Difference of Sets**

  The difference of two sets A and B includes elements that are present in A but not in B. This operation can be performed using the – operator or the difference() method.

  ```
  # Using the - operator
  A = {1, 2, 3}
  B = {3, 4, 5}
  difference_set = A - B
  print(difference_set)
  ```

  Output:
  {1, 2}

  ```
  # Using the difference() method
  A = {1, 2, 3}
  B = {3, 4, 5}
  difference_set = A.difference(B)
  print(difference_set)
  ```

  Output:
  {1, 2}

- **Symmetric Difference of Sets**

  The symmetric difference of two sets A and B includes elements that are in either A or B but not in both. The symmetric difference can be found using the ^ operator or the sym_diff() method.

  ```
  # Using the ^ operator
  A = {1, 2, 3}
  B = {3, 4, 5}
  sym_diff_set = A ^ B
  print(sym_diff_set)
  ```

  Output:
  {1, 2, 4, 5}

  ```
  # Using the symmetric_difference() method
  A = {1, 2, 3}
  B = {3, 4, 5}
  sym_diff_set = A.symmetric_difference(B)
  print(sym_diff_set)
  ```

  Output:
  {1, 2, 4, 5}

- **Subset and Superset Checks**

  Subset and superset operations are useful for determining hierarchical relationships between sets. A set A is a subset of set B if all

167

elements of A are also in B, which can be checked using the <= operator or the issubset() method. Conversely, B is a superset of A if it contains all elements of A, checked using the >= operator or the issuperset() method.

```
# Subset check using the <= operator
A = {1, 2}
B = {1, 2, 3}
is_subset = A <= B
print(is_subset)
```

Output:
True

```
# Subset check using the issubset() method
A = {1, 2}
B = {1, 2, 3}
is_subset = A.issubset(B)
print(is_subset)
```

Output:
True

```
# Superset check using the >= operator
A = {1, 2, 3}
B = {1, 2}
is_superset = A >= B
print(is_superset)
```

Output:
True

```
# Superset check using the issuperset() method
A = {1, 2, 3}
B = {1, 2}
is_superset = A.issuperset(B)
print(is_superset)
```

Output:
True

- **Disjoint Sets**

  Two sets are disjoint if they have no elements in common. This relationship can be verified using the isdisjoint() method in Python.

```
# Checking if two sets are disjoint
A = {1, 2, 3}
B = {4, 5, 6}
are_disjoint = A.isdisjoint(B)
print(are_disjoint)
```

Output:
True

The preceding sections covered the fundamental operations on sets, each integral for efficient data manipulation and processing. Understanding these operations allows developers to perform complex data-related tasks with clarity and precision, leveraging the full potential of sets in Python.

5.7 Dictionaries: Key-Value Pairs

Dictionaries in Python are powerful, efficient data structures that associate keys with values. They are akin to associative arrays or hash maps found in other programming languages and are designed for quick retrieval of values when the corresponding key is known. In this section, we will explore dictionary creation, access, modification, and common operations.

Dictionaries are created using curly braces {} with a series of key-value pairs, or by using the dict() constructor.

```
# Creating a dictionary with curly braces
student_grades = {
    'Alice': 85,
    'Bob': 92,
    'Charlie': 78
}

# Creating a dictionary with dict() constructor
employee_ids = dict(John=101, Jane=102, Jake=103)
```

Keys can be of any immutable data type such as integers, strings, or tuples, while values can be of any data type.

To access a value in a dictionary, use the key inside square brackets, or use the get() method to avoid a KeyError when the key does not exist.

```
# Accessing a value with a key
grade_of_alice = student_grades['Alice'] # Output: 85

# Accessing value using get() method
grade_of_david = student_grades.get('David', 'Not Found') # Output: 'Not Found'
```

Dictionaries are mutable, allowing for modification after creation. You can add new key-value pairs, update existing keys, or remove key-value pairs.

```
# Adding a new key-value pair
student_grades['David'] = 88

# Updating an existing key-value pair
student_grades['Alice'] = 90

# Removing a key-value pair using del
```

```
del student_grades['Bob']

# Removing a key-value pair using pop()
charlie_grade = student_grades.pop('Charlie')

# Checking the dictionary after modifications
print(student_grades) # Output: {'Alice': 90, 'David': 88}
```

Python provides several built-in methods to work with dictionaries effectively. Below are some frequently used methods.

keys() Returns a view object containing the dictionary's keys.

values() Returns a view object containing the dictionary's values.

items() Returns a view object containing key-value pairs as tuples.

update() Updates the dictionary with elements from another dictionary or an iterable of key-value pairs.

clear() Removes all items from the dictionary.

```
# Dictionary methods in action
keys = student_grades.keys() # Output: dict_keys(['Alice', 'David'])
values = student_grades.values() # Output: dict_values([90, 88])
items = student_grades.items() # Output: dict_items([('Alice', 90), ('David', 88)])

# Updating a dictionary with another dictionary
new_grades = {'Eve': 93, 'Frank': 80}
student_grades.update(new_grades)
print(student_grades) # Output: {'Alice': 90, 'David': 88, 'Eve': 93, 'Frank': 80}

# Clearing all items from the dictionary
student_grades.clear()
print(student_grades) # Output: {}
```

Iterating over dictionaries can be done directly over keys, values, or items depending on the use case.

```
# Iterating over keys
for key in employee_ids.keys():
    print(key) # Outputs: John, Jane, Jake

# Iterating over values
for value in employee_ids.values():
    print(value) # Outputs: 101, 102, 103

# Iterating over key-value pairs
for key, value in employee_ids.items():
    print(f'{key}: {value}') # Outputs: John: 101, Jane: 102, Jake: 103
```

The following chart demonstrates a visual representation of a dictionary's performance with the number of key-value pairs:

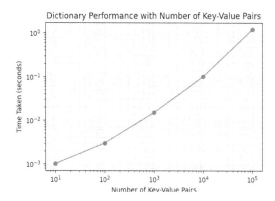

The code snippets demonstrate the versatility and efficiency of dictionaries in Python, enabling developers to manage key-value data structures seamlessly.

In the subsequent sections, we will delve into nested data structures and further explore advanced usage of dictionaries within these contexts.

5.8 Dictionary Methods and Operations

Python dictionaries are powerful data structures that store mappings of unique keys to values. They allow for efficient retrieval, insertion, and deletion of key-value pairs. This section provides an exhaustive overview of dictionary methods and operations, essential for leveraging the full potential of dictionaries in Python.

Creating and Accessing Dictionaries

A dictionary can be created using braces {} or the dict() constructor. Each key-value pair is separated by a colon (:), and pairs are separated by commas.

```
# Creating a dictionary using braces
person = {
    'name': 'Alice',
    'age': 30,
    'city': 'New York'
}

# Creating a dictionary using the dict() constructor
employee = dict(id=1234, name='Bob', department='HR')
```

Accessing dictionary values is performed using keys. The key is placed in square brackets following the dictionary's name, or the get method can be used.

```
# Accessing values using keys
name = person['name'] # 'Alice'
age = person.get('age') # 30

# Accessing a non-existing key using get() method with a default value
country = person.get('country', 'Unknown') # 'Unknown'
```

Adding and Updating Entries

To add or update a key-value pair, use the assignment operator with the desired key. If the key exists, the value will be updated; if not, a new key-value pair will be added.

```
# Adding a new key-value pair
person['occupation'] = 'Engineer'

# Updating an existing key-value pair
person['city'] = 'Boston'
```

Removing Entries

Dictionaries provide several methods to remove key-value pairs:

- pop(key) removes the specified key and returns the corresponding value.

- popitem() removes and returns the last inserted key-value pair as a tuple.

- del statement can remove a key-value pair by key or delete the entire dictionary.

```
# Remove a key-value pair and return its value
name = person.pop('name') # 'Alice'

# Remove and return the last inserted key-value pair
last_item = person.popitem() # ('occupation', 'Engineer')

# Remove a key-value pair using del
del person['city']

# Delete the entire dictionary
del person
```

172

Dictionary Methods

Python provides a suite of methods for performing various operations on dictionaries:

- `clear()` removes all key-value pairs.

- `copy()` returns a shallow copy of the dictionary.

- `fromkeys(seq, value)` creates a new dictionary with keys from seq and values set to `value`.

- `items()` returns a view object of key-value pairs.

- `keys()` returns a view object of dictionary keys.

- `values()` returns a view object of dictionary values.

- `update(other_dict)` updates the dictionary with elements from another dictionary or iterable.

```python
# Clearing all key-value pairs
person.clear()

# Creating a shallow copy
employee_copy = employee.copy()

# Creating a dictionary from keys with a default value
keys = ['name', 'age', 'city']
default_person = dict.fromkeys(keys, 'Unknown') # {'name': 'Unknown', 'age': '
    Unknown', 'city': 'Unknown'}

# Iterating over key-value pairs
for key, value in employee.items():
    print(f'{key}: {value}')

# Getting all keys and values
employee_keys = employee.keys() # dict_keys(['id', 'name', 'department'])
employee_values = employee.values() # dict_values(['HR'])

# Updating dictionary with another dictionary's items
employee.update({'name': 'Charlie', 'title': 'Manager'})
```

Iterating Over Dictionaries

Dictionaries can be iterated using loops. Common patterns include iterating over keys, values, or key-value pairs.

```python
# Iterating over keys
for key in employee.keys():
    print(f'Key: {key}')

# Iterating over values
```

```
for value in employee.values():
    print(f'Value: {value}')

# Iterating over key-value pairs
for key, value in employee.items():
    print(f'{key}: {value}')
```

Dictionary Comprehensions

Like list comprehensions, dictionary comprehensions provide a concise way to create dictionaries.

```
# Creating a dictionary with squares of numbers from 1 to 5
squares = {x: x**2 for x in range(1, 6)} # {1: 1, 2: 4, 3: 9, 4: 16, 5: 25}

# Filtering keys with a comprehension
filtered_dict = {k: v for k, v in employee.items() if v != 'HR'} # {'id': 1234, '
    name': 'Charlie', 'title': 'Manager'}
```

Merging Dictionaries

Starting with Python 3.9, the | operator merges dictionaries, and |= updates a dictionary with another dictionary's items.

```
# Merging two dictionaries
dict_a = {'a': 1, 'b': 2}
dict_b = {'b': 3, 'c': 4}
merged_dict = dict_a | dict_b # {'a': 1, 'b': 3, 'c': 4}

# Updating a dictionary in place
dict_a |= dict_b # {'a': 1, 'b': 3, 'c': 4}
```

Practical Considerations

While dictionaries are versatile, some considerations must be taken into account:

- Keys must be immutable and hashable types (e.g., strings, numbers, tuples). Mutable types like lists cannot be used as dictionary keys.

- Dictionary methods and operations run in average O(1) time complexity, ensuring efficient performance even with large datasets.

Python dictionaries provide a robust framework for managing key-value pairs with a wide range of methods and operations. Mastery of these techniques is essential for any proficient Python programmer.

5.9 Nested Data Structures

Nested data structures in Python refer to data structures that contain other data structures as their elements. Such nesting allows for the creation of complex, multi-dimensional collections, which can be used for a variety of advanced data handling tasks. This section covers the construction, manipulation, and practical applications of nested data structures, providing essential techniques for efficient data management.

Nested data structures can be created using Python's built-in data types such as list, tuple, set, and dict. Below are examples illustrating various forms of nesting:

Creation of Nested Data Structures

```python
# Nested Lists
nested_list = [[1, 2, 3], [4, 5, 6], [7, 8, 9]]

# Nested Tuples
nested_tuple = ((1, 2), (3, 4), (5, 6))

# Nested Sets
nested_set = {frozenset({1, 2}), frozenset({3, 4}), frozenset({5, 6})}

# Nested Dictionaries
nested_dict = {
    'first': {'a': 1, 'b': 2},
    'second': {'c': 3, 'd': 4},
    'third': {'e': 5, 'f': 6}
}
```

Accessing elements within a nested data structure requires index chaining or key chaining, depending on the type of elements contained.

Accessing Nested Data Structure Elements

```python
# Accessing elements in a nested list
element = nested_list[0][1] # Output: 2

# Accessing elements in a nested tuple
element = nested_tuple[1][0] # Output: 3

# Accessing elements in a nested dictionary
element = nested_dict['second']['d'] # Output: 4
```

Nested data structures can be modified by pointing to the specific nested element using appropriate indexing or key access methods.

Modifying Nested Data Structures

175

```
# Modifying an element in a nested list
nested_list[2][0] = 10

# Modifying an element in a nested dictionary
nested_dict['third']['e'] = 50
```

It is important to note that tuples and sets are immutable; thus, their elements themselves cannot be modified directly. However, the contents of mutable elements within nested tuples or sets can be changed.

Iteration over nested data structures generally involves nested loops or recursion.

Iterating Over Nested Data Structures

```
# Iterating over a nested list
for sublist in nested_list:
    for item in sublist:
        print(item)

# Iterating over a nested dictionary
for key, subdict in nested_dict.items():
    for subkey, value in subdict.items():
        print(f"{subkey}: {value}")
```

Nested data structures are crucial for representing grid-like structures, such as matrices in mathematical computations, hierarchical data like JSON responses, and complex relationships in graphs and trees.

```
Matrix Representation:
[
    [1, 2, 3],
    [4, 5, 6],
    [7, 8, 9]
]

Hierarchical Data (JSON):
{
    "name": "John",
    "address": {
        "street": "123 Maple St",
        "city": "Springfield"
    }
}
```

Nesting allows for more structured and readable code but can introduce higher computational complexity. Accessing deeply nested elements may be less efficient due to the multiple levels of dereferencing required. Therefore, it is essential to balance the need for structure against the performance characteristics of the resulting data structure.

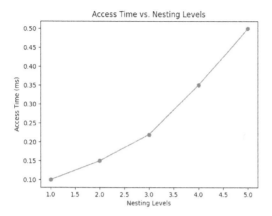

Nested data structures enhance the capability to represent complex data models, enabling more advanced and multi-dimensional data manipulation. Proper management of these structures allows for efficient data processing and storage solutions, vital for both simple applications and large-scale data systems.

5.10 Stacks: LIFO Structures

A stack is an abstract data structure that adheres to the Last-In, First-Out (LIFO) principle. In a stack, the most recently added element is the first to be removed. This behavior is akin to a stack of plates: you can only take from the top, and when you add a new plate, it goes on top of the existing stack.

Stack Operations

Stacks support a limited set of operations:

- **Push:** Add an element to the top of the stack.

- **Pop:** Remove and return the top element of the stack.

- **Peek (or Top):** Return the top element without removing it from the stack.

- **isEmpty:** Check whether the stack is empty.

177

An essential aspect of stack usage is efficient implementation. Here's how stacks can be realized in Python.

Stack Implementation in Python

Python does not have a built-in stack data structure, but the `list` type can be used to simulate stack behavior efficiently. The `append()` method of a list can be used as the push operation, and the `pop()` method can be used as the pop operation.

Here is a basic implementation of a stack using Python lists:

```python
class Stack:
    def __init__(self):
        self.items = []

    def push(self, item):
        self.items.append(item)

    def pop(self):
        if not self.is_empty():
            return self.items.pop()
        raise IndexError("pop from empty stack")

    def peek(self):
        if not self.is_empty():
            return self.items[-1]
        raise IndexError("peek from empty stack")

    def is_empty(self):
        return len(self.items) == 0

    def size(self):
        return len(self.items)
```

Example: Balanced Parentheses

One classic application of stacks is checking for balanced parentheses in an arithmetic expression. The algorithm involves iterating through each character in the string, pushing opening parentheses onto the stack and popping them when a matching closing parenthesis is found.

Algorithm 1: Balanced Parentheses

Data: String *expr*
Result: Boolean value indicating if parentheses are balanced
1 stack ← new Stack;
2 **for** *char ← each character in expr* **do**
3   **if** *char is '('* **then**
4   stack.push(char);
5   **if** *char is ')'* **then**
6   **if** *stack.is_empty()* **then**
7   **return** *False*;
8   stack.pop();

9 **return** *stack.is_empty()*;

Below is the Python implementation of the balanced parentheses algorithm using the `Stack` class:

```python
def is_balanced_parentheses(expr):
    stack = Stack()
    for char in expr:
        if char == '(':
            stack.push(char)
        elif char == ')':
            if stack.is_empty():
                return False
            stack.pop()
    return stack.is_empty()
```

Performance Considerations

The operations on a stack implemented using a Python list (append and pop) both have an average time complexity of $O(1)$, making them efficient for most applications.

Applications of Stacks

Stacks are used in numerous applications across various domains:

- **Function Call Management:** Programming languages use stacks to manage function calls and local variables.

- **Expression Evaluation:** Stacks assist in evaluating arithmetic expressions and syntax parsing for compilers.

- **Backtracking Algorithms:** In algorithms such as Depth-First Search (DFS), stacks help in traversing and backtracking through nodes.

Understanding and implementing stacks effectively aids in solving a variety of computational problems, forming a fundamental skill set for any software developer. Graph comprehension and data structure mastery, as illustrated by the stack, enhance logical organization and computational efficiency across both simple and complex systems.

5.11   Queues: FIFO Structures

In Python, a queue is a collection of elements that follows the First-In-First-Out (FIFO) principle. Queues are essential in various scenarios, such as task scheduling, breadth-first search in graphs, and real-time data processing systems. This section delves into the fundamentals of queues, their implementation, and their practical applications.

A queue operates by adding elements to the end (rear) and removing elements from the front. The primary operations on a queue are:

- **Enqueue**: Adding an element to the rear of the queue.

- **Dequeue**: Removing an element from the front of the queue.

- **Peek/Front**: Viewing the front element of the queue without removing it.

- **isEmpty**: Checking whether the queue is empty or not.

Python's `collections.deque` class provides an efficient way to implement a queue. The `deque` class is optimized for appending and popping elements from both ends, making it an ideal choice for queue operations. Below is an example implementation of a queue using `collections.deque`.

Queue Implementation using collections.deque

```
from collections import deque

class Queue:
    def __init__(self):
        self.queue = deque()

    def enqueue(self, item):
        self.queue.append(item)

    def dequeue(self):
        if not self.is_empty():
            return self.queue.popleft()
        raise IndexError("dequeue from an empty queue")
```

```python
    def front(self):
        if not self.is_empty():
            return self.queue[0]
        raise IndexError("peek from an empty queue")

    def is_empty(self):
        return len(self.queue) == 0

    def size(self):
        return len(self.queue)

# Example Usage
q = Queue()
q.enqueue(1)
q.enqueue(2)
print(q.dequeue()) # Outputs: 1
print(q.front()) # Outputs: 2
```

Queues are used in various real-world applications where tasks need to be executed in order of their arrival:

Task Scheduling

In operating systems, the CPU scheduler often uses queues to manage processes. Tasks are enqueued as they arrive and dequeued for execution.

```
Queue: [task1, task2, task3]
Dequeue task1 for execution.
Queue: [task2, task3]
Enqueue task4.
Queue: [task2, task3, task4]
```

Breadth-First Search (BFS) in Graphs

Breadth-First Search uses a queue to explore nodes level by level. The nodes adjacent to the current node are enqueued, ensuring that each level is processed before moving deeper into the graph.

Algorithm 2: Breadth-First Search Algorithm

Data: Graph G, starting node v
Result: Nodes visited in BFS order
1 Create a queue Q;
2 Enqueue v to Q;
3 Mark v as visited;
4 **while** *Q is not empty* **do**
5   node = Q.dequeue();
6   Process node;
7   **for** *each unvisited neighbor u of node* **do**
8   Mark u as visited;
9   Enqueue u to Q;

181

Real-Time Data Processing

Streams of data, such as log entries or network packets, can be buffered using queues. The consumer processes each item in the order it was received.

```
Incoming packets: [packet1, packet2, packet3]
Queue state: [packet1, packet2, packet3]
Processing packet1.
Queue state: [packet2, packet3]
```

A circular queue (or ring buffer) is a variation that improves upon the linear queue by reusing the empty space created by dequeuing elements. This is particularly useful in scenarios where fixed-size buffers are required.

The key operations on a circular queue include keeping track of two pointers, front and rear, and adjusting them modulo the size of the queue.

Circular Queue Implementation

```python
class CircularQueue:
    def __init__(self, capacity):
        self.queue = [None] * capacity
        self.capacity = capacity
        self.front = self.rear = -1

    def enqueue(self, item):
        if (self.rear + 1) % self.capacity == self.front:
            raise OverflowError("Queue is full")
        elif self.is_empty():
            self.front = self.rear = 0
        else:
            self.rear = (self.rear + 1) % self.capacity
        self.queue[self.rear] = item

    def dequeue(self):
        if self.is_empty():
            raise IndexError("Queue is empty")
        elif self.front == self.rear:
            temp = self.queue[self.front]
            self.front = self.rear = -1
        else:
            temp = self.queue[self.front]
            self.front = (self.front + 1) % self.capacity
        return temp

    def is_empty(self):
        return self.front == -1

    def is_full(self):
        return (self.rear + 1) % self.capacity == self.front
```

Queues are vital data structures in computer science, characterized by their FIFO behavior. Implemented efficiently in Python using the `collections.deque` class, queues support various crucial applications such as task scheduling, BFS, and real-time data processing. Additionally, circular queues offer a robust solution for fixed-size buffers. Understanding and mastering these structures enhances a developer's ability to design effective algorithms and systems.

5.12   Understanding Linked Lists

Linked lists are a fundamental data structure that allow for efficient insertion and deletion operations. Unlike arrays, which require contiguous memory allocation, linked lists consist of nodes that can be scattered throughout memory. Each node contains data and a reference (or pointer) to the next node in the sequence.

Node Structure

A linked list is composed of nodes, each of which can be represented as an object in Python. Here is a basic definition of a node in Python:

Node class definition

```
class Node:
    def __init__(self, data=None):
        self.data = data
        self.next = None
```

Singly Linked Lists

In a singly linked list, each node points to the next node and the final node points to None, signifying the end of the list.

Singly linked list definition

```
class SinglyLinkedList:
    def __init__(self):
        self.head = None

    def append(self, data):
        new_node = Node(data)
        if not self.head:
            self.head = new_node
            return
        last = self.head
```

183

```
    while last.next:
        last = last.next
    last.next = new_node

def display(self):
    curr = self.head
    while curr:
        print(curr.data, end=" -> ")
        curr = curr.next
    print("None")
```

```
# Creating and displaying a singly linked list
sll = SinglyLinkedList()
sll.append(1)
sll.append(2)
sll.append(3)
sll.display()
```

```
1 -> 2 -> 3 -> None
```

Insertion and Deletion in Singly Linked Lists

Insertion in a singly linked list can occur at the beginning, the end, or at any arbitrary position. Below are methods to perform these operations:

Insertion methods in singly linked lists

```
class SinglyLinkedList:
    # Existing methods...

    def insert_at_beginning(self, data):
        new_node = Node(data)
        new_node.next = self.head
        self.head = new_node

    def insert_at_position(self, position, data):
        if position < 0:
            raise ValueError("Position can't be negative")
        new_node = Node(data)
        if position == 0:
            new_node.next = self.head
            self.head = new_node
            return
        current = self.head
        for _ in range(position - 1):
            if not current:
                raise IndexError("Position out of bounds")
            current = current.next
        new_node.next = current.next
        current.next = new_node

    def delete_value(self, value):
        current = self.head
        if current and current.data == value:
            self.head = current.next
            return
        prev = None
        while current and current.data != value:
```

184

```
        prev = current
        current = current.next
    if not current:
        return # Value not found
    prev.next = current.next
```

```
# Insertion and deletion in a singly linked list
sll = SinglyLinkedList()
sll.append(1)
sll.append(3)
sll.insert_at_beginning(0)   # 0 -> 1 -> 3 -> None
sll.insert_at_position(2, 2) # 0 -> 1 -> 2 -> 3 -> None
sll.display()
sll.delete_value(2)          # 0 -> 1 -> 3 -> None
sll.display()

0 -> 1 -> 2 -> 3 -> None
0 -> 1 -> 3 -> None
```

Doubly Linked Lists

Doubly linked lists are an extension where each node not only points to the next node but also to the previous node. This bidirectional linkage allows for traversal in both directions.

Doubly linked list definition

```
class DoublyNode:
    def __init__(self, data=None):
        self.data = data
        self.next = None
        self.prev = None

class DoublyLinkedList:
    def __init__(self):
        self.head = None
        self.tail = None

    def append(self, data):
        new_node = DoublyNode(data)
        if not self.head:
            self.head = self.tail = new_node
            return
        self.tail.next = new_node
        new_node.prev = self.tail
        self.tail = new_node

    def display_forward(self):
        curr = self.head
        while curr:
            print(curr.data, end=" <-> ")
            curr = curr.next
        print("None")

    def display_backward(self):
        curr = self.tail
        while curr:
            print(curr.data, end=" <-> ")
```

185

```
        curr = curr.prev
      print("None")
```

```
# Creating and displaying a doubly linked list
dll = DoublyLinkedList()
dll.append(1)
dll.append(2)
dll.append(3)
dll.display_forward()
dll.display_backward()

1 <-> 2 <-> 3 <-> None
3 <-> 2 <-> 1 <-> None
```

Insertion and Deletion in Doubly Linked Lists

Much like singly linked lists, doubly linked lists support insertion and deletion at various positions:

Insertion and deletion in doubly linked lists

```
class DoublyLinkedList:
    # Existing methods...

    def insert_at_beginning(self, data):
        new_node = DoublyNode(data)
        new_node.next = self.head
        if self.head:
            self.head.prev = new_node
        self.head = new_node
        if not self.tail:
            self.tail = new_node

    def delete_value(self, value):
        current = self.head
        while current and current.data != value:
            current = current.next
        if not current:
            return # Value not found
        if current.prev:
            current.prev.next = current.next
        if current.next:
            current.next.prev = current.prev
        if current == self.head:
            self.head = current.next
        if current == self.tail:
            self.tail = current.prev
```

```
# Insertion and deletion in a doubly linked list
dll = DoublyLinkedList()
dll.append(1)
dll.append(3)
dll.insert_at_beginning(0) # 0 <-> 1 <-> 3 <-> None
dll.display_forward()
dll.delete_value(1)        # 0 <-> 3 <-> None
dll.display_forward()

0 <-> 1 <-> 3 <-> None
0 <-> 3 <-> None
```

186

Circular Linked Lists

In a circular linked list, the last node points back to the first node, forming a closed loop. This structure can be useful for applications that require circular iterations.

Circular linked list definition

```python
class CircularLinkedList:
    def __init__(self):
        self.head = None

    def append(self, data):
        new_node = Node(data)
        if not self.head:
            self.head = new_node
            new_node.next = self.head
            return
        curr = self.head
        while curr.next != self.head:
            curr = curr.next
        curr.next = new_node
        new_node.next = self.head

    def display(self):
        if not self.head:
            return
        curr = self.head
        while True:
            print(curr.data, end=" -> ")
            curr = curr.next
            if curr == self.head:
                break
        print(curr.data)
```

```python
# Creating and displaying a circular linked list
cll = CircularLinkedList()
cll.append(1)
cll.append(2)
cll.append(3)
cll.display()
```

```
1 -> 2 -> 3 -> 1
```

Linked lists are a versatile data structure with many variations—each offering unique advantages. Their non-contiguous memory allocation and efficient insertion/deletion operations make them a valuable tool in a programmer's toolkit. Understanding linked lists and their implementations in Python is crucial for performing foundational data structure manipulations and building more complex structures.

Chapter 6

File Handling

This chapter explains file handling in Python, covering how to open, read, write, and close files. It discusses different file modes and buffering, and provides techniques for working with both text and binary files. The chapter includes handling CSV and JSON files, file seeking operations, and the use of context managers with the with statement. Additionally, it addresses handling file exceptions and performing directory operations.

6.1 Introduction to File Handling

File handling is a fundamental aspect of Python programming, enabling the storage, retrieval, and manipulation of data in files. This capability is pivotal for a wide range of applications, including data analysis, logging, configuration management, and persistent storage solutions. Understanding how to efficiently and effectively manage files is essential for any software developer.

Python provides a comprehensive suite of tools for file handling, encapsulated within its standard library. These tools support operations such as opening, reading, writing, and closing files, as well as error handling. This section provides an overview of these capabilities and sets the stage for more detailed discussions in subsequent sections.

Basic File Operations

The primary file operations in Python are facilitated by built-in func-

189

tions and methods. The most fundamental operations include opening a file, performing read and write operations, and closing the file after the operations are complete. The basic syntax for these operations is as follows:

Basic File Operations

```python
# Open a file
file = open('example.txt', 'r')

# Read content from the file
content = file.read()

# Close the file
file.close()
```

Opening a File: The open() function is used to open a file. It takes at least one argument, the filename, and an optional second argument that specifies the mode in which the file is to be opened (e.g., read, write, append). The available modes will be discussed in more detail in a subsequent section.

Reading from a File: The read() method reads the entire content of the file and returns it as a string. Other methods such as readline() and readlines() can be used to read the file line-by-line or as a list of lines, respectively.

Writing to a File: Writing to a file involves similar steps, with the mode set to 'w', 'a', or other suitable options. For example:

Writing to a File

```python
# Open a file in write mode
file = open('example.txt', 'w')

# Write content to the file
file.write("Hello, World!")

# Close the file
file.close()
```

Closing a File: The close() method is used to close the file, ensuring that all the changes are saved and resources are released. It is crucial to close files to avoid memory leaks and other potential issues.

File Paths

Files can reside in different directories and locations, requiring the specification of a path to access them. Python provides support for both relative and absolute file paths.

Relative Path: A relative path specifies a file location in relation to

190

the current working directory.

Using Relative Path

```
# Relative path
file = open('data/example.txt', 'r')
```

Absolute Path: An absolute path specifies the full path to the file from the root of the file system.

Using Absolute Path

```
# Absolute path
file = open('/home/user/data/example.txt', 'r')
```

To handle file paths robustly, especially across different operating systems, the os and pathlib modules provide utilities for path manipulation.

Handling Paths with pathlib

```
from pathlib import Path

# Create a Path object
path = Path('/home/user/data/example.txt')

# Open the file
file = path.open('r')
```

File Modes

The mode in which a file is opened determines the operations that can be performed on the file. Common modes include:

- r: Read (default)
- w: Write (truncate)
- a: Append
- b: Binary mode
- t: Text mode (default)
- x: Exclusive creation

These modes can be combined, such as rb for reading in binary mode.

The Importance of Context Managers

Handling files without properly managing their lifecycle can lead to resource leaks and corrupted files. Python's with statement provides a context manager that ensures the file is properly closed after its suite finishes, even if an exception is raised.

Using Context Manager

```
# Using with statement
with open('example.txt', 'r') as file:
    content = file.read()
    # File is automatically closed at the end of this block
```

This introduction serves as a foundation for more advanced topics in file handling, such as file modes, buffering, binary file operations, and error handling mechanisms, which will be covered in subsequent sections. Mastery of these basics is essential for efficient and reliable file manipulation in Python.

6.2 Opening and Closing Files

File handling in Python begins with the fundamental operations of opening and closing files. Understanding these basic operations is crucial, as they form the foundation for more advanced file manipulations.

To open a file in Python, the built-in open() function is utilized. This function requires at least one argument—the name of the file to be opened. Additional optional arguments can specify the mode in which the file is to be opened, and the encoding if the file is a text file.

The basic syntax for opening a file is:

```
file_object = open(filename, mode, encoding)
```

Here, filename is the name of the file (including the path if not in the current directory), mode specifies the operation to be performed on the file, and encoding is relevant for text files.

File Modes

The mode argument determines the purpose for which the file is being opened:

- 'r': Opens the file for reading (default mode). The file must exist.

- 'w': Opens the file for writing. If the file already exists, it is truncated. If the file does not exist, it is created.

192

- 'a': Opens the file in append mode. New data will be written at the end of the file. If the file does not exist, it is created.

- 'b': Opens the file in binary mode.

- 't': Opens the file in text mode (default mode).

- 'x': Creates a new file and opens it for writing. If the file already exists, the operation fails.

- '+': Opens the file for both reading and writing.

In practice, these modes can be combined, e.g., 'rb' opens a file for reading in binary mode, and 'wt' opens a file for writing in text mode.

Example usage:

```
# Open an existing file for reading
f_read = open('example.txt', 'r')

# Open a file for writing (truncates if exists)
f_write = open('example.txt', 'w')

# Open a file for appending (creates if doesn't exist)
f_append = open('example.txt', 'a')

# Open a file for reading and writing in binary mode
f_rw_binary = open('example.bin', 'r+b')
```

Closing Files

Once file operations are completed, it is imperative to close the file using the close() method to free up system resources. Failure to close a file can lead to memory leaks and files remaining locked.

```
file_object.close()
```

Example:

```
# Open a file for reading
f = open('example.txt', 'r')

# Perform file operations
# ...

# Close the file
f.close()
```

Using with Statement

To simplify file handling and ensure that files are properly closed after their operations are complete, Python provides the with statement. The with statement ensures that the file is closed as soon as the block of code inside the with statement is exited, even if an exception is thrown.

Example:

```
with open('example.txt', 'r') as f:
    # Perform file operations
    content = f.read()

# The file is automatically closed outside the with block
```

Using the with statement eliminates the need to explicitly call close() and is generally considered best practice for file operations.

Error Handling During File Operations

Error handling is crucial when dealing with file operations. Common errors include attempting to open a file that does not exist, or lacking the necessary permissions. Python's exception handling try ... except block can be employed to handle such errors gracefully.

Example:

```
try:
    with open('non_existent_file.txt', 'r') as f:
        content = f.read()
except FileNotFoundError:
    print("The file does not exist.")
except IOError:
    print("An I/O error occurred.")
```

The try ... except structure allows the program to continue running even if an error occurs, thereby enhancing robustness and reliability.

Opening and closing files are fundamental operations in Python file handling. Mastery of these operations, including the use of file modes, proper resource management with the close() method, and error handling with the try ... except block, lays the groundwork for more advanced file manipulation techniques.

194

6.3 Reading from Files

Reading data from files is a fundamental operation in many Python programs. This section delves into various approaches and methods available for efficiently reading text and binary files. We will explore the open() function for initializing file objects, methods such as read(), readline(), and readlines(), and discuss how to handle large files to maintain optimal performance.

Opening a File for Reading

To read from a file, it must first be opened in an appropriate mode. The open() function facilitates this by providing a file object for subsequent operations. The syntax for opening a file in read mode is as follows:

Opening a file

```
file = open('sample.txt', 'r')
```

Here, 'r' denotes read mode. Attempting to read a file that does not exist will raise a FileNotFoundError. For safer code, use exception handling to manage this scenario.

Reading Entire File: read()

The read() method reads the entire content of a file into a single string. This approach is convenient for small files but can lead to high memory consumption for larger files.

Reading entire file content

```
try:
    with open('sample.txt', 'r') as file:
        content = file.read()
        print(content)
except FileNotFoundError:
    print("File not found.")
```

```
Output:
Line 1 of the file
Line 2 of the file
...
```

In this code, the with statement ensures the file is properly closed after reading.

Reading Line by Line: readline()

For scenarios where memory efficiency is critical, reading the file line by line with readline() is preferable. This method returns one line at a time, allowing for processing of each line independently.

195

Reading line by line

```
try:
    with open('sample.txt', 'r') as file:
        while True:
            line = file.readline()
            if not line:
                break
            print(line.strip())
except FileNotFoundError:
    print("File not found.")
```

```
Output:
Line 1 of the file
Line 2 of the file
...
```

In this example, strip() is used to remove any trailing newline characters.

Reading All Lines: readlines()

The readlines() method reads all lines in a file and returns them as a list. Each element of the list corresponds to a line in the file, maintaining line breaks.

Reading all lines

```
try:
    with open('sample.txt', 'r') as file:
        lines = file.readlines()
        for line in lines:
            print(line.strip())
except FileNotFoundError:
    print("File not found.")
```

```
Output:
Line 1 of the file
Line 2 of the file
...
```

This method is convenient when it is necessary to process lines collectively but can be resource-intensive for very large files.

Reading Large Files Efficiently

When dealing with large files, it is crucial to read data in manageable chunks to prevent excessive memory usage. The read(size) method supports reading a specific number of bytes at a time.

Reading large files in chunks

```
try:
    with open('large_file.txt', 'r') as file:
        while True:
            chunk = file.read(1024) # Read 1024 bytes at a time
            if not chunk:
                break
```

196

```
        print(chunk)
except FileNotFoundError:
    print("File not found.")
```

```
Output:
[First 1024 bytes of the file]
[Next 1024 bytes of the file]
...
```

This approach allows for processing large datasets without overwhelming system memory.

Binary File Reading

Binary files require handling raw data instead of text. Opening a file in binary read mode is achieved using `'rb'`.

Reading binary files

```
try:
    with open('sample.bin', 'rb') as file:
        binary_data = file.read()
        print(binary_data)
except FileNotFoundError:
    print("File not found.")
```

```
Output:
b'\x89PNG\r\n\x1a\n\x00\x00\x00\rIHDR\x00\x00\x00...'
```

Reading binary files is similar to reading text files but the data is returned as a bytes object, suitable for non-text content like images or executables.

Efficient file reading is essential for performance and resource management. Python provides a diverse set of methods for reading files, accommodating various needs from small, textual data to large, binary datasets. Each method comes with its own advantages and considerations, ensuring developers can choose the most appropriate technique for their specific use cases.

6.4 Writing to Files

Writing to files is a fundamental operation in Python, ensuring data persistence. This section provides comprehensive details on how to write to files, focusing on various file modes, methods, and handling textual and binary data. The ability to write efficiently and safely to files is crucial for a wide array of applications, from logging and configuration management to data storage and processing.

To write to a file in Python, the file must first be opened using the built-in open() function. The open() function creates a file object, which provides methods and attributes for interacting with the file. It requires at least one argument: the name of the file. Optionally, a second argument specifies the mode in which the file is opened.

Opening a File for Writing

```
# Opening a file for writing (this will create the file if it does not exist)
file = open('example.txt', 'w')
```

In the example above, example.txt is opened in write mode using the 'w' mode. If the file does not exist, it is created. If the file does exist, its contents are truncated, meaning the existing content is removed and replaced by what is written next.

Text data can be written using the write() method, which takes a string argument and returns the number of characters written. If an error occurs, an IOError exception is raised.

Writing Text to a File

```
# Writing a string to the file
file.write('Hello, world!\n')
file.close()
```

It is essential to close the file using the close() method to ensure that all data is physically written to the disk and resources are released.

To add content to an existing file without truncating it, open the file in append mode with the 'a' mode.

Appending Text to a File

```
# Appending a string to the file
with open('example.txt', 'a') as file:
    file.write('Appending this line.\n')
```

Using the 'a' mode ensures that new content is added to the end of the file. The with statement automatically closes the file after the block of code is executed, even if an exception occurs.

When dealing with non-text files, such as images or executables, the file must be opened in binary mode using 'wb' mode. This mode writes data as bytes.

Opening a File for Binary Writing

```
# Opening a file for binary writing
file = open('binary_example.bin', 'wb')
```

Writing binary data is performed using the `write()` method, but the data must be in bytes format.

Writing Binary Data

```
# Writing binary data to the file
data = b'\x00\xFF\x00\xFF'
file.write(data)
file.close()
```

Here, `data` is a bytes object containing binary data. It is crucial to ensure that non-text data is correctly converted to bytes before writing it to a file.

For structured data formats like CSV and JSON, Python provides specific libraries (`csv` and `json`), which are well-integrated with the standard file handling functions.

The `csv` module provides functionalities to write rows of data into a CSV file.

Writing CSV Data

```
import csv

# Writing rows to a CSV file
with open('data.csv', 'w', newline='') as csvfile:
    writer = csv.writer(csvfile)
    writer.writerow(['Name', 'Age', 'City'])
    writer.writerow(['Alice', 30, 'New York'])
```

The `json` module allows easy serialization and writing of JSON data.

Writing JSON Data

```
import json

# Writing a dictionary to a JSON file
data = {'name': 'Alice', 'age': 30, 'city': 'New York'}
with open('data.json', 'w') as jsonfile:
    json.dump(data, jsonfile, indent=4)
```

Closing a file is necessary to ensure data integrity and release system resources. This can be done explicitly using the `close()` method or implicitly using a `with` statement.

Explicitly Closing a File

```
file = open('example.txt', 'w')
file.write('Some data')
file.close()
```

It is best practice to use the `with` statement for opening files as it guarantees that the file is properly closed after its suite finishes, even if exceptions are raised. This method enhances code readability and maintenance.

By understanding these methods and practices, one can effectively write data to various file types in Python, ensuring data persistence and seamless data management for applications.

6.5 File Modes and Buffering

In file handling, understanding file modes and buffering is fundamental to managing how files are interacted with in Python. This section delves into the different file modes available in Python, followed by an exploration of buffering mechanisms and their implications on file operations.

File Modes

File modes determine the nature of operations that can be performed on a file. The basic file modes in Python are as follows:

- `'r'`: Opens a file for reading (default mode). If the file does not exist, an `FileNotFoundError` is raised.

- `'w'`: Opens a file for writing. If the file already exists, it is truncated. If the file does not exist, it is created.

- `'x'`: Opens a file for exclusive creation. If the file already exists, an `FileExistsError` is raised.

- `'a'`: Opens a file for appending. If the file does not exist, it is created. Writes are appended to the end of the file.

- `'b'`: Binary mode. This mode can be used in conjunction with other modes (e.g., `'rb'`, `'wb'`) to read or write binary files.

- `'t'`: Text mode (default mode). Typically used in conjunction with other modes (e.g., `'rt'`, `'wt'`) for reading or writing text files.

- `'+'`: Update mode. This mode allows simultaneous reading and writing. When combined with other modes such as `'r+'`, `'w+'` or `'a+'`, it provides additional flexibility.

To open a file in a specific mode, the `open()` function is utilized:

200

Opening a file in different modes

```
# Open a file for reading in text mode
with open('example.txt', 'r') as file:
    content = file.read()

# Open a file for writing in binary mode
with open('example.bin', 'wb') as file:
    file.write(b'\x00\x01\x02')
```

Buffering

Buffering plays a crucial role in file I/O operations by improving performance. It temporarily holds data in a buffer before writing it to or reading it from the file. The buffer acts as an intermediary storage area, reducing the number of direct I/O operations on the file system.

Types of Buffering

Python offers three types of buffering:

- **Fully Buffered**:

    - Default behavior for text files.

    - Data is buffered in larger chunks.

    - Good for reducing the number of read/write operations.

- **Line Buffered**:

    - Data is buffered until a newline character is encountered.

    - Commonly used for text files when line-by-line processing is preferred.

- **Unbuffered**:

    - Data is written or read directly without any intermediate buffering.

    - Can be less efficient but offers immediate data transfer.

Buffering behavior can be controlled using the open() function by setting the buffering parameter:

Controlling Buffering

```
# Fully buffered mode (default)
with open('example.txt', 'w', buffering=4096) as file:
    file.write("Data to be buffered")

# Line buffered mode
with open('example.txt', 'w', buffering=1) as file:
```

201

```
file.write("Line buffered data\n")

# Unbuffered mode
with open('example.txt', 'w', buffering=0) as file:
    file.write("Immediate data\n")
```

Buffer Flushing

Controlled flushing of the buffer can be essential to ensure data integrity. Flushing forces a buffer to write its content to the file before the buffer is filled. The flush() method can be utilized to manually flush the buffer:

Manual Buffer Flushing

```
with open('example.txt', 'w', buffering=4096) as file:
    file.write("Some data to buffer")
    file.flush() # Forces buffer to write data to file
```

Alternatively, the with statement can be employed for automatic flushing when the file is closed:

Using 'with' for Automatic Flushing

```
with open('example.txt', 'w') as file:
    file.write("Data is automatically flushed when file is closed")
```

Buffering in Binary Mode

When working with binary files, buffering operates similarly, but with raw bytes instead of text. Efficient binary operations can be performed using appropriate modes and buffering strategies:

Buffering in Binary Mode

```
# Writing binary data with manual flushing
with open('example.bin', 'wb', buffering=1024) as file:
    file.write(b'\x00\x01\x02\x03')
    file.flush()

# Reading binary data with default buffering
with open('example.bin', 'rb') as file:
    data = file.read()
```

Understanding and appropriately applying file modes and buffering techniques is integral to optimizing file I/O operations in Python. These methods influence both the performance and reliability of file interactions, ensuring data is handled efficiently and accurately.

6.6 Working with Binary Files

Binary files differ from text files in that they store data in a binary format, which is not human-readable. These files are used for storing images, videos, executables, and other non-text data. This section will detail the methods for reading from and writing to binary files using Python.

Reading Binary Files

To read from a binary file, open the file in binary read mode (rb). This mode ensures that the file is read as a sequence of bytes. The read() method can be used to read the entire content or a specified number of bytes from the file.

Reading from a binary file

```python
# Open the binary file in read-binary mode
with open('example.bin', 'rb') as file:
    # Read the entire content of the file
    data = file.read()
    # Print the read data
    print(data)
```

In the example above, the example.bin file is opened in binary read mode, and its content is read into the variable data. Using the with statement ensures that the file is automatically closed after the block of code is executed.

Writing Binary Files

Writing to a binary file requires opening the file in binary write mode (wb). Any data written to the file must be in bytes, which can involve encoding strings or directly writing byte objects.

Writing to a binary file

```python
# Open the binary file in write-binary mode
with open('example.bin', 'wb') as file:
    # Data to be written to the file
    data = b'This is binary data'
    # Write data to the file
    file.write(data)
```

In this example, a byte string b'This is binary data' is written to the file example.bin. The with statement is used to ensure proper handling and closing of the file.

Appending to Binary Files

Appending data to an existing binary file without overwriting it is possible using the append binary mode (ab). This mode appends the new data to the end of the file content.

Appending to a binary file

```
# Open the binary file in append-binary mode
with open('example.bin', 'ab') as file:
    # Data to be appended to the file
    additional_data = b' Additional binary data'
    # Append data to the file
    file.write(additional_data)
```

Here, example.bin is opened in append binary mode, and additional_data is appended to the file without affecting its existing content.

Using the struct Module

For more complex binary file operations, such as reading and writing structured binary data (e.g., fixed-size records), Python's struct module is useful. The struct module provides functions to interpret bytes as packed binary data.

Working with the struct module

```
import struct

# Define a format string for struct (e.g., an integer and a float)
format_string = 'if'

# Pack data into a binary format
binary_data = struct.pack(format_string, 1, 3.14)

# Open the file to write the packed data
with open('example_struct.bin', 'wb') as file:
    file.write(binary_data)

# Read and unpack the data from the binary file
with open('example_struct.bin', 'rb') as file:
    binary_data = file.read()
    unpacked_data = struct.unpack(format_string, binary_data)

print(unpacked_data)
```

This example utilizes struct.pack to convert an integer and a float into a binary format string according to format_string. The packed data is then written to example_struct.bin. Subsequently, struct.unpack is used to read and convert the binary data back to its original Python tuple.

Visualizing Binary Data

204

Understanding the structure of a binary file can be challenging. Visualization tools or custom scripts can aid in interpreting the data layout.

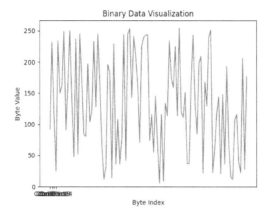

The above Python script simulates binary data and visualizes it using `matplotlib`, which can help in understanding patterns or verifying the integrity of data in binary files.

6.7 Reading and Writing CSV Files

The Comma-Separated Values (CSV) format is a widely-used file format for tabular data that facilitates the exchange of data between diverse applications. Python's standard library provides the `csv` module, which simplifies the process of reading from and writing to CSV files. This section details the methods and classes provided by the `csv` module to handle CSV files effectively.

Reading CSV Files

To read from a CSV file, Python offers the `csv.reader` class. This class reads and parses lines from a specified CSV file, allowing iteration over its rows. Each row is represented as a list of strings.

Reading a CSV file

```
import csv
```

```
with open('example.csv', mode='r', newline='') as file:
    csv_reader = csv.reader(file)
    for row in csv_reader:
        print(row)
```

In the above example, the open() function is used to open the CSV file in read mode. The newline parameter ensures that newline characters are handled correctly. The csv.reader() function creates a reader object which is then iterated over, printing each row.

Alternatively, the csv.DictReader class can be used for reading CSV files into a dictionary. In this case, each row is represented as an ordered dictionary, with the keys derived from the first row of the CSV file.

Reading a CSV file using DictReader

```
import csv

with open('example.csv', mode='r', newline='') as file:
    csv_reader = csv.DictReader(file)
    for row in csv_reader:
        print(row)
```

Writing to CSV Files

Writing to a CSV file involves the use of the csv.writer or csv.DictWriter classes provided by the csv module. The csv.writer class is utilized for writing a sequence of iterable values, such as lists, while the csv.DictWriter class writes dictionaries.

Writing to a CSV file

```
import csv

data = [
    ['Name', 'Age', 'Occupation'],
    ['John Doe', '28', 'Software Developer'],
    ['Jane Smith', '34', 'Data Analyst']
]

with open('example.csv', mode='w', newline='') as file:
    csv_writer = csv.writer(file)
    csv_writer.writerows(data)
```

In the example above, the writerows() method is used to write multiple rows to the CSV file at once. This method accepts a list of lists, where each inner list corresponds to a row in the CSV file.

For writing dictionaries, csv.DictWriter is appropriate, ensuring that dictionary keys are written as headers.

Writing to a CSV file using DictWriter

```
import csv

data = [
    {'Name': 'John Doe', 'Age': '28', 'Occupation': 'Software Developer'},
    {'Name': 'Jane Smith', 'Age': '34', 'Occupation': 'Data Analyst'}
]

with open('example.csv', mode='w', newline='') as file:
    fieldnames = ['Name', 'Age', 'Occupation']
    csv_writer = csv.DictWriter(file, fieldnames=fieldnames)

    csv_writer.writeheader()
    csv_writer.writerows(data)
```

In this case, the fieldnames parameter must be specified to denote the order of columns. The writerows() method writes each dictionary in the list to the CSV file, and the writeheader() method writes the header row.

CSV Dialects and Customization

The csv module supports customization through dialects, allowing the specification of different delimiters, quote characters, and other formatting parameters. A dialect is a subclass of the csv.Dialect class, which can be registered and then used to read or write CSV files that adhere to that specific format.

Defining and using a CSV dialect

```
import csv

csv.register_dialect('myDialect', delimiter=';', quoting=csv.QUOTE_ALL)

data = [
    ['Name', 'Age', 'Occupation'],
    ['John Doe', '28', 'Software Developer'],
    ['Jane Smith', '34', 'Data Analyst']
]

with open('example.csv', mode='w', newline='') as file:
    csv_writer = csv.writer(file, dialect='myDialect')
    csv_writer.writerows(data)
```

Here, the custom dialect myDialect is registered with a semicolon as the delimiter and quoting set to QUOTE_ALL. This dialect is then used to write the CSV file, ensuring that all fields are quoted.

Above we discussed the mechanisms provided by Python's csv module for reading from and writing to CSV files. The methods and classes discussed include csv.reader, csv.writer, csv.DictReader, csv.DictWriter, and the use of CSV dialects for customization. These tools provide robust support for handling CSV files in Python, accommodating a wide variety of formatting requirements and ensuring efficient data exchange.

6.8   File Seeking: Moving the File Pointer

File seeking allows for more controlled and flexible file I/O operations by enabling the movement of the file pointer to specific positions within a file. This capability is essential when dealing with large files or when specific portions of the file need to be accessed directly without sequential reads. This section explores the functions provided by Python for file seeking, including seek() and tell().

seek() Method

The seek() method is used to move the file pointer to a specific location within the file. Its syntax is as follows:

```
file_object.seek(offset, whence=0)
```

- offset: The number of bytes to move the file pointer.

- whence (optional): The reference point from which offset is calculated. The default value is 0.

The whence argument can take the following values:

- 0 (default): The offset is from the beginning of the file.

- 1: The offset is from the current file pointer position.

- 2: The offset is from the end of the file.

Consider the following example:

```
with open('example.txt', 'rb') as file:
    # Move pointer to the 5th byte from the beginning
    file.seek(5)
    print(file.read(10))

    # Move pointer to the 5th byte from the current position
    file.seek(5, 1)
    print(file.read(10))

    # Move pointer to the 5th byte from the end of the file
    file.seek(-5, 2)
    print(file.read(10))
```

In this example, the file pointer is manipulated using different reference points. The seek() method supports both positive and negative values for the offset, allowing movement in both forward and backward directions.

tell() Method

The tell() method returns the current file pointer position, measured in bytes from the beginning of the file. This method is particularly useful for debugging and understanding the current read/write position within a file.

```
with open('example.txt', 'rb') as file:
    file.seek(0, 2) # Move to end of file
    print(file.tell())
```

In the above example, using file.tell() after moving the pointer to the end of the file with seek(0, 2) returns the total number of bytes in the file.

Practical Use Cases

Skipping Headers in CSV Files

When dealing with CSV files, skipping headers is a common task. Using seek() and tell(), you can efficiently skip headers without reading the entire file.

```
with open('data.csv', 'r') as file:
    # Assume first line is the header
    file.readline()
    print(file.tell()) # Position after header
    for line in file:
        process(line)
```

In this scenario, readline() reads and skips the header, setting the file pointer to the beginning of the data rows.

Binary File Manipulation

File seeking is indispensable when dealing with binary files where specific byte offsets are critical.

```
with open('binary_file.dat', 'rb+') as file:
    # Navigate to a specific position
    file.seek(1024)

    # Read 16 bytes from this position
    data = file.read(16)
    print(data)

    # Modify the bytes starting from this position
    file.seek(1024)
    file.write(b'new_data')
```

209

This code demonstrates reading and writing binary data at specific locations, which is crucial in many systems programming tasks.

Limitations and Considerations

When using `seek()` with text files, it's essential to be aware that file seeking behaves differently in text mode and binary mode. In text mode, the offsets are interpreted in terms of characters rather than bytes, which can lead to unexpected results if the file contains multibyte characters.

Moreover, while `seek()` is powerful, inappropriate usage can lead to data corruption or misaligned reads/writes. It is paramount to handle file pointers properly, ensuring alignment corresponds to the file structure being manipulated.

The `seek()` and `tell()` methods are critical for efficient file handling in Python, offering precise control over file pointer movements. By understanding and utilizing these methods, developers can create more efficient and responsive applications that handle file I/O operations gracefully. Proper understanding and cautious application of file seeking can significantly optimize the performance and versatility of file operations in Python.

6.9   Context Managers and the `with` Statement

In Python, the management of resources such as files, network connections, or locks necessitates proper setup and teardown procedures to avoid resource leaks or unexpected behavior. The traditional approach involves explicitly opening a resource, performing operations, and then ensuring that the resource is closed or released. However, this can lead to verbose and error-prone code, particularly in the presence of exceptions. Context managers in Python provide a standardized way to encapsulate these setup and teardown operations, fostering cleaner and more reliable code. This section elucidates the usage and implementation of context managers, accentuating the utility of the `with` statement.

The `with` statement simplifies resource management by automatically handling the setup and teardown operations associated with context managers. It ensures that resources are correctly released, even if an exception occurs during the execution of the block. The general syntax of the `with` statement is as follows:

```
with expression as variable:
    # Code block using variable
```

In the context of file handling, the with statement is commonly used as follows:

```
with open('example.txt', 'r') as file:
    content = file.read()
    # Process content
# File is automatically closed here
```

The open function returns a file object that supports context management. The with statement ensures that the file is automatically closed when the block is exited, even if an exception is raised.

To create a custom context manager, a class must define two special methods: __enter__() and __exit__(). The __enter__() method is executed when the execution flow enters the with block and should return the resource to be managed. The __exit__() method is invoked upon exiting the block and is responsible for performing cleanup operations.

Consider the example of a custom context manager for handling database connections:

```
class DatabaseConnection:
    def __init__(self, dbname):
        self.dbname = dbname

    def __enter__(self):
        self.conn = self._connect_to_database(self.dbname)
        return self.conn

    def __exit__(self, exc_type, exc_val, exc_tb):.
        self._close_connection(self.conn)

    def _connect_to_database(self, dbname):
        # Logic to establish a database connection
        pass

    def _close_connection(self, conn):
        # Logic to close the database connection
        pass

# Usage with the with statement
with DatabaseConnection('test.db') as conn:
    # Perform operations using conn
    pass
# Connection is automatically closed here
```

In this example, the DatabaseConnection class encapsulates the logic for managing a database connection. The __enter__() method establishes the connection and returns it, while the __exit__() method en-

211

sures the connection is closed.

The `contextlib` module in Python provides utilities to facilitate the creation of context managers. The `@contextmanager` decorator allows a generator function to be used as a context manager, streamlining the implementation.

Here is an example using `contextlib.contextmanager` to create a context manager for temporary file manipulation:

```python
from contextlib import contextmanager
import os

@contextmanager
def temporary_file(filename, content):
    with open(filename, 'w') as file:
        file.write(content)
    try:
        yield filename
    finally:
        os.remove(filename)

# Usage with the with statement
with temporary_file('temp.txt', 'Temporary content') as temp_file:
    with open(temp_file, 'r') as file:
        print(file.read())
# Temporary file is automatically deleted here
```

The `@contextmanager` decorator transforms the `temporary_file` function into a context manager. The function executes the setup code before the `yield` statement and the teardown code in the `finally` block, ensuring the temporary file is created and subsequently deleted.

Context managers offer the following key benefits:

- Ensured Resource Cleanup: Resources are automatically released, reducing the likelihood of resource leaks.

- Exception Safety: Cleanup code is executed regardless of whether an exception is raised, enhancing robustness.

- Improved Readability: The `with` statement produces more concise and readable code by abstracting explicit setup and teardown.

- Reusability: Context managers can be reused across different parts of an application, promoting modular and maintainable design.

Adopting context managers and the `with` statement for resource management is a best practice in Python programming. It simplifies resource handling and ensures that resources are properly managed even in the face of exceptions, leading to more robust and maintainable code-bases.

6.10 Handling File Exceptions

Error handling is a critical aspect of robust file operations. Proper exception handling ensures that your program can gracefully manage unexpected conditions, such as missing files, permission issues, or errors in reading and writing operations. Python uses the `try-except` block to manage exceptions, providing a structured way to handle errors that may arise during file operations.

When dealing with file operations, you may encounter several types of exceptions. Common file exceptions include:

- `FileNotFoundError`: Raised when trying to open a file that does not exist.

- `PermissionError`: Raised when the program does not have the necessary permissions to access the file.

- `IsADirectoryError`: Raised when a file operation is attempted on a directory.

- `IOError`: A broader exception that encompasses many input/output-related errors.

Understanding and appropriately handling these exceptions will make your code more robust and user-friendly.

The `try-except` block allows you to test a block of code for errors and provides a way to handle them if they occur. Here is a basic example demonstrating its use with file operations:

Basic File Handling with try-except

```
try:
    with open('example.txt', 'r') as file:
        content = file.read()
    print(content)
except FileNotFoundError:
    print("The file was not found")
except PermissionError:
    print("You do not have permission to access this file")
except Exception as e:
    print(f"An unexpected error occurred: {e}")
```

In this example, the `try` block attempts to open and read from a file. If the file does not exist or the program lacks the necessary permissions, the respective except block will execute, providing a useful error message.

For production-quality applications, merely printing error messages may not be sufficient. Instead, logging detailed error information for later analysis is recommended. Python's `logging` module can be utilized to log exceptions:

Logging Exceptions using logging Module

```
import logging

logging.basicConfig(filename='file_operations.log', level=logging.ERROR)

try:
    with open('example.txt', 'r') as file:
        content = file.read()
    print(content)
except FileNotFoundError as e:
    logging.error("The file was not found: %s", e)
except PermissionError as e:
    logging.error("Permission denied: %s", e)
except Exception as e:
    logging.error("An unexpected error occurred: %s", e)
```

In this example, errors are logged to a file (`file_operations.log`), which can be reviewed to understand and diagnose issues.

The `try-except` construct can be augmented with `else` and `finally` clauses. The `else` block will execute if no exceptions are raised, while the `finally` block will execute irrespective of whether an exception was raised or not, typically used for cleanup operations.

Using else and finally with try-except

```
try:
    with open('example.txt', 'r') as file:
        content = file.read()
    print(content)
except FileNotFoundError as e:
    print(f"The file was not found: {e}")
except PermissionError as e:
    print(f"Permission denied: {e}")
except Exception as e:
    print(f"An unexpected error occurred: {e}")
else:
    print("File read successfully")
finally:
    print("Execution completed")
```

Here, if no exceptions are raised by the file operations, the `else` block executes, confirming successful file reading, and the `finally` block ex-

214

ecutes at the end, regardless of the outcome.

In some cases, you may need more specific control over the exceptions, necessitating custom error handling. Custom exceptions can be defined by subclassing the Exception class. This allows for more granular exception management.

Defining and Raising Custom Exceptions

```
class FileProcessError(Exception):
    pass

try:
    with open('example.txt', 'r') as file:
        content = file.read()
    if some_condition(content):
        raise FileProcessError("Custom error occurred while processing the file")
except FileProcessError as e:
    print(f"File processing error: {e}")
except Exception as e:
    print(f"An unexpected error occurred: {e}")
```

In this snippet, a custom exception FileProcessError is raised if a specific condition is met during file processing. Custom exceptions facilitate better error categorization and handling.

To ensure robust and maintainable code, follow these best practices for file exception handling:

- **Anticipate Common Exceptions**: Always anticipate and handle common file exceptions in your code.

- **Use Specific Exceptions**: Catch specific exceptions rather than a general Exception to provide clearer error messages and avoid masking issues.

- **Maintain Clean Log Files**: Use the logging module to keep detailed logs of errors.

- **Clean Up Resources**: Use finally blocks or context managers to ensure resources are cleaned up correctly.

- **Avoid Silent Exceptions**: Do not catch exceptions without handling them; provide meaningful messages or log entries.

By adhering to these practices, your file handling code will be more robust, maintainable, and user-friendly. Properly managing exceptions not only enhances the stability of your software but also improves the overall user experience by providing clear guidance when issues occur.

215

6.11 Directory Operations

Directory operations are crucial for efficiently managing the file system within your Python programs. This section details the mechanisms for performing directory operations using the os and shutil modules. These operations include creating, listing, changing, and removing directories. Additionally, we will review advanced directory manipulations such as copying and moving entire directory trees.

Creating Directories

To create a directory, use the os.mkdir() function for single directories, or os.makedirs() to create intermediate directories as needed.

Creating Directories

```python
import os

# Creating a single directory
os.mkdir('new_directory')

# Creating nested directories
os.makedirs('new_directory/sub_directory')
```

Listing Directory Contents

Listing the contents of a directory can be achieved using the os.listdir(). This function returns a list of the names of the entries in the directory given by path.

Listing Directory Contents

```python
import os

# List contents of a directory
contents = os.listdir('existing_directory')
print(contents)
```

```
['file1.txt', 'file2.txt', 'sub_directory']
```

For more detailed listing, including information about each entry, consider using os.scandir().

Detailed Directory Listing

```python
import os

# Scanning a directory for more detailed entry info
with os.scandir('existing_directory') as entries:
    for entry in entries:
        print(entry.name, entry.is_file(), entry.is_dir())
```

216

```
file1.txt True False
file2.txt True False
sub_directory False True
```

Changing the Current Working Directory

The current working directory can be changed using the os.chdir() function. It sets the current working directory to path.

Changing the Current Working Directory

```
import os

# Change the current working directory
os.chdir('new_directory')
```

Removing Directories

To remove a directory, use os.rmdir() for empty directories, or shutil.rmtree() for directories that might contain files or other directories.

Removing Directories

```
import os
import shutil

# Remove an empty directory
os.rmdir('new_directory/sub_directory')

# Remove a non-empty directory tree
shutil.rmtree('new_directory')
```

Copying and Moving Directories

The shutil module provides utilities to copy and move directories. To copy an entire directory tree, use shutil.copytree(). To move, use shutil.move().

Copying and Moving Directories

```
import shutil

# Copying a directory tree
shutil.copytree('source_directory', 'destination_directory')

# Moving a directory tree
shutil.move('source_directory', 'destination_directory')
```

Directory Walk

To traverse a directory tree, use the os.walk(). This generates the directory names, sub-directory names, and file names.

Traversing Directory Tree

```
import os

# Traversing the directory tree
for dirpath, dirnames, filenames in os.walk('root_directory'):
    print(f'Found directory: {dirpath}')
    for file_name in filenames:
        print(f'\t{file_name}')
```

```
Found directory: root_directory
    file1.txt
    file2.txt
Found directory: root_directory/sub_directory
    subfile1.txt
```

Permissions and Metadata

File and directory metadata, such as permissions, can be retrieved and modified using various methods in the os and stat modules.

Retrieving Directory Metadata

```
import os
import stat

# Retrieving metadata
metadata = os.stat('existing_directory')
print(stat.filemode(metadata.st_mode))
print(metadata.st_size)
print(metadata.st_mtime)
```

```
drwxr-xr-x
4096
1671032342.0
```

Permissions can be modified using the os.chmod() function.

Modifying Directory Permissions

```
import os

# Modifying directory permissions to read-only
os.chmod('existing_directory', 0o444)
```

Understanding directory operations is essential for effective file system management in Python. The os and shutil modules provide a comprehensive suite of functions to perform various directory manipulations, each crucial to the development of robust Python applications.

218

6.12   Working with JSON Files

JavaScript Object Notation (JSON) is a lightweight data interchange format that is easy for humans to read and write, and easy for machines to parse and generate. It is commonly used for transmitting data in web applications.

To effectively work with JSON data in Python, the json module is utilized. This section will explore reading, writing, parsing, generating, and handling complex JSON structures as well as addressing potential issues that may arise when working with JSON data.

- **Reading JSON Files**

JSON files can be read and converted into Python dictionaries or lists using the json.load() method. Below is an example demonstrating how to read a JSON file:

Reading a JSON file

```
import json

with open('data.json', 'r') as file:
    data = json.load(file)
print(data)
```

In this example, the open() function accesses the data.json file in read mode. The content is then loaded into the data variable as a Python dictionary.

- **Writing JSON Files**

To write data to a JSON file, the json.dump() method serializes a Python object into a JSON formatted stream:

Writing to a JSON file

```
import json

data = {
    "name": "John Doe",
    "age": 30,
    "city": "New York"
}

with open('output.json', 'w') as file:
    json.dump(data, file, indent=4)
```

In this example, the dictionary `data` is serialized to a JSON formatted string and written to `output.json`. The `indent` parameter is used for pretty-printing with an indentation of four spaces.

- **Parsing JSON Strings**

The `json` module also allows parsing JSON strings directly using the `json.loads()` method:

Parsing a JSON string

```
import json

json_string = '{"name": "Jane Doe", "age": 25, "city": "Los Angeles"}'
data = json.loads(json_string)
print(data)
```

Here, the `json.loads()` method parses the JSON string and converts it into a Python dictionary stored in the `data` variable.

- **Generating JSON Strings**

Generating JSON formatted strings from Python objects can be achieved using the `json.dumps()` method:

Generating a JSON string

```
import json

data = {
    "name": "Alice",
    "age": 28,
    "city": "San Francisco"
}

json_string = json.dumps(data, indent=4)
print(json_string)
```

The `json.dumps()` method converts the Python dictionary `data` into a JSON string. The `indent` parameter is used for pretty-printing.

- **Complex Data Structures**

The `json` module supports complex data structures, including lists, tuples, and nested dictionaries:

Complex data structure in JSON

```
import json
```

220

```
complex_data = {
    "name": "Bob",
    "roles": ["developer", "tester"],
    "projects": [
        {
            "name": "Project A",
            "status": "ongoing"
        },
        {
            "name": "Project B",
            "status": "completed"
        }
    ]
}

json_string = json.dumps(complex_data, indent=4)
print(json_string)
```

This example demonstrates the serialization of a more complex Python data structure into a JSON string. The structure includes a top-level dictionary, a list of strings, and a list of dictionaries.

- **Error Handling**

When working with JSON files, it is crucial to handle exceptions such as json.JSONDecodeError during parsing of an invalid JSON or IOError when accessing a file:

Handling JSON exceptions

```
import json

try:
    with open('invalid.json', 'r') as file:
        data = json.load(file)
except json.JSONDecodeError as e:
    print(f"Error decoding JSON: {e}")
except IOError as e:
    print(f"Error reading file: {e}")
```

In this example, a try-except block handles JSONDecodeError and IOError exceptions to ensure the program responds gracefully to errors.

Leveraging the json module, developers can efficiently manage various JSON data interchange operations in their applications, thereby enhancing data utilization and processing capabilities.

Chapter 7

Exception Handling

This chapter details Python's exception handling mechanisms, focusing on the try, except, else, and finally blocks. It explains how to raise exceptions, create custom exception classes, and handle multiple exceptions. The chapter also covers the assert statement, best practices for exception handling, logging exceptions, and clean-up actions to ensure robust and error-resistant code.

7.1   Introduction to Exceptions

In software development, an exception represents an unscheduled event that considerably affects the normal flow of the program's execution. Typically, exceptions indicate conditions that a program may not be able to handle during its operation, such as invalid inputs, file access errors, or network issues. Understanding and appropriately managing these exceptions is crucial in developing robust and reliable Python applications.

Python includes a well-defined mechanism for detecting and responding to exceptions, which promotes the creation of efficient error-handling routines. In this section, we will delve into the foundational concepts of Python exceptions and provide a groundwork for implementing exception handling in Python code.

What are Exceptions?

An exception in Python is an object encapsulating an error condition that arose during the execution of a program. When such an error condition is detected, also known as an exception being "raised" or "thrown," it disrupts the standard flow of the program, transferring control to the nearest exception handler capable of managing the error.

Python maintains a rich set of built-in exceptions that cater to various standard error situations. Here are a few commonly encountered ones:

- **ValueError** - Raised when an operation or function receives an argument of the right type but inappropriate value.

- **TypeError** - Raised when an operation or function is applied to an object of inappropriate type.

- **IndexError** - Raised when a sequence subscript is out of range.

- **KeyError** - Raised when a dictionary key is not found.

- **FileNotFoundError** - Raised when attempting to open a file that does not exist.

The ability to delineate various types of exceptions allows developers to implement fine-grained error handling strategies.

Raising and Handling Exceptions

An exception can be explicitly raised using the `raise` statement. This is particularly useful for signaling errors detected during program execution. The basic syntax for raising an exception is as follows:

```
raise ExceptionType("Error message")
```

Where `ExceptionType` is one of the built-in exception types or any user-defined exception type.

To ensure a program can respond to exceptions, Python provides the `try` and `except` blocks. The `try` block encompasses the code that might raise an exception, while the `except` block contains the code to handle the exception. Here is a simple example illustrating this concept:

```
try:
    result = 10 / 0
except ZeroDivisionError as e:
    print(f"Error occurred: {e}")
```

224

When the division by zero is attempted, a `ZeroDivisionError` is raised. The control is immediately transferred to the `except` block where the error is managed.

The Exception Hierarchy

Python's exceptions are organized into a hierarchy, where all exceptions are derived from the `BaseException` class. This hierarchy allows a consistent structure for exception handling and enables catching exceptions at appropriate granularity. Below is a simplified representation of the Python exception hierarchy:

```
BaseException
 +-- SystemExit
 +-- KeyboardInterrupt
 +-- Exception
        +-- ArithmeticError
        |     +-- ZeroDivisionError
        |     +-- OverflowError
        |     +-- FloatingPointError
        +-- LookupError
        |     +-- IndexError
        |     +-- KeyError
        +-- Other specific exceptions
```

Understanding this hierarchy helps in implementing more nuanced and specific exception handling routines. For instance, catching an `ArithmeticError` would handle both zero division and overflow errors:

```
try:
    result = some_complex_operation()
except ArithmeticError as e:
    print(f"Arithmetic error occurred: {e}")
```

Exceptions are a powerful construct in Python that effectively signal and handle error conditions during program execution. Familiarity with built-in exceptions, the syntax for raising errors, and the structure of the exception hierarchy forms the granular foundation necessary for robust error handling. The subsequent sections of this chapter will build on this introductory knowledge, exploring more complex scenarios and detailed mechanisms for managing exceptions in Python, leading to resilient and maintainable code.

7.2 The `try` and `except` Block

Exception handling in Python is primarily managed through the use of the `try` and `except` blocks. The `try` block allows you to test a block of code for errors, while the `except` block enables you to handle those errors gracefully if they occur. This mechanism is crucial for creating robust applications that can handle unexpected situations without crashing.

Syntax and Basic Usage

The basic syntax for the `try` and `except` blocks is as follows:

```python
try:
    # Code that might raise an exception
except SomeException:
    # Code that runs if the exception occurs
```

Here, the code inside the `try` block is executed first. If no exception occurs, the `except` block is skipped. If an exception of type `SomeException` occurs, the code inside the `except` block is executed.

Handling Specific Exceptions

It is often necessary to handle different types of exceptions in a specific manner. Python allows for the creation of multiple `except` blocks to handle various exceptions individually:

```python
try:
    # Code that might raise multiple types of exceptions
except ValueError:
    print("A ValueError occurred")
except TypeError:
    print("A TypeError occurred")
```

In this example, if a `ValueError` occurs, the message "A ValueError occurred" is printed. If a `TypeError` occurs, the message "A TypeError occurred" is printed.

Catching All Exceptions

To catch all exceptions, one can use the generic `Exception` class. This approach, however, should be used cautiously, as it can mask problems that are better solved by fixing the underlying code rather than catching every exception indiscriminately.

```python
try:
    # Code that might raise any exception
except Exception as e:
    print(f"An exception occurred: {e}")
```

226

In this case, any exception that occurs within the try block will be caught, and the message containing the exception details will be printed.

Exception Handling with Multiple Statements

A try block can contain multiple statements, enabling the handling of exceptions that may arise from any of those statements.

```
try:
    statement1
    statement2
    # Additional statements that might raise exceptions
except SomeException:
    # Handle the exception if one occurs
```

This structure ensures that if any of the statements within the try block raise an exception, control is immediately passed to the corresponding except block.

Accessing Exception Details

When an exception is caught, the exception object provides information about the error. This object can be accessed using the as keyword:

```
try:
    # Code that might raise an exception
except SomeException as e:
    print(f"An exception occurred: {e}")
```

Here, the variable e holds the exception object, which can then be used to obtain information about the error.

Nested try and except Blocks

It is possible to nest try and except blocks to handle exceptions at different levels of code execution. This approach is particularly useful in complex functions where different parts of the code may require distinct exception handling mechanisms.

```
try:
    try:
        # Code that might raise an exception
    except SomeException:
        # Handle specific exception
except AnotherException:
    # Handle another type of exception
```

Example

Consider the following example, which demonstrates the use of try and except blocks to handle potential errors when performing division:

227

```
def divide(a, b):
    try:
        result = a / b
    except ZeroDivisionError as e:
        print(f"Error: {e}")
        return None
    except TypeError as e:
        print(f"Error: {e}")
        return None
    else:
        return result

print(divide(10, 2)) # Output: 5.0
print(divide(10, 0)) # Output: Error: division by zero, None
print(divide(10, 'a')) # Output: Error: unsupported operand type(s) for /: 'int'
    and 'str', None
```

In this example, the try block attempts to perform division. If a ZeroDivisionError or TypeError occurs, the corresponding except block handles the error and prints an appropriate message. The presence of the else block ensures that if no exception occurs, the result of the division is returned.

The try and except blocks are fundamental components of Python's exception handling framework. They provide a structured way to address errors and ensure that programs can gracefully recover from unexpected conditions. By understanding and effectively utilizing these constructs, developers can enhance the reliability and robustness of their code.

7.3 Multiple Except Clauses

Handling different types of exceptions with specific responses is facilitated by using multiple except clauses within a single try block. This approach enables developers to address varying error conditions with tailored exception-handling routines, ensuring more accurate and controlled program behavior.

The syntax for employing multiple except clauses is straightforward. Each except clause is followed by an exception type and an optional variable to hold the exception object. Here's the basic structure:

```
try:
    # Block of code that may raise exceptions
except ExceptionType1 as e1:
    # Handle ExceptionType1
except ExceptionType2 as e2:
    # Handle ExceptionType2
# Potential additional except clauses
```

228

```
except ExceptionTypeN as eN:
    # Handle ExceptionTypeN
```

In this structure, the try block contains code that may raise exceptions. The subsequent except blocks catch and handle specific exception types, if they occur.

The order in which except clauses are written is significant. Python evaluates these clauses sequentially, from top to bottom. When an exception is raised, the first matching except clause is executed. Therefore, more specific exceptions should precede more general ones to prevent them from being preempted.

Consider the following example, where ZeroDivisionError and ValueError are handled:

```
try:
    result = 10 / int(input("Enter a number: "))
except ZeroDivisionError as zde:
    print("Error: Division by zero is not allowed.")
except ValueError as ve:
    print("Error: Invalid input, please enter a numeric value.")
```

In this example, if the user inputs a non-numeric value, the ValueError clause will handle it. If the user inputs zero, the ZeroDivisionError clause will manage the exception.

To illustrate the utility of multiple except clauses further, consider a function that reads a file and processes its content. This function can raise various exceptions, including FileNotFoundError, IOError, and ValueError. Handling each of these exceptions appropriately enhances the robustness of the function.

```
def process_file(file_path):
    try:
        with open(file_path, 'r') as file:
            content = file.read()
            # Process file content
    except FileNotFoundError as fnf_error:
        print(f"Error: File not found. Detail: {fnf_error}")
    except IOError as io_error:
        print(f"Error: I/O error occurred. Detail: {io_error}")
    except ValueError as val_error:
        print(f"Error: Value error encountered. Detail: {val_error}")

# Example usage
file_path = 'example.txt'
process_file(file_path)
```

In this sample, the process_file function attempts to open and read a file. If the file specified by file_path does not exist, a FileNotFoundError is raised and handled. If an I/O error occurs, it is managed by the IOError clause. Lastly, a ValueError is caught and handled if raised.

Python also allows handling multiple exception types within a single except clause using a tuple. This can be useful when you want to execute the same handling code for different exceptions:

```
try:
    result = 10 / int(input("Enter a number: "))
except (ZeroDivisionError, ValueError) as error:
    print(f"Error: {error}")
```

In this example, both ZeroDivisionError and ValueError are handled by the same except block, where the error message is printed regardless of the specific exception type.

When using multiple except clauses, consider the following best practices to ensure clarity and maintainability:

- **Order Specific to General Exceptions:** Always place specific exception types before general ones, such as Exception, to prevent the latter from overriding the former.

- **Clear and Descriptive Handles:** Provide clear and concise handling for each exception type to facilitate debugging and maintenance.

- **Avoid Overusing General Exceptions:** Refrain from using overly broad exception clauses, which can obscure the nature of errors and lead to harder-to-debug code.

- **Document Exception Handling:** Document the intention behind catching specific exceptions, particularly for more complex handling logic.

By adhering to these guidelines, developers can leverage multiple except clauses to create robust and error-resilient Python applications.

7.4 The else Clause

In Python's exception handling framework, the else clause plays a pivotal role in managing code that must run only if no exceptions are raised within the try block. This clause provides a systematic approach to separating the normal, non-exceptional path of execution from the

230

error handling routines. The structure of including an `else` clause is as follows:

```
try:
    # Code that might raise an exception
    risky_operation()
except SomeException as e:
    # Code that handles the exception
    handle_exception(e)
else:
    # Code to run if no exceptions were raised
    subsequent_operation()
```

Purpose and Usage

The `else` clause is executed only if the `try` block terminates successfully, meaning no exceptions were raised. It enhances code clarity by cleanly demarcating the normal flow of logic from exception handling procedures. This separation can be particularly beneficial for readability and maintainability, ensuring that the core logic is not intertwined with error management code.

Consider the following practical example:

```
try:
    with open('data.txt', 'r') as file:
        content = file.read()
except FileNotFoundError:
    print("File not found. Please check the file path.")
else:
    print("File read successfully. Processing content...")
    process_content(content)
```

In this scenario, the `else` block handles the operations dependent on the successful execution of the `try` block. It ensures that `process_content(content)` is called only if no `FileNotFoundError` is raised.

Comparison with the `finally` Clause

To provide comprehensive understanding, it is crucial to differentiate between the `else` and `finally` clauses. The `finally` clause is executed regardless of whether an exception occurred, typically used for cleanup actions. In contrast, the `else` clause runs only in the absence of exceptions. The following example elucidates their differing roles:

```
try:
    data = fetch_data()
except DataFetchException:
    print("An error occurred while fetching data.")
else:
    validate_data(data)
finally:
    close_connection()
```

Here, `validate_data(data)` executes only if `fetch_data()` succeeds without exceptions, while `close_connection()` runs regardless of the outcome, to ensure no resources are left unutilized.

Best Practices

Employing the `else` clause effectively contributes to more readable and maintainable code. Below are some best practices:

- **Distinct Logic**: Use the `else` clause for code that should only execute when the `try` block has completed successfully. This reduces the risk of conflating normal operation code with error-handling logic.

- **Minimal Dependency**: Keep the `else` clause independent. Avoid placing code that relies on specific exception handling outcomes, as `else` should only depend on the successful execution of the `try` block.

Common Pitfalls

While the `else` clause is beneficial, misuse can lead to ambiguity and maintenance challenges:

- **Overuse**: Avoid overusing the `else` clause for trivial operations. Reserve it for significant tasks that logically follow a successful `try` block.

- **Obscured Logic**: Ensure the purpose of the `else` clause remains clear and logical within the context of the `try-except` block. Avoid scenarios where the relationship between the `try` block and the `else` clause is not immediately obvious.

The `else` clause in Python's exception handling mechanism offers a structured and legible way to handle conditional logic that should occur only in the absence of exceptions. It enhances the readability and maintainability of the code by distinctly separating the primary logic from error handling. By adhering to best practices and avoiding common pitfalls, developers can effectively utilize the `else` clause to write robust and clean code.

7.5 The `finally` Clause

The `finally` clause in Python is instrumental in ensuring that certain actions are always executed, regardless of whether an exception occurs within a `try` block. This clause is particularly valuable for operations that must be completed to maintain program integrity, such as the release of resources, closing files, or cleanup activities that should not be omitted under any circumstance.

The structure of a `try-finally` block is as follows:

```
try:
    # Code that may raise an exception
finally:
    # Code that will execute irrespective of an exception
```

Execution of `finally` Clause

When a `finally` clause is used in conjunction with a `try` block, the code within the `finally` block is guaranteed to run even if an unhandled exception is raised, or a `return`, `break`, or `continue` statement is encountered. This ensures that necessary cleanup activities are performed.

Consider the following example:

```
def read_file(file_path):
    try:
        file = open(file_path, 'r')
        # Perform file operations
    finally:
        file.close()
```

In this example, the `file.close()` method is called within the `finally` block. This ensures that the file is properly closed, even if an error occurs during the file operations within the `try` block. Failure to close the file could result in resource leaks and potential data corruption.

Combined Usage with `except` Clause

In practice, a `try` block often includes both `except` and `finally` clauses. The following example illustrates such a composite structure:

```
def divide_numbers(a, b):
    try:
        result = a / b
    except ZeroDivisionError:
        print("Error: Division by zero")
        result = None
    finally:
        print("Execution of finally clause")
    return result
```

Here, if an attempt to divide by zero is made, a ZeroDivisionError is caught by the except block, and an appropriate message is printed. Regardless of whether an exception is caught, the finally block will execute, ensuring that the clean-up action—or any other essential operation denoted within it—occurs.

Interaction with return Statements

One nuance when working with the finally block is its interaction with the return statement. If a return statement is encountered in the try or except block, the finally block will still execute prior to the actual return. This can be illustrated as follows:

```
def example_function():
    try:
        return 'from try'
    finally:
        print('finally block executed')

result = example_function()
print(result)
```

The output of this code will be:

```
finally block executed
from try
```

As exhibited, the message from the finally block is printed before the function returns its value. This behavior ensures that the finally block is honored, even in the presence of an imminent return.

Practical Considerations

In designing robust software systems, using the finally clause becomes indispensable for resource management, particularly when dealing with files, network connections, and other I/O operations. For example, consider the context of network connections which must be closed gracefully to avoid resource leaks:

```
import socket

def connect_to_server(server_address):
    s = socket.socket(socket.AF_INET, socket.SOCK_STREAM)
    try:
        s.connect(server_address)
        # Perform data exchange with server
    except socket.error as e:
        print(f"Socket error: {e}")
    finally:
        s.close()
```

In this snippet, the s.close() method in the finally block ensures the socket is closed, even if an exception is raised during the connection process or data exchange. Without this safeguard, the program might exhaust system resources or leave connections hanging.

The `finally` clause's role extends beyond error handling; it fortifies programs against unforeseen circumstances, ensuring that critical operations are not skipped, thus contributing to the stability and reliability of the software. Understanding and leveraging the `finally` clause is essential for writing resilient and maintainable Python code.

7.6 Raising Exceptions

In Python, raising exceptions is a fundamental technique for enforcing correct program behavior, signaling error conditions, or interrupting normal program flow when a particular condition is met. This section delves into the mechanics of raising exceptions, demonstrating its syntax and providing examples of effective usage.

Syntax of Raising Exceptions

Exceptions are raised using the `raise` statement, which can be followed by specifying an exception class or an instance of an exception class. The general syntax is:

```
raise [ExceptionClass[(optional_argument)]]
```

The above syntax outlines that the `ExceptionClass` is a placeholder for Python's built-in exception classes (e.g., `ValueError`, `TypeError`) or user-defined exception classes. The `optional_argument` can be used to provide more context or information about the exception.

Raising Built-in Exceptions

To raise a built-in exception, one specifies the desired exception class, optionally followed by an argument that provides additional details about the error:

```
raise ValueError("Invalid input provided")
```

In this example, a `ValueError` is raised with a message indicating the nature of the error.

```
Traceback (most recent call last):
  ...
ValueError: Invalid input provided
```

Raising User-Defined Exceptions

Python allows the creation of custom exceptions to encapsulate specific

235

error conditions relevant to the program. Custom exceptions typically derive from the base Exception class.

```
class CustomError(Exception):
    pass

raise CustomError("An error specific to the application occurred")
```

In the above example, a custom exception class CustomError is defined and subsequently raised with a descriptive message.

Chaining Exceptions

Python 3 supports exception chaining, which is the practice of associating a raised exception with another exception. This is particularly useful for tracking the sequence of errors. Exception chaining is achieved using the from keyword:

```
try:
    1 / 0
except ZeroDivisionError as e:
    raise ValueError("A division error occurred") from e
```

In this code snippet, a ValueError is raised in response to a caught ZeroDivisionError, effectively chaining the two exceptions.

```
Traceback (most recent call last):
  ...
ZeroDivisionError: division by zero

The above exception was the direct cause of the following exception:

Traceback (most recent call last):
  ...
ValueError: A division error occurred
```

Re-Raising Exceptions

Situations may arise where an exception is caught and then re-raised to propagate it to higher levels of the program. This can be achieved using the bare raise statement:

```
try:
    # Code that may raise an exception
    pass
except SomeException as e:
    # Perform any cleanup actions or logging
    raise
```

By using raise alone, the original context and traceback of the exception are preserved.

Best Practices for Raising Exceptions

The following best practices should be adhered to when raising exceptions in Python:

- **Use Meaningful Messages:** Always provide informative and clear messages when raising exceptions. This facilitates debugging and understanding the error context.

- **Avoid Raising Generic Exceptions:** Raise specific exceptions relevant to the error condition rather than using the base `Exception` class.

- **Leverage Exception Chaining:** Utilize exception chaining to maintain the original context of exceptions, making it easier to trace the sequence of errors.

- **Adopt Custom Exceptions Judiciously:** When built-in exceptions are not adequate, create custom exception classes to encapsulate specific error conditions, thereby enhancing readability and maintainability of the code.

Raising exceptions is a pivotal aspect of robust error handling in Python. It allows for the identification, signaling, and management of error conditions, making it possible to write resilient programs that are both easier to debug and maintain. By following the syntactical guidelines and best practices outlined in this section, developers can ensure that their use of exceptions is both effective and efficient.

7.7   Custom Exception Classes

In most programming scenarios, the built-in exceptions provided by Python suffice for error handling. However, there are situations where defining custom exception classes can greatly enhance the clarity and specificity of exception handling in your code. Custom exceptions allow developers to tailor error messages and handling procedures, making code more robust and readable.

Creating a Custom Exception Class

Creating a custom exception class in Python is straightforward. Custom exception classes are generally subclasses of the `Exception` base class. By inheriting from `Exception`, your custom exception will integrate smoothly with Python's existing exception handling framework.

237

Defining a Custom Exception Class

```
class InvalidInputError(Exception):
    def __init__(self, message="Invalid input provided"):
        self.message = message
        super().__init__(self.message)
```

In the example above, we define a custom exception class called InvalidInputError. The __init__ method initializes the exception with a default error message. By calling super().__init_(self.message), we ensure that the base Exception class is properly initialized.

Raising Custom Exceptions

Once defined, custom exceptions can be raised using the raise keyword. This can be particularly useful for enforcing specific validation rules or handling particular error conditions that are unique to your application.

Raising a Custom Exception

```
def process_input(value):
    if not isinstance(value, int):
        raise InvalidInputError("Only integers are allowed")
    # Proceed with processing the valid input
    return value * 2

try:
    result = process_input("abc")
except InvalidInputError as e:
    print(f"Error: {e}")
```

In the above code, the function process_input raises an InvalidInputError if the provided value is not of integer type. The raised exception is then caught by the except block, which handles the error appropriately by printing the custom error message.

Custom Exception Hierarchies

For more complex applications, it is often useful to define a hierarchy of custom exceptions. This allows for more granular error handling, as well as the ability to catch multiple related exceptions under a common base exception. To achieve this, simply create multiple custom exceptions that inherit from a common parent class.

Defining a Hierarchy of Custom Exceptions

```
class ApplicationError(Exception):
    """Base class for all application-specific errors"""
    pass

class ConfigurationError(ApplicationError):
    """Raised for errors in configuration settings"""
    pass
```

```
class ConnectionError(ApplicationError):
    """Raised for network connection errors"""
    pass
```

Here, `ApplicationError` serves as the base class for all custom exceptions in this hypothetical application. `ConfigurationError` and `ConnectionError` are specific exceptions that inherit from `ApplicationError`. This design allows catching all application-specific errors with a single except block if needed:

Catching Custom Exception Hierarchies

```
try:
    # Code that may raise ConfigurationError or ConnectionError
    raise ConfigurationError("Invalid configuration detected")
except ApplicationError as e:
    print(f"An application error occurred: {e}")
```

By catching `ApplicationError`, the except block will handle any exceptions that are instances of `ApplicationError` or its subclasses, enabling more flexible and maintainable error handling.

Best Practices for Custom Exception Classes

When designing custom exception classes, adhere to the following best practices:

- **Naming conventions:** Use clear and descriptive names ending with "Error" to indicate exception classes.

- **Documentation:** Provide comprehensive docstrings for custom exception classes to explain their usage and purpose.

- **Hierarchy:** Structure custom exceptions hierarchically to allow grouped handling of related errors.

- **Minimalism:** Define custom exceptions sparingly. Only create new exceptions when the built-in ones are insufficient.

Adhering to these guidelines ensures that custom exception classes remain effective tools for handling errors uniquely tied to the specifics of the application while maintaining code readability and robustness.

7.8 Handling Multiple Exceptions

In robust Python programs, it is common to anticipate various types of exceptions that may arise during execution. This section elucidates how to handle multiple exceptions within a single block, ensuring comprehensive error management.

Python enables the handling of multiple exceptions using a single except clause by grouping the exceptions in a tuple. This approach is particularly useful when identical handling logic applies to various exception types.

Combining Multiple Exceptions

```
try:
    result = operation()
except (TypeError, ValueError) as e:
    handle_exception(e)
```

In this example, if either a TypeError or ValueError is raised, it is caught and passed to the handle_exception function for unified processing.

When distinct handling for different exceptions is necessary, multiple except clauses can be employed, each tailored to a specific exception type.

Multiple Except Clauses for Different Exceptions

```
try:
    result = operation()
except TypeError as te:
    handle_type_error(te)
except ValueError as ve:
    handle_value_error(ve)
```

Here, TypeError and ValueError exceptions are managed independently, allowing for precise control over the program's response to each type of error.

To catch fallback exceptions that are not anticipated in specific clauses, the base Exception class can be used. This ensures that any unforeseen errors are also addressed, preventing unintended program termination.

Catching a Base Exception

```
try:
    result = operation()
except (TypeError, ValueError) as e:
    handle_exception(e)
```

```
except Exception as ex:
    log_unexpected_exception(ex)
```

In this structure, `TypeError` and `ValueError` are processed together, and any other unexpected exceptions are logged for further investigation.

There are scenarios where specific exceptions need to be caught, logged, and subsequently re-raised for higher-level exception handling. This technique provides layered error management.

Re-raising Exceptions

```
try:
    result = operation()
except SpecificException as se:
    log_specific_exception(se)
    raise
except GeneralException as ge:
    log_general_exception(ge)
    raise
```

In this setup, each captured exception is logged appropriately and then re-raised, ensuring that the higher-level logic is aware of the occurrence.

Handling multiple exceptions may also require nested `try-except` blocks, which allow for specific exceptions to be managed within progressively broader scopes.

Nested Try-Except Blocks

```
try:
    try:
        result = operation()
    except TemporaryException as te:
        handle_temporary_exception(te)
except PermanentException as pe:
    handle_permanent_exception(pe)
```

Here, `TemporaryException` is managed within the inner block, while PermanentException is handled by the outer block, facilitating detailed error categorization and resolution.

In certain cases, the `else` clause, which executes when no exceptions are raised, can be used in combination with multiple exception handling to streamline the logical flow.

Utilizing the Else Clause

```
try:
    result = operation()
except (IOError, OSError) as ioe:
```

```
    handle_io_error(ioe)
else:
    process_result(result)
```

The `else` clause here ensures that `process_result` is only called if no `IOError` or `OSError` occurs, logically separating the main operation from its exception handling.

For comprehensive programs, constructing a cumulative strategy that combines all discussed techniques can ensure robust exception handling across different modules and functionalities.

In summary, handling multiple exceptions in Python is facilitated through a variety of techniques ranging from combining exceptions in tuples to utilizing nested `try-except` blocks, re-raising exceptions, and employing the `else` clause. Each method provides flexibility in ensuring robust and resilient code, catering to the intricacies of diverse error scenarios.

7.9   The assert Statement

Assertions in Python serve as a debugging aid that tests a condition as an internal self-check within the program. They are often employed to ensure that the program is operating as expected. The `assert` statement is used to verify that a certain condition holds true. If the condition evaluates to false, an `AssertionError` exception is thrown, halting program execution unless the exception is caught. This section elucidates the syntactical structure, usage, and practical considerations associated with the `assert` statement.

Syntax

The `assert` statement in Python has the following syntax:

```
assert condition, error_message
```

Here, `condition` is a boolean expression that the program expects to be true. If the condition evaluates to false, the optional `error_message` is provided, which is displayed as part of the `AssertionError`.

Usage

Assertions should be used to catch situations that should never happen if the code is correct. They are typically used in the following scenarios:

- To check internal invariants in the code

- To validate argument types and values

- To ensure that critical preconditions and postconditions are met

Example

Consider a function that calculates the average of a list of numbers. An assertion can ensure that the input list is not empty.

```
def calculate_average(numbers):
    assert len(numbers) > 0, "The list of numbers is empty"
    return sum(numbers) / len(numbers)
```

In the example above, the assertion verifies that the `numbers` list has at least one element. If the list is empty, the assertion throws an `AssertionError` with the message, "The list of numbers is empty."

Disabling Assertions

Assertions are a debugging tool and can be globally disabled with the `-O` (optimize) and `-OO` options when running the Python interpreter. This would remove all `assert` statements and their associated error messages, effectively treating assertions as no-operation (NO-OP).

```
python -O your_script.py
```

Therefore, it is prudent not to rely on assertions for implementing critical program logic. Assertions are not a replacement for proper error handling with exceptions but a complementary tool to ensure sanity checks during development.

Caveats

Care should be taken when using assertions, particularly with mutable data structures or function calls that have side effects. Consider the following example:

```
def func_with_side_effect():
    # side effect
    return True

assert func_with_side_effect()
```

In this case, if assertions are disabled with `-O`, the function `func_with_side_effect()` will not be called, potentially leading to unintended consequences.

Another caveat is the use of complex logic in assertions. Assertions should remain simple, focusing on testing conditions without incorporating elaborate logic that could obscure the primary functionality of the code.

Best Practices

Adhering to best practices when using assertions can enhance code reliability and maintainability:

- **Simplicity**: Keep assertions straightforward and readable.

- **Descriptive Messages**: Provide clear and concise error messages to help diagnose issues quickly when assertions fail.

- **Non-invasive**: Ensure assertions do not alter the state or flow of the program.

- **Supplementary Use**: Utilize assertions primarily for debugging purposes, not for critical runtime checks.

The `assert` statement in Python is a powerful feature for adding internal checks during program development. While it can help identify problems early by enforcing assumptions about the code, it should be used judiciously and not substitute for regular error handling mechanisms. Properly utilized, assertions can contribute significantly to ensuring program correctness and robustness, especially during the early phases of development and testing.

By embedding sanity checks directly into the code, developers can catch erroneous conditions promptly, improving code quality and reliability.

7.10   Best Practices for Exception Handling

Efficient and effective exception handling is essential to maintain the robustness of Python applications. Adhering to best practices ensures that exceptions do not lead to unmanageable states or security vulnerabilities, and that they provide meaningful feedback for debugging and user interaction. This section outlines several key principles to achieve reliable and maintainable exception handling.

Catch Only Exceptions You Can Handle

Catching exceptions without appropriate handling can obscure errors and result in nondeterministic behavior. Always catch exceptions specific to the anticipated error conditions. For example, avoid using a bare except clause:

```
# Avoid this
try:
    risky_operation()
except:
    print("An error occurred.")
```

Instead, handle specific exceptions:

```
try:
    risky_operation()
except ValueError:
    print("ValueError occurred.")
except TypeError:
    print("TypeError occurred.")
```

Follow the "Easier to Ask for Forgiveness than Permission" (EAFP) Principle

Python supports the EAFP coding style, which promotes trying an operation directly and catching permissible exceptions rather than using conditional checks to prevent the error. This technique can lead to cleaner and more readable code.

```
# EAFP approach
try:
    result = my_dict[key]
except KeyError:
    result = default_value
```

Conversely, the Look Before You Leap (LBYL) approach requires additional conditional logic, which can clutter the code:

```
# LBYL approach
if key in my_dict:
    result = my_dict[key]
else:
    result = default_value
```

Do Not Silence Exceptions

Silencing exceptions can make debugging difficult. Unless an exception is expected and specific handling logic is implemented, always propagate exceptions. Avoid constructs that consume exceptions silently:

```
try:
    execute_operation()
except Exception:
    pass # Avoid this
```

A better approach is to log the exception or re-raise it with additional context:

```
import logging

try:
    execute_operation()
except Exception as e:
    logging.error("An error occurred: %s", e)
    raise
```

Use the `finally` Block for Resource Management

The `finally` block should be used for clean-up actions that must be executed regardless of whether an exception occurred. This is particularly important for operations involving external resources, such as file handles or network connections.

```
try:
    file = open("data.txt")
    # Perform file operations
except IOError as e:
    logging.error("File error: %s", e)
finally:
    file.close()
```

In modern Python code, using context managers (the `with` statement) is preferred for such resource management:

```
try:
    with open("data.txt") as file:
        # Perform file operations
except IOError as e:
    logging.error("File error: %s", e)
```

Leveraging Custom Exception Classes

Creating custom exception classes allows for more precise and context-aware error handling. Custom exceptions can inherit from base exception classes and can include additional attributes or methods for enhanced functionality.

```
class MyCustomError(Exception):
    def __init__(self, message, errors=None):
        super().__init__(message)
        self.errors = errors

try:
    raise MyCustomError("An error occurred", errors={"code": 123})
except MyCustomError as e:
    logging.error("Custom error: %s with errors: %s", e, e.errors)
```

Documenting Exception Behavior

246

Properly documenting which exceptions a function or method can raise is essential for maintainable code. This can be achieved using docstrings.

```python
def parse_integer(value):
    """
    Parses a string to an integer.

    :param value: String to parse
    :type value: str
    :raises ValueError: If the string cannot be converted to an integer
    :return: Parsed integer
    :rtype: int
    """
    return int(value)
```

Utilizing Asserts for Debugging, Not for Logic

The assert statement is a valuable tool for debugging, used to check logical conditions that should be met within the code. It is not intended for regular error handling and should not be used where recoverable exceptions are required.

```python
def compute_percentage(part, whole):
    assert whole != 0, "Whole cannot be zero"
    return (part / whole) * 100
```

Assertions are stripped out when Python is run in optimized mode, making them unsuitable for runtime logic.

Consistent and Informative Logging

Logging exceptions is a best practice for auditing and monitoring. Ensure that all relevant information, including stack traces and error messages, is logged to aid in diagnosing issues.

```python
import logging

logger = logging.getLogger(__name__)

def process_data(data):
    try:
        # Process data
    except Exception as e:
        logger.exception("Processing error")
        raise
```

By following the above guidelines, Python developers can construct robust, maintainable, and clear error handling mechanisms, thereby enhancing the overall quality and reliability of their applications.

7.11 Logging Exceptions

Effective exception handling in Python involves not only catching and managing exceptions but also appropriately logging them to provide invaluable insights during debugging and application monitoring. Logging exceptions can help developers track issues, understand error patterns, and maintain non-intrusive record-keeping of operational anomalies. The `logging` module in Python's standard library facilitates this process by offering a flexible framework for emitting log messages from Python programs. This section delves into best practices and methodologies for logging exceptions effectively.

The Logging Module

The `logging` module allows for hierarchical logging that includes multiple loggers, handlers, filters, and formatters. It supports different levels of severity, namely DEBUG, INFO, WARNING, ERROR, and CRITICAL, providing a fine-grained control over what is logged and how it is handled. First, we need to set up a basic configuration for the logging system:

Basic Logging Configuration

```
import logging

logging.basicConfig(level=logging.DEBUG,
             format='%(asctime)s - %(name)s - %(levelname)s - %(message)s',
             handlers=[logging.FileHandler("application.log"),
                     logging.StreamHandler()])
```

In the example above, the `basicConfig` method configures the logging system with a specific format and assigns both a file handler and a stream handler to the root logger.

Logging an Exception

When an exception occurs, it is crucial to log the details to aid in diagnosis. The `logging.exception()` method is specifically designed for this purpose. It records a message along with the traceback of the exception, thus providing comprehensive information for postmortem analysis.

Logging an Exception Example

```
import logging

def divide(a, b):
    try:
        result = a / b
    except ZeroDivisionError as e:
        logging.exception("Exception occurred")
```

```
    else:
        return result

divide(10, 0)
```

In this example, if a division by zero occurs, the message "Exception occurred" will be logged along with the traceback. The `exception` method must be called within an except block to catch any exceptions and log the relevant information effectively.

Custom Loggers and Handlers

Creating custom loggers and handlers provides greater control over logging configurations and allows different parts of an application to have distinct logging behaviors.

Configuring Custom Logger and Handler

```
import logging

# Creating a custom logger
logger = logging.getLogger('customLogger')
logger.setLevel(logging.INFO)

# Creating handler
handler = logging.FileHandler('custom.log')
handler.setLevel(logging.INFO)

# Creating a logging format
formatter = logging.Formatter('%(name)s - %(levelname)s - %(message)s')
handler.setFormatter(formatter)

# Adding the handler to the logger
logger.addHandler(handler)

def divide(a, b):
    try:
        result = a / b
    except ZeroDivisionError as e:
        logger.exception("Division by zero exception occurred")
    else:
        return result

divide(10, 0)
```

In the above snippet, a custom logger named `customLogger` is defined. A file handler associated with the logger writes the log messages to `custom.log`. The formatter specifies the structure of the log messages.

Logging Best Practices

Adhering to best practices ensures that logging provides meaningful, actionable insights into the runtime behavior of applications. Key recommendations include:

249

- **Set appropriate log levels**: Utilize different log levels (DEBUG, INFO, WARNING, ERROR, CRITICAL) judiciously to categorize the severity of messages.

- **Avoid excessive logging**: Over-logging can flood log files, complicating diagnosis. Ensure that the logged information is pertinent.

- **Log meaningful messages**: Include relevant context in log messages to enhance their utility (e.g., variable values, user IDs).

- **Secure log files**: Log files may contain sensitive information; enforce proper access controls and consider redacting sensitive data.

- **Use structured logging**: Structure logs in a consistent format, perhaps JSON, to improve their parsability and queryability.

Logging exceptions is an indispensable aspect of robust application monitoring and debugging. Leveraging the capabilities of the Python `logging` module, developers can capture detailed exception information, facilitate real-time monitoring, and maintain more traceable codebases. By following best practices, developers ensure their logging strategy is efficient, secure, and effective in providing valuable insights into the runtime behavior of their applications.

7.12 Clean-Up Actions

In Python, clean-up actions are essential for ensuring that resources are properly released and systems maintain their integrity, even when errors occur. These actions typically involve closing files, releasing locks, and cleaning up temporary resources. The `finally` clause is the primary mechanism in Python for executing clean-up actions, and it is guaranteed to run regardless of whether an exception is raised in the `try` block.

Using the `finally` Clause

The `finally` clause ensures that specific clean-up code runs whether an exception is raised or not. The following is the syntax for using the `finally` clause:

```
try:
    # Code that may raise an exception
```

```
    pass
except SomeException as e:
    # Exception handling code
    pass
finally:
    # Clean-up code
    pass
```

The finally block is executed after the try and except blocks, irrespective of whether an exception was caught. Consider an example where a file is opened and needs to be closed:

```
try:
    file = open('example.txt', 'r')
    # Process file
except IOError as e:
    print(f"An I/O error occurred: {e}")
finally:
    file.close()
```

In this example, file.close() is called within the finally block, ensuring that the file is closed no matter what happens during the file processing.

Context Managers

While the finally clause is effective, Python provides a more elegant and often preferred way to handle resource management using context managers via the with statement. The with statement abstracts the boilerplate code involved with resource management, providing an automatic clean-up mechanism.

The basic syntax for using the with statement is as follows:

```
with resource_management_expression as resource:
    # Code that makes use of the resource
    pass
```

Here's how you would use the with statement to manage a file:

```
with open('example.txt', 'r') as file:
    # Process file
    pass
# No need to explicitly close the file
```

In this instance, the file is automatically closed when the block inside the with statement is exited, whether it is exited normally or via an exception. This not only simplifies the code but also makes it less error-prone.

Creating Custom Context Managers

Custom context managers can be created by defining a class with

__enter__ and __exit__ methods, or by using the
contextlib.contextmanager decorator.

Using the Class-Based Approach

A class-based context manager should implement __enter__ and
__exit__ methods as shown below:

```python
class ManagedResource:
    def __enter__(self):
        # Acquire resource
        return self

    def __exit__(self, exc_type, exc_value, traceback):
        # Release resource
        pass

with ManagedResource() as resource:
    # Use the resource
    pass
```

Using the contextlib Module

The contextlib module simplifies the creation of context managers by
using a generator decorated with @contextlib.contextmanager:

```python
from contextlib import contextmanager

@contextmanager
def managed_resource():
    try:
        # Acquire resource
        yield
    finally:
        # Release resource
        pass

with managed_resource():
    # Use the resource
    pass
```

Both methods ensure that your resources are properly managed and
cleaned up.

Best Practices for Clean-Up Actions

- **Always Close Resources**: Ensure that all open files, network connections, and database connections are properly closed.

- **Prefer with Statement**: Use the with statement for managing resources when possible. It simplifies the code and ensures clean-
  up actions are performed correctly.

- **Use Finally for Critical Clean-Up**: When the with statement is not applicable, use the `finally` block to handle crucial clean-up actions.

- **Handle Exceptions in Clean-Up**: Ensure that clean-up actions account for any potential exceptions that may occur during the process.

By adhering to these best practices, you can write robust Python programs that manage resources efficiently and handle exceptions gracefully.

Chapter 8

Object-Oriented Programming

This chapter introduces object-oriented programming in Python, covering the creation and use of classes and objects, instance variables and methods, and the concepts of constructors and destructors. It explains inheritance, method overriding, and the use of the super() function, as well as encapsulation, polymorphism, and special methods for operator overloading. The chapter also discusses the differences between composition and inheritance, along with abstract classes and methods.

8.1 Introduction to Object-Oriented Programming

Object-Oriented Programming (OOP) is a programming paradigm that uses objects and classes as fundamental components. This section delves into the core concepts and principles of OOP, emphasizing their implementation and significance in Python programming.

OOP offers a structured framework for designing and organizing software, promoting code reuse, scalability, and maintainability. It is predicated on the abstraction of real-world entities into computational objects, enabling clear and intuitive modeling of complex systems.

Principles of Object-Oriented Programming

OOP is underpinned by four primary principles: encapsulation, abstraction, inheritance, and polymorphism. Each principle contributes uniquely to the simplification of software development and the enhancement of code efficiency.

Encapsulation

Encapsulation refers to the bundling of data (attributes) and methods (functions) that manipulate the data into a single unit, known as a class. This principle also enforces information hiding, restricting direct access to some of an object's components and protecting the object's internal state from unintended interference.

In Python, encapsulation is implemented through class definitions and access specifiers such as public, protected, and private attributes. While Python's attribute visibility is not enforced by language syntax, naming conventions (e.g., a single underscore for protected and double underscore for private) informally signal intended access levels.

Encapsulation Example in Python

```
class BankAccount:
    def __init__(self, balance=0):
        self.__balance = balance # Private attribute

    def deposit(self, amount):
        if amount > 0:
            self.__balance += amount

    def withdraw(self, amount):
        if 0 < amount <= self.__balance:
            self.__balance -= amount

    def get_balance(self):
        return self.__balance

account = BankAccount()
account.deposit(100)
account.withdraw(50)
print(account.get_balance()) # Output: 50
```

Abstraction

Abstraction simplifies complexity by providing a simplified model of a system, highlighting the essential features while hiding irrelevant details. Classes and objects serve as abstractions, allowing developers to focus on high-level operations rather than intricate implementation details.

Abstract classes and methods in Python are defined using the abc module, which enables the creation of abstract base classes (ABCs) that out-

256

line methods to be implemented by subclasses.

Abstract Classes and Methods in Python

```python
from abc import ABC, abstractmethod

class Animal(ABC):
    @abstractmethod
    def make_sound(self):
        pass

class Dog(Animal):
    def make_sound(self):
        return "Bark"

dog = Dog()
print(dog.make_sound()) # Output: Bark
```

Inheritance

Inheritance allows a class (derived class) to inherit attributes and methods from another class (base class), fostering code reuse and the creation of hierarchical relationships. It enables the derived class to inherit and extend the functionalities of the base class, promoting modularity and reducing redundancy.

In Python, inheritance is denoted by specifying the base class in parentheses after the derived class name.

Single Inheritance Example in Python

```python
class Vehicle:
    def __init__(self, brand, model):
        self.brand = brand
        self.model = model

    def start_engine(self):
        return "Engine started"

class Car(Vehicle):
    def open_trunk(self):
        return "Trunk opened"

car = Car("Toyota", "Corolla")
print(car.start_engine()) # Output: Engine started
print(car.open_trunk()) # Output: Trunk opened
```

Polymorphism

Polymorphism allows objects of different classes to be treated as objects of a common superclass. It supports the ability to call the same method on different objects and have each of them respond in their own way. This is typically achieved through method overriding and interfaces in Python, where a derived class provides a specific implementation of a method that is also defined in its base class.

Polymorphism Example in Python

```python
class Bird:
    def make_sound(self):
        return "Chirp"

class Duck(Bird):
    def make_sound(self):
        return "Quack"

class Owl(Bird):
    def make_sound(self):
        return "Hoot"

def make_animal_sound(animal):
    print(animal.make_sound())

duck = Duck()
owl = Owl()

make_animal_sound(duck) # Output: Quack
make_animal_sound(owl) # Output: Hoot
```

Advantages of Object-Oriented Programming

The adoption of OOP brings numerous benefits to software development:

- **Modularity:** OOP encourages modular design, where software is divided into discrete units (classes and objects). This facilitates maintenance, debugging, and collaborative development.

- **Code Reuse:** Through inheritance and composition, OOP minimizes redundancy by reusing existing code, reducing development time and effort.

- **Scalability:** OOP supports the extension and scalability of software systems. New functionalities can be integrated seamlessly by extending existing classes or creating new subclasses.

- **Maintainability:** Encapsulation and abstraction allow for changes to be made internally within classes without affecting the external code that interfaces with these classes. This leads to better maintainability.

Object-Oriented Programming offers a robust framework for developing organized, maintainable, and scalable software architectures. The principles of encapsulation, abstraction, inheritance, and polymorphism collectively empower developers to create sophisticated and efficient programs.

258

8.2 Classes and Objects

In Python, the core tenets of object-oriented programming are achieved through the use of classes and objects. Classes serve as blueprints for creating objects (instances), encapsulating data for the object in the form of attributes and providing mechanisms for behaviors through methods.

Defining a Class

A class in Python is defined using the class keyword, followed by the class name and a colon. The class name should conventionally use CamelCase. Attributes and methods are defined within the class body.

Defining a simple class

```
class MyClass:
    """A simple example class"""

    def __init__(self, data):
        self.data = data

    def display_data(self):
        print(f'Data: {self.data}')
```

The above example shows a basic class definition. The class MyClass includes:

- A docstring providing a brief description.

- An __init__ method that initializes instances of the class with a data attribute.

- A display_data method to print the data attribute.

Creating Objects

Objects are instances of a class. Creation of an object involves calling the class with its necessary arguments.

Creating an instance of MyClass

```
obj = MyClass('Some data')
obj.display_data()
```

259

Data: Some data

The above code snippet instantiates the class MyClass with the string 'Some data', assigns it to the variable obj, and calls the display_data method to print the stored data.

Instance Variables and Methods

Instance variables are unique to each instance and are typically defined within the __init__ method. Instance methods operate on these variables and can modify the object's state or perform operations using instance data.

Using instance variables and methods

```
class Rectangle:
    """A class to represent a rectangle"""

    def __init__(self, width, height):
        self.width = width
        self.height = height

    def area(self):
        return self.width * self.height

    def perimeter(self):
        return 2 * (self.width + self.height)
```

Creating and using an instance of the Rectangle class:

Instantiating Rectangle object

```
rect = Rectangle(4, 5)
print(f'Area: {rect.area()}')
print(f'Perimeter: {rect.perimeter()}')
```

Output:
Area: 20
Perimeter: 18

Class Variables and Methods

Class variables are shared across all instances of a class, while instance variables are unique to each instance. Class methods, marked with the @classmethod decorator, operate on class variables and are called on the class itself rather than on instances.

Class variables and methods

```
class Circle:
```

260

```
"""A class to represent a circle"""
pi = 3.14159 # Class variable

def __init__(self, radius):
    self.radius = radius

@classmethod
def circumference(cls, radius):
    return 2 * cls.pi * radius
```

Accessing class methods:

Calling class method

```
circumference = Circle.circumference(5)
print(f'Circumference: {circumference}')
```

```
Output:
Circumference: 31.4159
```

Encapsulation

Encapsulation is the concept of limiting the exposure of data and methods from outside interference and misuse. In Python, this is commonly implemented using private attributes and methods, denoted by a leading underscore _.

Encapsulation with private attributes

```
class BankAccount:
    """A simple bank account class"""

    def __init__(self, balance):
        self._balance = balance # Private attribute

    def deposit(self, amount):
        if amount > 0:
            self._balance += amount

    def get_balance(self):
        return self._balance
```

Using an instance of BankAccount:

Accessing private attributes through methods

```
account = BankAccount(100)
account.deposit(50)
print(f'Balance: {account.get_balance()}')
```

```
Output:
Balance: 150
```

Classes and objects form the cornerstone of object-oriented programming in Python, providing a structured approach to coding by bundling data and behavior. This section has covered defining classes and creating objects, managing instance and class variables and methods, and ensuring encapsulation of data. These principles collectively enable the development of organized, modular, and reusable code.

8.3   Defining and Using Classes

In Python, classes serve as blueprints for creating objects, encapsulating both data and behavior. This section details the procedures for defining and utilizing classes, complete with syntax and practical examples.

A class in Python is defined using the `class` keyword, followed by the class name and a colon. The body of the class contains method definitions and attributes. Here, we define a simple class named `Person`:

Defining a Person class

```
class Person:
    pass
```

The above class contains no methods or attributes and uses the `pass` statement as a placeholder.

Instance variables are data attributes specific to each instance of a class, while methods define the behaviors of the class. Below, we expand the `Person` class to include instance variables and a method:

Person class with attributes and method

```
class Person:
    def __init__(self, name, age):
        self.name = name
        self.age = age

    def greet(self):
        return f'Hello, my name is {self.name} and I am {self.age} years old.'
```

Here, the `__init__` method initializes the instance variables `name` and `age`, while the `greet` method returns a greeting string that includes these attributes.

To utilize the defined class, create instances by calling the class name with the requisite arguments for its `__init__` method:

Creating instances of the Person class

```
person1 = Person("Alice", 30)
person2 = Person("Bob", 25)
```

Each instance person1 and person2 now has its own name and age attributes.

Instance attributes and methods are accessed using the dot notation. Below, we demonstrate how to call the greet method for an instance of the Person class:

Accessing attributes and methods

```
print(person1.greet()) # Output: Hello, my name is Alice and I am 30 years old.
print(person2.greet()) # Output: Hello, my name is Bob and I am 25 years old.
```

```
Hello, my name is Alice and I am 30 years old.
Hello, my name is Bob and I am 25 years old.
```

Instance attributes can be modified directly:

Modifying instance attributes

```
person1.age = 31
print(person1.greet()) # Output: Hello, my name is Alice and I am 31 years old.
```

```
Hello, my name is Alice and I am 31 years old.
```

Private attributes are intended to be inaccessible from outside the class. In Python, this is conventionally achieved by prefixing the attribute name with a double underscore:

Person class with a private attribute

```
class Person:
    def __init__(self, name, age):
        self.name = name
        self.__age = age

    def greet(self):
        return f'Hello, my name is {self.name} and I am {self.__age} years old.'

    def get_age(self):
        return self.__age
```

Attempting to access __age directly will result in an attribute error, promoting encapsulation by restricting direct access to crucial data. Access can be granted through a method like get_age.

Class attributes are shared among all instances of the class and are defined outside of the __init__ method. Similarly, class methods use the @classmethod decorator and take cls as their first parameter:

Person class with a class attribute and method

263

```
class Person:
    species = "Homo sapiens"

    def __init__(self, name, age):
        self.name = name
        self.__age = age

    @classmethod
    def species_info(cls):
        return f'Humans are classified as {cls.species}'
```

Class attributes can be accessed using either the class name or an instance:

Accessing class attributes and methods

```
print(Person.species) # Output: Homo sapiens
print(person1.species) # Output: Homo sapiens
print(Person.species_info()) # Output: Humans are classified as Homo sapiens
```

```
Homo sapiens
Homo sapiens
Humans are classified as Homo sapiens
```

By adhering to these conventions and practices, one ensures the proper definition and utilization of classes in Python, fostering clear and maintainable code.

8.4   Instance Variables and Methods

In Python, instance variables and methods are foundational elements of object-oriented programming, providing the primary means for storing and manipulating object-specific data. This chapter delves into the mechanics of instance variables and methods, elucidating their role and implementation within a class context.

Instance Variables

Instance variables are attributes that belong to an instance of a class. Each object instance created from a class has its own copy of instance variables, which can be used to store data specific to that instance.

Instance variables are typically defined within the __init__ method (the constructor) of a class. The __init__ method is called when an instance of the class is created, and it is used to initialize instance variables.

264

Defining Instance Variables

```
class Employee:
    def __init__(self, name, age, salary):
        self.name = name
        self.age = age
        self.salary = salary
```

In this example, the Employee class has three instance variables: name, age, and salary. These variables are initialized with the values passed to the __init__ method.

Instance variables can be accessed and modified using dot notation. This allows for direct interaction with the attributes of an object.

Accessing and Modifying Instance Variables

```
emp1 = Employee("John Doe", 30, 50000)
print(emp1.name) # Output: John Doe

emp1.age = 31
print(emp1.age) # Output: 31
```

Here, emp1 is an instance of the Employee class. The instance variable name is accessed and printed, and the age instance variable is modified and then printed.

Instance Methods

Instance methods are functions defined within a class that operate on instances of that class. They have access to the instance variables and can modify the object's state.

An instance method is defined using the def keyword within a class. It must take self as its first parameter, which represents the instance of the class.

Defining Instance Methods

```
class Employee:
    def __init__(self, name, age, salary):
        self.name = name
        self.age = age
        self.salary = salary

    def give_raise(self, amount):
        self.salary += amount
```

In this example, the Employee class includes an instance method give_raise, which takes an amount parameter and adds it to the salary instance variable.

265

Instance methods are called on instances of a class using dot notation, similar to accessing instance variables.

Calling Instance Methods

```
emp1 = Employee("John Doe", 30, 50000)
emp1.give_raise(5000)
print(emp1.salary) # Output: 55000
```

Here, emp1 calls the give_raise method with an amount of 5000, which modifies the salary instance variable.

Best Practices for Instance Variables and Methods

Understanding how to effectively use instance variables and methods is crucial for designing robust and maintainable classes.

Instance variables should be encapsulated to protect the internal state of an object. In Python, this can be achieved by using private variables (prefixed with a double underscore) and providing public methods to access and modify these variables.

Encapsulation and Data Hiding

```
class Employee:
    def __init__(self, name, age, salary):
        self.__name = name
        self.__age = age
        self.__salary = salary

    def get_salary(self):
        return self.__salary

    def give_raise(self, amount):
        self.__salary += amount
```

In this example, the instance variables __name, __age, and __salary are private. Public methods get_salary and give_raise provide controlled access to these variables.

Ensure that all instance variables are initialized within the __init__ method to maintain consistency. Avoid defining and using instance variables outside of this method, as it can lead to unpredictable behavior.

Consistency in Initialization

```
class Employee:
    def __init__(self, name, age, salary):
        self.name = name
        self.age = age
        self.salary = salary
```

266

```
        self.bonus = 0 # Initializing with a default value

    def add_bonus(self, bonus_amount):
        self.bonus += bonus_amount
```

Here, bonus is initialized with a default value of 0 within the `__init__` method, ensuring that it exists for every instance of the Employee class.

This chapter provided an in-depth understanding of instance variables and methods, including their definition, access, and best practices. These concepts are integral to developing well-structured and efficient object-oriented programs in Python.

8.5   Constructor and Destructor

Constructors and destructors are core concepts in object-oriented programming, essential for managing object lifetimes. This section explores their definitions, usage, and importance within Python classes.

Constructor

A constructor is a special method triggered upon the instantiation of an object. Its primary function is to initialize the object's state or conduct setup procedures. In Python, the constructor method is recognized by `__init__`.

The `__init__` method is automatically invoked when a class instance is created. It can accept arguments to initialize the object's attributes. The example below illustrates defining and using a constructor in a Python class:

Defining a Constructor in a Python Class

```
class Vehicle:
    def __init__(self, make, model, year):
        self.make = make
        self.model = model
        self.year = year

# Creating an instance of the Vehicle class
car = Vehicle("Toyota", "Camry", 2022)
print(car.make)
print(car.model)
print(car.year)
```

```
Toyota
Camry
2022
```

Here, the Vehicle class constructor initialize the attributes make, model, and year. When a `Vehicle` object is instantiated, these attributes are assigned the provided values ("Toyota", "Camry", 2022).

Destructor

A destructor is a special method triggered when an object is about to be destroyed. Its main purpose is to manage clean-up operations such as resource release or other termination tasks. In Python, the destructor method is represented by `__del__`.

The `__del__` method is invoked when the object's reference count drops to zero, and it is garbage collected. The example below demonstrates implementing and invoking a destructor:

Defining a Destructor in a Python Class

```
class Vehicle:
    def __init__(self, make, model, year):
        self.make = make
        self.model = model
        self.year = year

    def __del__(self):
        print(f"The vehicle {self.make} {self.model} from {self.year} is being
            destroyed.")

# Creating and deleting an instance of the Vehicle class
car = Vehicle("Toyota", "Camry", 2022)
del car
```

```
The vehicle Toyota Camry from 2022 is being destroyed.
```

In this example, the destructor of the `Vehicle` class prints a message when the `Vehicle` object is destroyed. The explicit call to `del car` triggers this event.

Note that Python's garbage collector handles memory de-allocation, and the `__del__` method is not always reliable for resource management in complex applications. Context managers and the `with` statement are generally recommended for handling resources like files and network connections.

Best Practices

Using constructors and destructors wisely enhances code robustness and maintainability. Some best practices include:

- **Initialize All Attributes:** Ensure that the constructor initializes all necessary attributes of the class.

- **Resource Management:** Prefer context managers for resource management rather than relying solely on destructors.

- **Avoid Complex Logic in Destructors:** Restrict destructors to clean-up tasks. Avoid complex logic to prevent unpredictable behavior.

- **Explicit Clean-Up:** Provide explicit clean-up methods for resources, and clearly document their usage to prevent resource leaks.

Following these best practices helps manage object lifecycles effectively, ensuring application stability and maintaining readable, maintainable codebases.

8.6 Class Variables and Methods

In object-oriented programming, class variables and methods play pivotal roles in defining behaviors and attributes that pertain to the class itself, rather than any individual instance of the class. This section explores the concept of class variables and class methods, elucidating their syntax, uses, and implications in Python.

Class variables are defined within a class but outside any instance methods. They are shared across all instances of the class, meaning that a single copy of the variable exists, and it is accessible to every instance. Modifications to a class variable affect all instances that access it.

```python
class Employee:
    company_name = "Tech World Inc." # class variable

    def __init__(self, name, position):
        self.name = name # instance variable
        self.position = position # instance variable
```

Here, `company_name` is a class variable, while `name` and `position` are instance variables. All instances of the `Employee` class share the `company_name` variable.

Class variables can be accessed either through the class itself or through any instance of the class. However, it is recommended to access class variables using the class name to maintain clarity.

```python
# Accessing via class name
print(Employee.company_name)

# Accessing via instance
emp1 = Employee("John Doe", "Developer")
print(emp1.company_name)
```

To modify a class variable, one should ideally do so through the class itself to avoid unintended behavior:

```
# Modifying via class name
Employee.company_name = "Tech Universe Inc."
print(Employee.company_name) # Outputs: Tech Universe Inc.
print(emp1.company_name) # Outputs: Tech Universe Inc.
```

It is important to note that modifying the class variable through an instance rebinds the variable for that particular instance, creating an instance variable with the same name.

```
# Modifying via instance
emp1.company_name = "Tech One Inc."
print(emp1.company_name) # Outputs: Tech One Inc.
print(Employee.company_name) # Outputs: Tech Universe Inc.
```

Here, emp1.company_name now refers to an instance variable specific to emp1 and does not affect the class variable company_name.

Class methods are methods that are bound to the class, not to an instance. They can access and modify class state that applies across all instances of the class. Python denotes class methods using the @classmethod decorator. A class method takes the class itself as the first argument, typically named cls.

A class method is defined using the classmethod decorator and can access class variables and class methods. Consider the following example:

```
class Employee:
    company_name = "Tech Future Inc."

    def __init__(self, name, position):
        self.name = name
        self.position = position

    @classmethod
    def change_company_name(cls, new_name):
        cls.company_name = new_name
```

Here, the change_company_name method is a class method that updates the company_name class variable.

Class methods can be invoked through the class itself or an instance of the class. However, invoking them through the class name is considered best practice to avoid confusion.

```
# Invoking via class name
Employee.change_company_name("Future Tech Solutions")
print(Employee.company_name) # Outputs: Future Tech Solutions

# Invoking via instance
```

270

```
emp2 = Employee("Jane Smith", "Manager")
emp2.change_company_name("Global Tech")
print(Employee.company_name) # Outputs: Global Tech
```

In this example, regardless of how `change_company_name` is called, it affects the `company_name` for all instances of the `Employee` class.

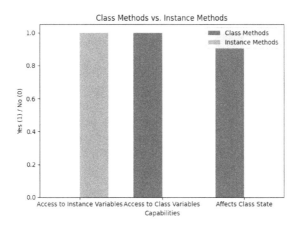

Class methods have the ability to operate on class-wide data, whereas instance methods can manipulate data specific to the instance. The provided comparison chart visually reinforces these distinctions. The chart illustrates the access and impact spectrum of class methods versus instance methods, emphasizing their respective domains of influence within the class structure.

While not a direct focus, it is worth briefly noting static methods, marked with the `@staticmethod` decorator, which do not access or modify class or instance variables. They are utility functions grouped within the class for logical organization.

```
class Employee:
    company_name = "Tech Dynamic Inc."

    def __init__(self, name, position):
        self.name = name
        self.position = position

    @staticmethod
    def is_valid_position(position):
        return position in ["Developer", "Manager", "Designer"]
```

Static methods provide functionality related to the class without the need to interact with class or instance-specific data.

271

Class variables and methods are crucial tools for maintaining and manipulating state and behavior at the class level. Proper understanding and utilization of these attributes and methods enable more efficient and organized object-oriented programming practices in Python.

8.7   Inheritance and Subclasses

Inheritance is a fundamental concept in object-oriented programming (OOP) wherein a new class, referred to as the *subclass*, is derived from an existing class, known as the *base class* or *superclass*. The primary advantage of inheritance is its ability to promote code reuse and establish a natural hierarchical relationship among classes. This chapter delves into the mechanics of inheritance in Python, the syntax involved, and best practices for implementing and utilizing subclasses.

Defining a Subclass

In Python, a subclass is defined by specifying the base class as a parameter within the class definition. The subclass inherits all the attributes and methods of the base class. Consider the following example:

Defining a Subclass

```
class BaseClass:
    def __init__(self, base_attr):
        self.base_attr = base_attr

    def base_method(self):
        return f"Base attribute: {self.base_attr}"

class SubClass(BaseClass):
    def __init__(self, base_attr, sub_attr):
        super().__init__(base_attr)
        self.sub_attr = sub_attr

    def sub_method(self):
        return f"Sub attribute: {self.sub_attr}"
```

In this example, `SubClass` inherits from `BaseClass`. The `__init__` method of `SubClass` calls the `super()` function to initialize the `base_attr` from `BaseClass`, ensuring the base class is properly initialized before extending its functionality.

272

Using Inherited Members

A subclass can access the methods and attributes of its superclass directly. This allows the subclass to leverage existing functionality and add or modify behavior as needed:

Using Inherited Members

```
base_instance = BaseClass(base_attr="base_value")
print(base_instance.base_method()) # Output: Base attribute: base_value

sub_instance = SubClass(base_attr="base_value", sub_attr="sub_value")
print(sub_instance.base_method()) # Output: Base attribute: base_value
print(sub_instance.sub_method()) # Output: Sub attribute: sub_value
```

Here, sub_instance can call base_method() inherited from BaseClass as well as sub_method() defined in SubClass.

Overriding Methods

Subclasses can provide specific implementations of methods by overriding methods defined in the base class. Method overriding allows the subclass to modify or enhance the behavior of the inherited methods:

Overriding Methods

```
class SubClass(BaseClass):
    def base_method(self):
        base_output = super().base_method()
        return f"{base_output} - Extended in SubClass"
```

In this example, SubClass overrides the base_method() of BaseClass. The override calls the base class method using super() and enhances its output.

Multiple Inheritance

Python supports multiple inheritance, allowing a class to inherit from more than one base class. This can lead to complex hierarchies and the *diamond problem*, which Python resolves using the *Method Resolution Order* (MRO) and the C3 linearization algorithm:

Multiple Inheritance Example

```
class ClassA:
    def method_A(self):
        return "Method A from ClassA"
```

273

```
class ClassB:
    def method_B(self):
        return "Method B from ClassB"

class ClassC(ClassA, ClassB):
    pass

instance_c = ClassC()
print(instance_c.method_A()) # Output: Method A from ClassA
print(instance_c.method_B()) # Output: Method B from ClassB

print(ClassC.mro()) # Output: [<class '__main__.ClassC'>, <class '__main__.ClassA'>,
        <class '__main__.ClassB'>, <class 'object'>]
```

Here, ClassC inherits from both ClassA and ClassB. The mro() method reveals the method resolution order, ensuring a predictable structure for resolving method calls.

Best Practices

- **Use Inheritance Judiciously**: Ensure that inheritance represents a true "is-a" relationship. Avoid forcing a subclass relationship where composition might be more appropriate.

- **Constructor Chaining**: Always call the superclass's constructor in the subclass using super() to ensure proper initialization.

- **Method Overrides**: Explicitly use super() when overriding methods to maintain clarity and ensure the correct base method is called.

- **Avoid Overcomplicating with Multiple Inheritance**: Use multiple inheritance sparingly. Prefer single inheritance and interfaces to maintain simplicity and clarity.

By adhering to these principles, developers can harness the power of inheritance to create efficient, understandable, and maintainable code.

Inheritance and subclasses form the backbone of code reuse in object-oriented programming, allowing for the creation of hierarchies that mirror real-world relationships. Understanding how to effectively define and utilize subclasses, along with managing method overrides and multiple inheritance, equips developers with the tools needed to build robust and scalable Python applications.

8.8 Method Overriding

Method overriding in object-oriented programming is a critical mechanism that allows a subclass to provide a specific implementation of a method that is already defined in its superclass. The primary purpose of method overriding is to adapt or extend the functionality of an inherited method without modifying the superclass, thereby promoting code reusability and flexibility.

When a method in a subclass has the same name, return type, and parameters as a method in its superclass, the method in the subclass is said to override the method in the superclass. Method overriding enables polymorphism and is fundamental for implementing dynamic method dispatch, where the method to be executed is determined at runtime based on the object's actual type.

To override a method in Python, simply define a method in the subclass with the same name and parameters as the method in the superclass. Consider the following example:

Example of Method Overriding

```
class Animal:
    def sound(self):
        return "Some generic sound"

class Dog(Animal):
    def sound(self):
        return "Bark"

# Create instance of Dog
dog = Dog()
print(dog.sound()) # Outputs: Bark
```

In this example, the Dog class overrides the sound method of the Animal class. When the sound method is called on an instance of Dog, the overridden version in the Dog class is invoked, producing the output Bark.

The super() function provides a way to call a method from the superclass in the context of the subclass. This is particularly useful when the overridden method in the subclass needs to extend rather than completely replace the functionality of the superclass method. The super() function ensures that the call is properly routed to the next class in the method resolution order (MRO).

Using the super() function to call superclass method

```
class Animal:
    def sound(self):
        return "Some generic sound"
```

```
class Dog(Animal):
    def sound(self):
        # Call the superclass method
        superclass_sound = super().sound()
        return f"Bark and also {superclass_sound}"

# Create instance of Dog
dog = Dog()
print(dog.sound()) # Outputs: Bark and also Some generic sound
```

In this example, the Dog class extends the functionality of the sound method by incorporating the output of the superclass method using super(). The overridden method produces a combined output.

When overriding methods, it is important to adhere to certain best practices to ensure code maintainability and clarity:

- Maintain consistency in method signatures between the superclass and subclass to avoid unexpected behavior.

- Use the super() function judiciously to leverage the functionality of the superclass rather than rewriting existing logic.

- Document overridden methods clearly to convey the intent and differences from the superclass method.

- Ensure that overridden methods respect the contract of the superclass method, particularly with regard to input parameters and return types.

Method overriding is a cornerstone of achieving polymorphic behavior in object-oriented systems. It allows a single interface to dynamically resolve to different implementations based on the object's actual type. This capability is demonstrated in the following example:

Polymorphism with method overriding

```
class Animal:
    def sound(self):
        return "Some generic sound"

class Dog(Animal):
    def sound(self):
        return "Bark"

class Cat(Animal):
    def sound(self):
        return "Meow"

# Function that demonstrates polymorphic behavior
def make_sound(animal: Animal):
```

```
    return animal.sound()

animals = [Dog(), Cat(), Animal()]

for animal in animals:
    print(make_sound(animal))
```

```
Bark
Meow
Some generic sound
```

In this example, the `make_sound` function accepts an object of type `Animal` and calls its `sound` method. The actual method executed depends on the runtime type of the object passed to the function, demonstrating polymorphism.

Method overriding is a powerful feature that enables subclasses to customize or enhance the behavior of methods inherited from a superclass. By understanding and applying method overriding correctly, developers can create flexible and maintainable object-oriented systems that leverage polymorphism and code reuse effectively.

8.9 The super() Function

In Python's object-oriented programming paradigm, the `super()` function plays a crucial role in facilitating cooperative multiple inheritance and invoking methods from a superclass. It ensures that inherited methods are called appropriately, thereby aiding in the development of maintainable and predictable class hierarchies.

Basic Usage

The primary purpose of the `super()` function is to return a proxy object that delegates method calls to a parent or sibling class of the type. This method enables developers to call a method from a superclass without explicitly referencing the parent class's name.

Basic usage of super()

```
class Parent:
    def __init__(self):
        self.value = 5

    def display(self):
        print("Parent Value:", self.value)

class Child(Parent):
    def __init__(self):
        super().__init__()
        self.value *= 2
```

277

```
    def display(self):
        print("Child Value:", self.value)
        super().display()

c = Child()
c.display()
```

This Python script demonstrates fundamental usage. In this example, the Child class inherits from the Parent class. The super() function in the Child's __init__ method calls the __init__ method of the Parent, enabling proper initialization. Similarly, the super().display() statement in the Child's display method calls the display method from the Parent class.

Cooperative Multiple Inheritance

In the context of multiple inheritance, the super() function is indispensable for maintaining a cooperative method resolution order (MRO). It ensures methods from all ancestor classes are invoked appropriately.

Using super() in multiple inheritance

```
class A:
    def method(self):
        print("Method in A")

class B(A):
    def method(self):
        print("Method in B")
        super().method()

class C(A):
    def method(self):
        print("Method in C")
        super().method()

class D(B, C):
    def method(self):
        print("Method in D")
        super().method()

d = D()
d.method()
```

This script illustrates the use of the super() function in a multiple inheritance hierarchy with classes A, B, C, and D. The call to super().method() in each class ensures that every relevant method in the MRO is executed. The output will reflect the sequence dictated by the MRO, validating cooperative inheritance behavior.

278

```
Method in D
Method in B
Method in C
Method in A
```

In this process, Python ensures that all classes' methods are called in the correct order, avoiding the redundancy and complexity that arise from explicitly calling a superclass method.

Method Resolution Order (MRO)

Understanding the MRO is pivotal to leveraging the super() function effectively. The MRO determines the order in which base classes are traversed when searching for a method. Python uses the C3 linearization algorithm (also known as the C3 superclass linearization) to compute the MRO.

To view a class's MRO, the .mro() method can be employed:

Viewing the Method Resolution Order

```
print(D.mro())
```

```
[<class '__main__.D'>, <class '__main__.B'>, <class '__main__.C'>, <class '__main__.A'>, <class 'object'>]
```

This illustrates that class D follows the MRO sequence: D, B, C, A, and finally the base object class. The consistency in this order is imperative for reliable multiple inheritance behavior.

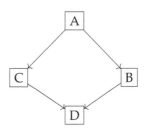

The super() function is a fundamental feature in Python for managing complex inheritance structures. It not only simplifies the invocation of superclass methods but also ensures conformance to the method resolution order, thereby enabling maintainable and efficient class hierarchies. Proper utilization of super() fosters better collaboration among base classes and mitigates potential issues in large-scale, multi-inheritance applications.

279

8.10   Encapsulation and Data Hiding

Encapsulation and data hiding are cornerstone concepts in object-oriented programming (OOP). They enable the bundling of data (attributes) and methods (functions) that operate on the data into a single unit, known as a class. This section delves into these concepts, demonstrating proper usage and implementation within Python.

Encapsulation refers to the practice of restricting access to certain parts of an object and only exposing a public API. This encapsulation mechanism controls the internal state of an object and shields its complexity from the outside world, promoting modular programming.

To implement encapsulation in Python, use access modifiers to define the visibility of class attributes. Python supports three types of access modifiers:

- **Public** attributes and methods can be accessed from anywhere.

- **Protected** attributes and methods are meant to be accessed within the class and its subclasses.

- **Private** attributes and methods are not accessible from outside the class, ensuring that internal representation can be hidden from external users.

Public attributes are defined without any prefix, protected attributes with a single underscore (_), and private attributes with double underscores (__).

Example of Encapsulation in Python

```
class ExampleClass:
    def __init__(self, public_attr, protected_attr, private_attr):
        self.public_attr = public_attr
        self._protected_attr = protected_attr
        self.__private_attr = private_attr

    def public_method(self):
        return 'Public Method'

    def _protected_method(self):
        return 'Protected Method'

    def __private_method(self):
        return 'Private Method'

    def access_private_method(self):
        return self.__private_method()
```

280

```
# Create an instance of ExampleClass
example = ExampleClass(1, 2, 3)

# Accessing public attribute
print(example.public_attr)   # Output: 1

# Accessing protected attribute (conventionally discouraged)
print(example._protected_attr)   # Output: 2

# Accessing private attribute (will raise AttributeError)
print(example.__private_attr)   # Output: AttributeError

# Accessing public method
print(example.public_method())   # Output: Public Method

# Accessing protected method (conventionally discouraged)
print(example._protected_method())   # Output: Protected Method

# Accessing private method (will raise AttributeError)
print(example.__private_method())   # Output: AttributeError

# Accessing private method via a public interface
print(example.access_private_method())   # Output: Private Method
```

Data hiding underpins the principle of restricting direct access to some of an object's attributes and methods. This is particularly important for maintaining the integrity of the data stored within objects, preventing unintended interference and ensuring encapsulation.

Private attributes and methods, as demonstrated earlier, provide a means to hide the internal workings of a class. Through data hiding, a class can maintain a clear boundary between its internal implementation and the external interface it presents to other components.

Data hiding offers several significant advantages:

- **Enhanced Security:** By restricting access to internal data, you can prevent unauthorized modification, safeguarding the integrity and consistency of the object's state.

- **Reduced Complexity:** By exposing only necessary components, data hiding simplifies the interface of the class, making it easier to use and understand.

- **Increased Flexibility:** It allows for changes in the internal implementation without affecting external code that relies on the object, promoting maintenance and scalability.

The use of double underscores (__) to define private attributes and methods effectively enables data hiding. However, Python's name mangling mechanism makes it feasible to access private attributes when necessary, albeit not recommended.

Example of Data Hiding

```
class SecureClass:
    def __init__(self, sensitive_data):
        self.__sensitive_data = sensitive_data

    def get_sensitive_data(self):
        return self.__sensitive_data

    def set_sensitive_data(self, data):
        self.__sensitive_data = data

# Create an instance of SecureClass
secure_instance = SecureClass('Secret')
print(secure_instance.get_sensitive_data()) # Output: Secret

# Trying to access private attribute directly (not recommended)
print(secure_instance._SecureClass__sensitive_data) # Output: Secret
```

While accessing _SecureClass__sensitive_data directly is possible through name mangling, it violates encapsulation principles and is not advised in practice.

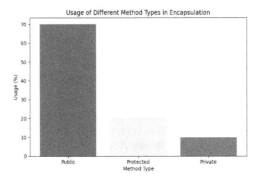

This chart exemplifies a hypothetical usage distribution of different method types in encapsulation, explaining their prevalence in a typical programming environment.

Encapsulation and data hiding are pivotal for preserving the integrity and clarity of an object-oriented design. By restricting access to internal data and exposing a clean and manageable interface, these principles facilitate the creation of resilient and maintainable software.

282

8.11 Polymorphism

Polymorphism is a fundamental concept in object-oriented programming that allows objects of different classes to be treated as instances of a common superclass. It enables the same interface to present different underlying forms (data types). In Python, polymorphism is often exploited through class inheritance, where child classes extend their parent classes' functionalities.

Polymorphism allows for a unified interface to interact with objects of different types. The principle behind polymorphism is that the same operation can behave differently on different classes. This is achieved by method overriding in subclasses. When a method is called on an object, the Python interpreter looks up the method in the class of that object. If subclass objects override the superclass methods, the subclass method gets executed.

Consider the following example demonstrating polymorphism through method overriding:

Polymorphism with Method Overriding

```python
class Animal:
    def sound(self):
        return "Some generic sound"

class Dog(Animal):
    def sound(self):
        return "Bark"

class Cat(Animal):
    def sound(self):
        return "Meow"

def make_sound(animal):
    print(animal.sound())

animals = [Dog(), Cat(), Animal()]

for animal in animals:
    make_sound(animal)
```

This example introduces three classes: Animal, Dog, and Cat. Each subclass (Dog and Cat) overrides the sound() method inherited from the Animal superclass. The function make_sound() accepts an instance of Animal (or any of its subclasses) and calls its sound() method. When make_sound() is called within the loop for instances of Dog, Cat, and Animal, the method suitable to the class of the object is invoked.

283

```
Bark
Meow
Some generic sound
```

Python's built-in functions also exploit polymorphism to handle objects of different types uniformly. For instance, the len() function can return the length of strings, lists, tuples, and various other types.

Polymorphism with Built-in Functions

```
print(len("Hello"))
print(len([1, 2, 3, 4]))
print(len((10, 20, 30)))
```

```
5
4
3
```

Here, the len() function is polymorphic as it can process sequences of different types.

Abstract classes and interfaces are critical for implementing polymorphism, especially in larger systems. By defining a common interface, polymorphism ensures that different classes can be used interchangeably.

Polymorphism with Abstract Base Class

```
from abc import ABC, abstractmethod

class AbstractAnimal(ABC):
    @abstractmethod
    def sound(self):
        pass

class Dog(AbstractAnimal):
    def sound(self):
        return "Bark"

class Cat(AbstractAnimal):
    def sound(self):
        return "Meow"

def make_sound(animal):
    print(animal.sound())

animals = [Dog(), Cat()]

for animal in animals:
    make_sound(animal)
```

In this code, AbstractAnimal is an abstract base class that defines an abstract method sound(). The classes Dog and Cat inherit from AbstractAnimal and implement the sound() method, thus achieving polymorphism. The function make_sound() can now uniformly handle any subclass of AbstractAnimal.

284

- **Improved Code Maintainability**: By using polymorphism, application logic can be written in a more abstract and general manner, reducing code redundancy and improving maintainability.

- **Scalability and Extensibility**: Software components can be extended and reused with minimal changes in existing code.

- **Interface Consistency**: It ensures a consistent interface for different types, simplifying the interaction between different objects.

Polymorphism enhances the flexibility and maintainability of Python applications. By allowing the same interface to interact with objects of different types, it supports the creation of more scalable and extensible codebases. Understanding and effectively applying polymorphism is essential for leveraging the full potential of object-oriented programming in Python.

8.12 Special Methods and Operator Overloading

In Python, special methods, also known as magic methods, enable the behavior of built-in operations with user-defined objects. These methods allow objects to be employed with standard operators and functions, simplifying code comprehensibility and maintenance. This section delves into the essentials and applications of special methods and operator overloading in Python.

Special methods in Python are identified by double underscores at the beginning and end of their names, such as `__init__`, `__str__`, and `__add__`. These methods are invoked implicitly by Python when corresponding operations are performed on objects, allowing custom behaviors and enhancing the expressiveness of classes.

Common Special Methods

Some commonly used special methods include:

- `__init__`: Called when an instance is created.

- `__str__`: Defines the human-readable string representation of an object.

- `__repr__`: Defines the official string representation of an object.

- `__eq__`: Called for the equality operator (==).

- `__lt__, __le__, __gt__, __ge__`: Implement comparison operators.

To illustrate the implementation of special methods, consider the following class definition:

Definition of a Vector Class with Special Methods

```
class Vector:
    def __init__(self, x, y):
        self.x = x
        self.y = y

    def __str__(self):
        return f'Vector({self.x}, {self.y})'

    def __repr__(self):
        return f'Vector({self.x}, {self.y})'

    def __eq__(self, other):
        return self.x == other.x and self.y == other.y

    def __lt__(self, other):
        return (self.x**2 + self.y**2) < (other.x**2 + other.y**2)

    def __add__(self, other):
        return Vector(self.x + other.x, self.y + other.y)
```

```
# Example usage
v1 = Vector(2, 4)
v2 = Vector(3, 1)
print(v1)              # Output: Vector(2, 4)
print(repr(v2))        # Output: Vector(3, 1)
print(v1 == v2)        # Output: False
print(v1 < v2)         # Output: False
print(v1 + v2)         # Output: Vector(5, 5)
```

This class definition includes several special methods:

- `__init__` initializes vector components.

- `__str__` and `__repr__` provide human-readable and official string representations, respectively.

- `__eq__` checks for equality by comparing vector components.

- `__lt__` defines the less-than comparison based on vector magnitude.

- `__add__` performs vector addition by adding corresponding components.

286

Operator overloading utilizes special methods to define custom behavior for standard operators, enabling intuitive application on user-defined types. Python supports overloading for arithmetic, comparison, and unary operators.

Arithmetic Operators

Special methods for arithmetic operators include:

- `__add__`: Addition (+) operator.

- `__sub__`: Subtraction (-) operator.

- `__mul__`: Multiplication (*) operator.

- `__truediv__`: True division (/) operator.

- `__floordiv__`: Floor division (//) operator.

- `__mod__`: Modulo (%) operator.

Consider adding multiplication to the `Vector` class:

Implementing Multiplication in the Vector Class

```
class Vector:
    # Existing methods...

    def __mul__(self, scalar):
        return Vector(self.x * scalar, self.y * scalar)
```

```
# Example usage
v = Vector(1, 2)
scaled_v = v * 3
print(scaled_v)        # Output: Vector(3, 6)
```

Comparison Operators

Special methods for comparison operators include:

- `__lt__`: Less-than (<) operator.

- `__le__`: Less-than or equal-to (<=) operator.

- `__gt__`: Greater-than (>) operator.

- `__ge__`: Greater-than or equal-to (>=) operator.

- `__eq__`: Equality (==) operator.

- `__ne__`: Inequality (!=) operator.

287

These enable fine-grained control over object comparison, as shown previously in the Vector class.

Unary Operators

Special methods for unary operators include:

- __neg__: Negation (-) operator.

- __pos__: Unary plus (+) operator.

- __abs__: Absolute value (abs()) function.

Adding negation to the Vector class:

Implementing Unary Negation in the Vector Class

```
class Vector:
    # Existing methods...

    def __neg__(self):
        return Vector(-self.x, -self.y)
```

```
# Example usage
v = Vector(2, -3)
neg_v = -v
print(neg_v)            # Output: Vector(-2, 3)
```

String Representation Methods

String representation methods (__str__ and __repr__) offer a way to control how objects are represented as strings. While __str__ is meant for creating output that is readable by end-users, __repr__ is intended for generating output that could be used to recreate the object.

Consider the following enhancements to the Vector class:

Enhanced String Representation Methods

```
class Vector:
    def __init__(self, x, y):
        self.x = x;
        self.y = y

    def __str__(self):
        return f'({self.x}, {self.y})'

    def __repr__(self):
        return f'Vector({self.x}, {self.y})'
```

```
# Example usage
v = Vector(2, 3)
print(str(v))          # Output: (2, 3)
print(repr(v))         # Output: Vector(2, 3)
```

288

By implementing special methods and operator overloading using these techniques, developers can create more intuitive and user-friendly interfaces for custom classes, enhancing both readability and functionality.

Special methods and operator overloading empower Python classes to integrate seamlessly with Python's syntax and built-in operations, enhancing the language's flexibility. By understanding and implementing these methods, developers can create robust, intuitive, and highly maintainable code structures that leverage the full expressive power of Python's object-oriented capabilities.

8.13   Composition vs. Inheritance

In object-oriented programming, both composition and inheritance are fundamental techniques for creating complex types by combining objects. Although they share similarities, these two paradigms solve different problems and have distinct impacts on design and architecture.

Inheritance allows a class (subclass) to inherit attributes and methods from another class (superclass). This relationship is often described as an "is-a" relationship, signifying that the subclass is a type of the superclass.

Example of Inheritance

```python
class Animal:
    def __init__(self, name):
        self.name = name

    def speak(self):
        raise NotImplementedError("Subclasses must implement this method")

class Dog(Animal):
    def speak(self):
        return f"{self.name} says Woof!"

class Cat(Animal):
    def speak(self):
        return f"{self.name} says Meow!"
```

In the example, `Dog` and `Cat` both inherit from `Animal`, implementing their versions of the speak method. Here, inheritance promotes polymorphism, allowing each subclass to be treated uniformly via their common interface.

Composition involves constructing complex classes by associating them with other classes. Unlike inheritance, which describes a hierarchical relationship, composition is a "has-a" relationship.

Example of Composition

```
class Engine:
    def start(self):
        return "Engine started"

class Car:
    def __init__(self):
        self.engine = Engine()

    def start(self):
        return self.engine.start()
```

In this example, Car class has an Engine object. The Car relies on the Engine to perform specific functionality, such as starting. This approach promotes high cohesion and low coupling, as each class maintains a single responsibility.

Deciding whether to use inheritance or composition requires careful consideration of the design and maintenance implications. Below are some guidelines to help achieve this:

- *Flexibility and Reusability*: Composition tends to offer greater flexibility and reusability. Components can be replaced or reused without affecting the dependent classes, leading to better maintainability.

Flexibility with Composition

```
class ElectricEngine:
    def start(self):
        return "Electric engine started"

class Car:
    def __init__(self, engine):
        self.engine = engine

    def start(self):
        return self.engine.start()

# Reusability
engine = ElectricEngine()
car = Car(engine)
print(car.start()) # Output: Electric engine started
```

In the snippet above, the Car class is flexible enough to use any engine type, thus enhancing reusability.

- *Hierarchy and Relationships*: Inheritance is best suited for representing logical hierarchies and relationships where subclasses naturally extend the behavior of a base class. It models an "is-a" relationship clearly and succinctly.

- *Encapsulation*: Composition improves encapsulation and adheres to the Single Responsibility Principle (SRP). Each class handles a specific aspect of functionality, promoting a clear separation of concerns.

- *Extensibility*: Composition allows easier modification and extension of systems. New functionalities can be added by creating new components and combining them, without altering existing hierarchies.

In practice, both inheritance and composition are often used in tandem to build extensible and maintainable systems. A common pattern is to use inheritance for creating core base classes and composition for assembling complex behaviors from simpler components.

Combining Composition and Inheritance

```python
class Animal:
    def __init__(self, name):
        self.name = name

    def speak(self):
        raise NotImplementedError("Subclasses must implement this method")

class Engine:
    def start(self):
        return "Engine started"

class RoboticDog(Animal):
    def __init__(self, name, engine):
        super().__init__(name)
        self.engine = engine

    def speak(self):
        return f"{self.name} says Beep Boop!"

    def start_engine(self):
        return self.engine.start()

# Usage
robot_dog = RoboticDog("Rover", Engine())
print(robot_dog.speak()) # Output: Rover says Beep Boop!
print(robot_dog.start_engine()) # Output: Engine started
```

Here, the RoboticDog class inherits from Animal and uses composition to provide engine functionalities, illustrating a hybrid approach.

Both composition and inheritance are powerful tools in object-oriented design. Inheritance helps in expressing hierarchical relationships naturally, while composition provides flexibility and modularity. Mak-

291

ing an informed choice between them depends on the specific requirements of the design, the need for reusability, maintainability, and the nature of relationships within the system. Employing the correct technique ensures that the design is robust, scalable, and easy to maintain.

8.14   Abstract Classes and Methods

In object-oriented programming, abstract classes and methods serve a critical role in defining interfaces and enforcing class design. An abstract class cannot be instantiated directly and typically includes one or more abstract methods. Abstract methods are declared in the base class and must be implemented by any subclass that inherits from the abstract class. This section delves into the purpose, creation, and usage of abstract classes and methods.

Purpose and Use Cases

Abstract classes and methods are fundamental for defining a common interface for a group of related classes. They allow you to specify methods that must be created within any child classes built from the abstract class. This ensures a consistent API and facilitates polymorphism by enabling code that works uniformly across different subclasses.

Use cases for abstract classes and methods include:

- Defining a common interface for a family of subclasses.

- Enforcing certain methods to be implemented in every subclass.

- Allowing partial implementation of functionalities that can be shared across subclasses.

Creating Abstract Classes

In Python, abstract classes are created using the ABC (Abstract Base Class) module from the abc package. To define an abstract class, derive it from ABC and use the @abstractmethod decorator to specify abstract methods.

Defining an abstract class

```
from abc import ABC, abstractmethod

class Shape(ABC):

    @abstractmethod
```

```
    def area(self):
        pass

    @abstractmethod
    def perimeter(self):
        pass
```

In this example, Shape is an abstract class with two abstract methods, area() and perimeter().

Implementing Abstract Methods in Subclasses

Any subclass inheriting from an abstract class must implement all abstract methods. Failure to do so will result in a TypeError.

Implementing abstract methods in a subclass

```
class Rectangle(Shape):

    def __init__(self, width, height):
        self.width = width
        self.height = height

    def area(self):
        return self.width * self.height

    def perimeter(self):
        return 2 * (self.width + self.height)
```

Here, Rectangle implements the area and perimeter methods required by the Shape abstract class.

Partial Implementation in Abstract Classes

Abstract classes can also provide concrete methods that are common across all subclasses, in addition to abstract methods.

Partial implementation in an abstract class

```
class Shape(ABC):

    @abstractmethod
    def area(self):
        pass

    @abstractmethod
    def perimeter(self):
        pass

    def describe(self):
        return "This is a shape."
```

In this modified example, the describe method is a concrete method that any subclass of Shape can use without modification.

Benefits of Abstract Classes and Methods

293

The utilization of abstract classes and methods offers several benefits:

- **Code Reusability:** By defining common functionality in the abstract class, subclasses can reuse this code, reducing duplication.

- **Maintability:** Abstract classes can serve as a single point of update and modification, promoting easier maintenance.

- **Extensibility:** New subclasses can be added with minimal changes to existing code, adhering to the Open/Closed Principle.

- **Enforcement of Interface:** Guarantees that all subclasses adhere to a specified interface, allowing polymorphic behavior.

Practical Example

Consider a situation where we need to represent different types of employees with specific methods to calculate their pay. We can model this scenario using an abstract class.

Abstract class for employees

```
from abc import ABC, abstractmethod

class Employee(ABC):

    def __init__(self, name):
        self.name = name

    @abstractmethod
    def calculate_pay(self):
        pass

    def employee_details(self):
        return f"Employee: {self.name}"
```

Subclasses such as `SalariedEmployee` and `HourlyEmployee` will implement the `calculate_pay` method.

Implementation of salaried and hourly employees

```
class SalariedEmployee(Employee):

    def __init__(self, name, annual_salary):
        super().__init__(name)
        self.annual_salary = annual_salary

    def calculate_pay(self):
        return self.annual_salary / 12

class HourlyEmployee(Employee):

    def __init__(self, name, hourly_rate, hours_worked):
        super().__init__(name)
```

294

```
        self.hourly_rate = hourly_rate
        self.hours_worked = hours_worked

    def calculate_pay(self):
        return self.hourly_rate * self.hours_worked
```

This setup ensures that every type of employee has a `calculate_pay` method while allowing customization based on the employee type.

Abstract classes and methods are a vital part of object-oriented programming, enabling developers to define consistent APIs and share common functionality among related classes, while ensuring that subclasses implement necessary specialized behaviors. They enhance code organization, maintenance, and extensibility, thereby making software robust and scalable.

Chapter 9

Modules and Packages

This chapter explains the use of modules and packages in Python for organizing and structuring code. It covers creating and using modules, different ways to import them, and utilizing built-in modules. The chapter also discusses the creation and importing of packages, the role of the __init__.py file, namespace packages, and distributing modules and packages. Practical examples and techniques for effective module and package management are provided.

9.1 Introduction to Modules and Packages

Modules and packages are fundamental constructs in Python that facilitate the organization, modularization, and reuse of code. This section provides a comprehensive overview of these constructs, explaining their definitions, uses, and the mechanics of their implementation and utilization.

A **module** in Python is a file containing Python code, which can include functions, classes, and variables. Modules allow for logical organization and segmentation of code into manageable and reusable components. By encapsulating related functionalities within a module, developers can enhance code maintainability and readability.

Creating a Module

Creating a module in Python is straightforward. Save the following Python code in a file named `mymodule.py`:

Example of a Simple Python Module

```
# mymodule.py

def add(a, b):
    return a + b

def subtract(a, b):
    return a - b

class Calculator:
    def multiply(self, a, b):
        return a * b

    def divide(self, a, b):
        if b == 0:
            raise ValueError("Cannot divide by zero")
        return a / b
```

This module defines two functions and a class with additional methods. Such a module can be imported and utilized in other Python scripts or modules.

Using a Module

To use the module `mymodule`, it must be imported within another Python file or an interactive environment. Example usage is shown below:

Importing and Using a Custom Module

```
# Example file or interactive environment

import mymodule

result_add = mymodule.add(5, 3)
result_subtract = mymodule.subtract(5, 3)

calc = mymodule.Calculator()
result_multiply = calc.multiply(5, 3)
result_divide = calc.divide(5, 3)

print("Addition:", result_add)
print("Subtraction:", result_subtract)
print("Multiplication:", result_multiply)
print("Division:", result_divide)
```

The `import` statement makes all the functions and classes defined in `mymodule` available for use.

Packages

A **package** is a collection of Python modules organized under a directory hierarchy. Packages enable a structured and scalable organization for large codebases, promoting reusability and modularity in a hierarchical manner. The presence of an `__init__.py` file in a directory indicates that it is a Python package.

Creating a Package

Consider a package named `mypackage` with the following structure:

```
mypackage/
    __init__.py
    module1.py
    module2.py
```

The `__init__.py` file can be empty or can initialize the package. Its existence makes `mypackage` a package.

Content of `module1.py`:

Example of a Python Module within a Package

```
# module1.py

def greet(name):
    return f"Hello, {name}!"
```

Content of `module2.py`:

Another Python Module within a Package

```
# module2.py

def farewell(name):
    return f"Goodbye, {name}!"
```

The `__init__.py` file could contain initialization code, such as:

Example __init__.py File

```
# __init__.py

from .module1 import greet
from .module2 import farewell
```

This `__init__.py` file allows for the direct import of the `greet` and `farewell` functions from `mypackage`.

Using a Package

To use the package mypackage, import it as follows:

Importing and Using a Package

```
# Example file or interactive environment

import mypackage

print(mypackage.greet("Alice"))
print(mypackage.farewell("Alice"))
```

The import statement loads the package and makes the functions greet and farewell available for use, demonstrating the modularity and convenience provided by packages.

Advantages of Modules and Packages

The modular design introduced by using modules and packages offers several key advantages:

- **Organization:** Code is more logically organized into separate files or directories based on functionality.

- **Reusability:** Functions, classes, and variables in modules and packages can be reused across different projects.

- **Maintainability:** Well-structured modules and packages make code easier to understand, debug, and modify.

- **Namespace Management:** Modules and packages help avoid naming conflicts by encapsulating identifiers.

By employing modules and packages effectively, a Python developer can enhance the comprehensibility, maintainability, and scalability of their codebase. This section has introduced the concepts and basic usage patterns of these constructs, setting the foundation for more advanced topics in subsequent sections.

9.2 Creating and Using Modules

In Python, a module is a file containing Python definitions and statements. The file name is the module name with the suffix .py added.

Modules serve as a fundamental structure for organizing code into manageable and reusable units. This section elaborates on creating, importing, and using modules efficiently in Python.

Creating a Module

Creating a module is straightforward. You simply define your functions, classes, or variables in a Python file and save it with a .py extension. Consider the following example:

example_module.py

```
# example_module.py

def add(a, b):
    return a + b

def subtract(a, b):
    return a - b

class SimpleMath:
    def multiply(self, a, b):
        return a * b

    def divide(self, a, b):
        if b == 0:
            raise ValueError("Cannot divide by zero.")
        return a / b
```

In this example, the file example_module.py contains the definitions for two functions, add and subtract, and a class SimpleMath with two methods, multiply and divide.

Importing Modules

Once you have a module, you can access its functionalities by importing it. Python provides several ways to import modules, which offer varying degrees of flexibility.

Basic Import

The most common way to import a module is using the import statement. This imports the module as a whole, and you can access its attributes using dot notation.

Basic module import

```
import example_module

result_add = example_module.add(5, 3)
print(result_add) # Output: 8
```

Importing Specific Attributes

You can import specific functions, classes, or variables directly from

301

a module using the `from` keyword. This allows you to use these attributes without prefixing them with the module name.

Importing specific attributes from a module

```
from example_module import add, SimpleMath

result_add = add(5, 3)
calculator = SimpleMath()
result_multiply = calculator.multiply(4, 6)
print(result_add) # Output: 8
print(result_multiply) # Output: 24
```

Renaming Module on Import

To avoid naming conflicts or to simplify access, you can alias a module or its attributes using the as keyword.

Renaming module on import

```
import example_module as em

result_subtract = em.subtract(10, 5)
print(result_subtract) # Output: 5
```

Renaming attributes on import

```
from example_module import SimpleMath as SM

calculator = SM()
result_divide = calculator.divide(20, 4)
print(result_divide) # Output: 5.0
```

Using __name__ and __main__

In Python, when a module is run as the main program, the module's `__name__` attribute is set to `"__main__"`. This allows you to conditionally execute code only when the module is run directly, and not when it is imported as a module in another script.

Using __name__ and __main__

```
# example_module.py

def main():
    print("This is a script that performs simple math operations.")

if __name__ == "__main__":
    main()
```

When you run `example_module.py` directly, it will execute the `main` function. However, if you import `example_module` in another script, the `main` function will not be executed.

Reloading Modules

During development, you might need to reload a module after modifying it. The `importlib` library provides utilities to reload a module:

Reloading a module

```
import importlib
import example_module

# Assume example_module was modified
importlib.reload(example_module)
```

This ensures that the latest version of the module is used without restarting the Python interpreter.

The Module Search Path

When importing a module, Python searches for the module in a sequence of directories given by the `sys.path` variable. This variable contains the current directory, PYTHONPATH environment variable directories, and default directories depending on the installation.

To examine the module search path:

Examining the module search path

```
import sys
print(sys.path)
```

The output will be a list of directory strings where Python looks for modules.

```
['', '/usr/lib/python3.8', ..., '/path/to/your/module']
```

Understanding the module search path is crucial to resolving module import issues effectively.

Creating and using modules in Python is vital for structuring large codebases in a manageable and maintainable manner. Modules enhance reusability and encapsulation, reducing redundancy and promoting clean code practices. The import mechanisms discussed provide flexibility in how modules are utilized, enabling clear and efficient code integration.

9.3 Importing Modules: Different Ways

Python provides several ways to import modules, each with distinct syntax and usage nuances. Understanding these methods is crucial for effective module utilization and can significantly impact the readability and maintenance of code.

Basic Import

The most straightforward way to import a module is using the `import` statement. This method imports the entire module, and its functions or classes can be accessed using the module's name as a prefix.

```
import math

radius = 5
area = math.pi * (radius ** 2)
print(area)
```

In this example, the `math` module is imported, and the `pi` constant is accessed using the `math` namespace.

Importing Specific Attributes

To import specific functions, classes, or variables from a module, the `from ... import ...` syntax is employed. This method allows direct access to the imported attributes, avoiding the need for the module's prefix.

```
from math import pi, sqrt

radius = 5
area = pi * (radius ** 2)
diagonal = sqrt(2 * (radius ** 2))
print(area, diagonal)
```

Here, only the `pi` and `sqrt` attributes are imported, thus simplifying their usage.

Renaming Imports

Modules or attributes can be imported with aliases using the as keyword. This is particularly useful for handling naming conflicts or for convenience when working with modules with long names.

```
import numpy as np
from datetime import datetime as dt

array = np.array([1, 2, 3, 4])
current_time = dt.now()
print(array, current_time)
```

The `numpy` module is aliased as `np`, and the `datetime` class is aliased as dt for brevity.

Importing All Attributes from a Module

To import all the attributes of a module into the current namespace, the `from ... import *` syntax can be used. While this method offers convenience, it is generally discouraged due to the risk of name collisions and reduced code clarity.

```
from math import *

radius = 5
area = pi * (radius ** 2)
print(area)
```

In this case, all functions and constants from the `math` module are imported, making `pi` directly accessible.

Conditional Import

Modules can be imported conditionally within a function or a specific block of code. This technique can optimize performance by loading modules only when they are needed.

```
def calculate_area(radius):
    if radius > 0:
        import math
        return math.pi * (radius ** 2)
    else:
        return 0

print(calculate_area(5))
```

Here, the `math` module is imported only when `radius` is greater than zero.

Importing from Packages

When working with packages, individual modules within the package can be imported using dot notation. This allows structured access to the package's modules and submodules.

```
import os.path

path_exists = os.path.exists('/some/directory')
print(path_exists)
```

In this example, the `path` module within the `os` package is imported to use the `exists` method.

Importing Dynamic Modules

Python also supports dynamic imports using the `importlib` module. This method is useful for scenarios where the modules to be imported are determined at runtime.

```
import importlib

module_name = 'math'
```

```
math_module = importlib.import_module(module_name)

result = math_module.sqrt(16)
print(result)
```

In this instance, the math module is imported dynamically based on the value of module_name.

Best Practices

When selecting an import method, consider code readability and maintainability. Importing specific attributes or using module aliases can enhance clarity, whereas importing all attributes from a module is typically best avoided. Additionally, conditional and dynamic imports should be used judiciously to optimize performance without sacrificing code simplicity.

Adhering to these practices will facilitate the effective organization and structuring of Python code, aligning with the overarching goals of leveraging modules and packages.

9.4   Built-in Modules

Python's standard library is replete with built-in modules that provide a wealth of functionality out of the box. These modules are integral to Python's utility and versatility, enabling developers to efficiently handle a myriad of common programming tasks without needing to write custom code from scratch. This section delves into some of the most frequently used built-in modules, examining their primary functions and providing practical examples to illustrate their utility.

The os Module

The os module provides a way of using operating system dependent functionality such as reading or writing to the file system. It offers a rich API to interact with the underlying operating system.

Here is an example of using the os module to list all files in a directory:

```
import os

# List all files and directories in the current directory
entries = os.listdir('.')
print(entries)
```

```
['file1.txt', 'file2.txt', 'dir1', 'script.py']
```

Other notable functions include os.path.join() for path manipulation and os.environ for accessing environment variables.

The sys Module

The sys module provides access to some variables used or maintained by the Python interpreter and to functions that interact strongly with the interpreter.

An illustrative example of using the sys module is to read command-line arguments:

```
import sys

# Print command-line arguments
print("Arguments passed:", sys.argv)
```

If invoked as python script.py arg1 arg2, the output would be:

```
Arguments passed: ['script.py', 'arg1', 'arg2']
```

The sys module also includes sys.exit() for terminating a program and sys.path for manipulating the module search path.

The json Module

The json module is used to parse JSON (JavaScript Object Notation), a popular data interchange format. It allows easy conversion between JSON strings and Python dictionaries.

For example, converting a Python dictionary to a JSON string and back:

```
import json

data = {
    'name': 'John Doe',
    'age': 30,
    'is_student': False
}

# Convert Python dictionary to JSON string
json_str = json.dumps(data)
print(json_str)

# Convert JSON string back to Python dictionary
parsed_data = json.loads(json_str)
print(parsed_data)
```

```
{"name": "John Doe", "age": 30, "is_student": false}
{'name': 'John Doe', 'age': 30, 'is_student': False}
```

The json module is indispensable for applications that need to exchange data over a network or interface with web APIs.

The re Module

The re module provides regular expression matching operations. It is a powerful tool for searching and manipulating text based on patterns.

Consider the following example for validating an email address using a regular expression:

```
import re

# Define the regex pattern for a basic email validation
pattern = r'^[a-zA-Z0-9_.+-]+@[a-zA-Z0-9-]+\.[a-zA-Z0-9-.]+$'

def validate_email(email):
    return re.match(pattern, email) is not None

# Test the function
print(validate_email('example@example.com')) # True
print(validate_email('invalid-email')) # False
```

In this example, the regex pattern specifies the allowed characters and structure for a valid email address. The re.match() function checks if the input string conforms to this pattern.

The time Module

The time module provides various time-related functions. It includes functions for time manipulation, formatting, and delays.

For instance, to measure the execution time of a code block:

```
import time

start_time = time.time()

# Code block whose execution time is to be measured
time.sleep(1) # Introduce a delay of 1 second

end_time = time.time()
execution_time = end_time - start_time
print(f"Execution Time: {execution_time} seconds")
```

```
Execution Time: 1.0012311935424805 seconds
```

The time.sleep() function is used to introduce a delay in the execution. This module is essential for applications that require precise time measurements or need to pause execution.

The `logging` Module

The `logging` module provides a flexible framework for emitting log messages from Python programs. It is highly configurable, allowing log messages to be directed to different destinations (e.g., console, files).

Here is an example demonstrating basic logging configuration:

```python
import logging

# Configure the logging
logging.basicConfig(level=logging.INFO, format='%(asctime)s - %(levelname)s - %(
    message)s')

# Example log messages
logging.debug("This is a debug message")
logging.info("This is an info message")
logging.warning("This is a warning message")
logging.error("This is an error message")
logging.critical("This is a critical message")
```

```
2023-05-01 10:00:00,000 - INFO - This is an info message
2023-05-01 10:00:00,000 - WARNING - This is a warning message
2023-05-01 10:00:00,000 - ERROR - This is an error message
2023-05-01 10:00:00,000 - CRITICAL - This is a critical message
```

The `logging` module supports extensive customization options, including different log levels (DEBUG, INFO, WARNING, ERROR, CRITICAL) and log handlers.

The `math` Module

The `math` module provides mathematical functions defined by the C standard. It includes functions for arithmetic, trigonometry, logarithms, and more.

For example, computing the factorial of a number and the value of π:

```python
import math

# Calculate factorial
factorial_of_five = math.factorial(5)
print(f"Factorial of 5: {factorial_of_five}")

# Value of
value_of_pi = math.pi
print(f"Value of  : {value_of_pi}")
```

```
Factorial of 5: 120
Value of  : 3.141592653589793
```

The math module is useful for tasks that require precise mathematical computations and is widely used in scientific and engineering applications.

The random Module

The random module implements pseudo-random number generators for various distributions. It includes functions to generate random numbers, select a random element from a sequence, and shuffle sequences.

Here is an example of generating a random number and shuffling a list:

```
import random

# Generate a random number between 1 and 10
random_number = random.randint(1, 10)
print(f"Random number between 1 and 10: {random_number}")

# Shuffle a list
sample_list = [1, 2, 3, 4, 5]
random.shuffle(sample_list)
print(f"Shuffled list: {sample_list}")
```

```
Random number between 1 and 10: 7
Shuffled list: [3, 1, 4, 2, 5]
```

The random module is essential for applications in fields such as data analysis, simulations, and games.

Understanding and effectively utilizing Python's built-in modules can significantly enhance productivity and code quality. This section covered some of the most commonly used modules, providing examples of their core functionalities. By leveraging these modules, developers can perform a wide array of tasks with simplicity and efficiency, relying on the robust features provided by Python's standard library.

9.5 Random Module and its Uses

The random module in Python is a robust toolkit for generating pseudo-random numbers and random sequences. It is widely used in scenarios requiring randomization, such as simulations, probabilistic algorithms, and games. This module relies on the Mersenne Twister as its core generator, which has an extensive period of $2^{19937} - 1$ and a robust distribution profile suitable for most applications.

The random module offers several fundamental functions for generating random values:

Basic Random Number Generation

```
import random

# Generate a random float between 0.0 and 1.0
random_float = random.random()
print(random_float)

# Generate a random integer between two given values
random_integer = random.randint(1, 10)
print(random_integer)

# Choose a random element from a non-empty sequence
choices = ['apple', 'banana', 'cherry']
random_choice = random.choice(choices)
print(random_choice)
```

```
0.3745401188473625
5
banana
```

The random.random() function returns a floating-point number in the range $[0.0, 1.0)$, providing a basic means of obtaining random decimal values. The random.randint(a, b) function is used to generate an integer N such that $a \leq N \leq b$, and random.choice(seq) selects a random element from a non-empty sequence seq.

In addition to basic random number generation, the random module extends its capabilities with more advanced functionalities:

Advanced Random Number Generation

```
# Generate a random float within a specified range
random_uniform = random.uniform(1.5, 3.5)
print(random_uniform)

# Shuffle a sequence randomly
sequence = [1, 2, 3, 4, 5]
random.shuffle(sequence)
print(sequence)

# Generate a random sample from a population
population = range(100)
sample = random.sample(population, 10)
print(sample)
```

```
2.4568276340075337
[3, 1, 5, 4, 2]
[34, 43, 28, 19, 95, 69, 0, 67, 30, 37]
```

- random.uniform(a, b) produces a random floating-point number N such that $a \leq N \leq b$. - random.shuffle(x) shuffles

311

the sequence x in place, altering its order pseudo-randomly. - random.sample(population, k) returns a k-length list of unique elements chosen from the population sequence or set.

To produce reproducible results, the random module allows seeding of the random number generator:

Seeding the Random Number Generator

```
# Seed the random number generator
random.seed(42)

# Generate reproducible random numbers
print(random.random())
print(random.randint(1, 10))
```

```
0.6394267984578837
1
```

By setting random.seed(a=None), the generator can be initialized to a predetermined state based on the seed value a. This technique is essential for debugging and scenarios requiring consistent random data.

The random module is integral in various practical applications:

- **Simulations:** Simulating stochastic processes such as Monte Carlo simulations for predicting future events.

- **Games:** Implementing random events, shuffles, or distributions in game mechanics.

- **Sampling:** Extracting random samples for statistical analysis or creating bootstrap datasets.

- **Randomized Algorithms:** Enhancing algorithmic performance through probabilistic methods.

The random module is a key component of Python's standard library, providing a plethora of options for random number generation and manipulation. Its versatility and ease of use make it a critical tool for developers engaged in tasks that necessitate randomness and variability.

9.6 Math and Statistics Modules

Python's standard library includes comprehensive modules for performing mathematical and statistical operations, namely the math and statistics modules. These modules provide a wide array of functions and utilities, enabling efficient execution of complex computations.

The math Module

The math module supplies mathematical functions defined by the C standard. The following example demonstrates the importation and fundamental use of the math module:

```
import math
```

Basic Arithmetic Functions

The math module includes essential arithmetic functions such as:

- math.sqrt(x): Returns the square root of x.

- math.pow(x, y): Returns x raised to the power of y.

- math.fabs(x): Returns the absolute value of x.

```
# Example of basic arithmetic functions
import math

print(math.sqrt(16)) # Output: 4.0
print(math.pow(2, 3)) # Output: 8.0
print(math.fabs(-5)) # Output: 5.0
```

Trigonometric Functions

The math module also offers a wide range of trigonometric functions, such as:

- math.sin(x), math.cos(x), math.tan(x): Compute the sine, cosine, and tangent of x, respectively.

- math.asin(x), math.acos(x), math.atan(x): Compute the arc sine, arc cosine, and arc tangent of x, respectively.

- math.atan2(y, x): Returns atan(y / x), considering the signs of both arguments to determine the correct quadrant.

```
# Example of trigonometric functions
import math

angle = math.radians(45) # Convert 45 degrees to radians
print(math.sin(angle)) # Output: 0.7071067811865476
print(math.cos(angle)) # Output: 0.7071067811865476
print(math.tan(angle)) # Output: 0.9999999999999999
```

Exponential and Logarithmic Functions

Key exponential and logarithmic functions include:

- `math.exp(x)`: Returns e raised to the power of x.

- `math.log(x, base)`: Returns the logarithm of x to the given base. If the base is not specified, returns the natural logarithm.

- `math.log10(x)`: Returns the base-10 logarithm of x.

- `math.log2(x)`: Returns the base-2 logarithm of x.

```
# Example of exponential and logarithmic functions
import math

print(math.exp(1)) # Output: 2.718281828459045
print(math.log(math.e)) # Output: 1.0
print(math.log10(100)) # Output: 2.0
print(math.log2(8)) # Output: 3.0
```

The `statistics` Module

The `statistics` module provides functions for calculating mathematical statistics of numeric data. It supports both Python lists or tuples of real-valued numbers and objects that can be converted to such sequences.

Measures of Central Tendency

Functions for central tendency include:

- `statistics.mean(data)`: Returns the sample arithmetic mean of data.

314

- `statistics.median(data)`: Returns the median (middle value) of data.

- `statistics.mode(data)`: Returns the most common value in data.

```
# Example of central tendency functions
import statistics

data = [1, 2, 2, 3, 4]

print(statistics.mean(data)) # Output: 2.4
print(statistics.median(data)) # Output: 2
print(statistics.mode(data)) # Output: 2
```

Measures of Spread

Functions for statistical dispersion include:

- `statistics.variance(data)`: Returns the sample variance of data.

- `statistics.stdev(data)`: Returns the sample standard deviation of data.

- `statistics.pvariance(data)`: Returns the population variance of data.

- `statistics.pstdev(data)`: Returns the population standard deviation of data.

```
# Example of measures of spread functions
import statistics

data = [1, 2, 2, 3, 4]

print(statistics.variance(data)) # Output: 1.3
print(statistics.stdev(data)) # Output: 1.140175425099138
print(statistics.pvariance(data)) # Output: 1.04
print(statistics.pstdev(data)) # Output: 1.019803902718557
```

Examples of Advanced Statistical Computations

Combining functions from both `math` and `statistics` modules can facilitate more sophisticated statistical analyses. For instance, to compute the coefficient of variation:

315

```
# Example of advanced statistical computation: coefficient of variation
import statistics
import math

data = [1, 2, 2, 3, 4]

mean = statistics.mean(data)
stdev = statistics.stdev(data)
cv = stdev / mean

print(cv) # Output: 0.47507308129130746
```

Coefficient of Variation (CV) indicates the ratio of the standard deviation to the mean.

Understanding and implementing the functionalities provided by the math and statistics modules is essential for executing both elementary and advanced mathematical and statistical operations in Python. By utilizing these modules, developers can perform efficient and accurate calculations, which is imperative in diverse applications ranging from basic data processing to complex scientific research.

9.7 Datetime Module

The datetime module in Python provides classes for manipulating dates and times. This section delves into its key components and common use cases to enable effective date and time handling within your applications.

The module consists of several classes, the most notable being date, time, datetime, timedelta, and tzinfo. Each serves a distinct purpose, allowing for comprehensive manipulation and arithmetic operations with temporal data.

Importing the datetime module

```
import datetime
```

The date Class

The date class handles calendar dates. You can instantiate it using the date(year, month, day) constructor. It features methods such as today(), fromtimestamp(), and instance methods like weekday().

Basic date usage

```
from datetime import date

# Create a specific date
```

316

```
d = date(2023, 10, 5)

# Get today's date
today = date.today()

# Get the day of the week (0=Monday, 6=Sunday)
day_of_week = d.weekday()
```

The time Class

The time class handles time of day independent of any particular date. Initialize it with time(hour, minute, second, microsecond=0, tzinfo=None).

Basic time usage

```
from datetime import time

# Create a specific time
t = time(14, 30, 45)

# Accessing time attributes
hour = t.hour # 14
minute = t.minute # 30
second = t.second # 45
```

The datetime Class

The datetime class combines date and time attributes. It can be instantiated using datetime(year, month, day, hour=0, minute=0, second=0, microsecond=0, tzinfo=None), providing a comprehensive timestamp representation.

Basic datetime usage

```
from datetime import datetime

# Create a specific datetime
dt = datetime(2023, 10, 5, 14, 30, 45)

# Get the current date and time
now = datetime.now()

# Access datetime attributes
year = dt.year # 2023
month = dt.month # 10
day = dt.day # 5
hour = dt.hour # 14
```

Timely Calculations

Perform arithmetic with datetime objects using the timedelta class, which represents differences between dates or times.

Using timedelta

317

```
from datetime import datetime, timedelta

# Define timedelta for 5 days
delta = timedelta(days=5)

# Add timedelta to a datetime object
new_date = datetime(2023, 10, 5) + delta # 2023-10-10

# Subtracting timedelta
previous_date = datetime(2023, 10, 5) - delta # 2023-09-30
```

Time Zones

The `tzinfo` abstract base class enables time zone handling. It is recommended to use third-party libraries like `pytz` to leverage comprehensive time zone data.

Using `pytz` for time zone conversion

```
import pytz
from datetime import datetime

# Define time zones
tz_utc = pytz.utc
tz_est = pytz.timezone('US/Eastern')

# Assigning time zone to datetime object
dt = datetime(2023, 10, 5, 14, 30, 45, tzinfo=tz_utc)

# Convert datetime to another time zone
dt_est = dt.astimezone(tz_est)
```

Formatting and Parsing

Use `strftime()` and `strptime()` methods of the `datetime` class to format dates and times to and from strings.

Formatting and parsing dates and times

```
from datetime import datetime

# Formatting datetime object to string
dt = datetime(2023, 10, 5, 14, 30, 45)
formatted_date = dt.strftime('%Y-%m-%d %H:%M:%S') # '2023-10-05 14:30:45'

# Parsing string to datetime object
date_string = '2023-10-05 14:30:45'
parsed_date = datetime.strptime(date_string, '%Y-%m-%d %H:%M:%S')
```

Practical Example: Calculating Age

A practical example involves calculating age using the `datetime` and `date` classes.

Calculating age

```
from datetime import datetime, date
```

318

```
def calculate_age(birth_date):
    today = date.today()
    age = today.year - birth_date.year - ((today.month, today.day) < (birth_date.
        month, birth_date.day))
    return age

# Example usage
birth_date = date(1990, 4, 18)
age = calculate_age(birth_date) # Calculate age
```

The datetime module is an essential component for any application requiring date and time manipulation. Its robust framework handles various temporal operations comprehensively and efficiently.

9.8 Custom Modules

Custom modules are essential tools for organizing and managing larger codebases in Python. By breaking down complex programs into smaller, manageable, and reusable components, custom modules promote code reusability and maintainability. This section outlines the creation, use, and management of custom modules, providing technical guidance and illustrative examples.

Creating a custom module in Python is straightforward. A module is simply a file containing Python definitions and statements. For instance, consider the module mymodule.py:

mymodule.py

```
# mymodule.py

def add(a, b):
    return a + b

def subtract(a, b):
    return a - b

PI = 3.14159
```

This module contains two functions, add and subtract, and a constant PI.

To use the functions and variables defined in mymodule.py, it must be imported into another script or interactive session. The import statement is used for this purpose:

main.py

```
# main.py
```

319

```
import mymodule

# Using the add function from mymodule
result = mymodule.add(5, 3)
print(f"The result of addition is: {result}")

# Using the PI constant
print(f"The value of PI is: {mymodule.PI}")
```

When main.py is executed, it produces the following output:

```
The result of addition is: 8
The value of PI is: 3.14159
```

Python provides flexibility in how modules are imported. If only specific elements from a module are needed, they can be imported directly using the from...import statement:

importing specific elements

```
from mymodule import add, PI

result = add(5, 3)
print(f"The result of addition is: {result}")
print(f"The value of PI is: {PI}")
```

Here, only the add function and the PI constant are imported, which can make the code cleaner and more readable.

To avoid naming conflicts or improve code clarity, imported modules and their functions can be renamed using the as keyword:

Renaming imports

```
import mymodule as mm

result = mm.add(5, 3)
print(f"The result of addition is: {result}")

from mymodule import subtract as sub

result = sub(10, 5)
print(f"The result of subtraction is: {result}")
```

When a module is imported, Python searches for the module in the directories listed in the sys.path variable. The following code displays the module search path:

Displaying sys.path

```
import sys
print(sys.path)
```

The sys.path includes the directory containing the input script (or

320

the current directory), PYTHONPATH (a list of directory names), and the installation-dependent default directories. To include additional directories in the module search path, they can be appended to sys.path:

Modifying sys.path

```
import sys
sys.path.append('/path/to/my/modules')
```

This allows Python to locate and import modules from the specified directory.

When a module is imported, the code at the top level of the module is executed only once. Subsequent imports do not re-execute the module's code. To demonstrate this, consider the following module initexample.py:

initexample.py

```
# initexample.py

print("Initializing the initexample module.")

def greet(name):
    return f"Hello, {name}!"
```

When this module is imported, the print statement is executed:

main.py

```
# main.py

import initexample
import initexample # Importing second time

print(initexample.greet("Alice"))
```

The output is:

```
Initializing the initexample module.
Hello, Alice!
```

Notably, the module initialization message is printed only once.

Creating and managing custom modules is a powerful technique to structure and reuse code in Python. By understanding how to create, import, and organize modules effectively, developers can build scalable and maintainable applications. This section has provided the foundational knowledge required to work with custom modules, enabling developers to leverage Python's modularity to its fullest potential.

321

9.9 Understanding Packages

In Python, a package is a collection of modules that are grouped together within a directory hierarchy. This organization facilitates modular programming by dividing large codebases into smaller, manageable, and reusable components. Unlike individual modules, packages provide a structured namespace and help resolve potential name conflicts, making the codebase more maintainable and scalable.

`Package Structure`

A package is essentially a directory that contains a special file named `__init__.py`. This file can be empty or can include initialization code for the package. The directory may also contain sub-packages and module files. A typical package structure might look like this:

```
package_name/
    __init__.py
    module1.py
    module2.py
    subpackage/
        __init__.py
        submodule1.py
```

In this example, `package_name` is a package that contains two modules (`module1.py` and `module2.py`) and a sub-package `subpackage`, which itself contains additional modules (`submodule1.py`).

`Importing from Packages`

Python provides several ways to import modules from a package, enhancing flexibility in how you utilize package components within your code. Consider the following examples:

Importing an entire package

```
import package_name
```

This statement imports the entire package. To access functions or classes from the package, you need to use the package name as a prefix:

Accessing package contents

```
package_name.module1.some_function()
```

Alternatively, you can import specific modules from a package:

Importing a specific module

```
from package_name import module1
```

322

Then, use the module name directly to call its functions:

Calling functions of a module

```
module1.some_function()
```

Moreover, importing directly from sub-packages is also straightforward:

Importing from a sub-package

```
from package_name.subpackage import submodule1
```

This method is useful for reducing namespace pollution and enhancing code readability.

Advantages of Using Packages

Utilizing packages provides several advantages:

- **Namespace Management:** Packages help avoid name clashes by encapsulating modules within a distinct namespace.

- **Modularization:** Packages facilitate dividing a large codebase into smaller, more manageable, and reusable components.

- **Code Organization:** Packages impose a directory structure that encourages better organization of your code.

- **Distributed Development:** Teams can work on different modules or sub-packages independently, enhancing collaboration and parallel development.

Best Practices for Packages

To effectively leverage packages, consider the following best practices:

- **Meaningful Names:** Use descriptive names for packages, modules, and functions to improve code readability and maintainability.

- **Documentation:** Include docstrings and comments within your package modules to explain their purpose and usage.

- **Init Files:** Utilize the __init__.py file wisely to initialize package-level variables or import sub-modules as needed.

323

- **Consistent Structure:** Maintain a consistent directory and module structure across your project to simplify navigation and encourage uniformity.

Example: Creating and Using a Package

We will create a simple package named mymath with modules for basic arithmetic operations. The package directory structure will be as follows:

```
mymath/
    __init__.py
    addition.py
    subtraction.py
```

The addition.py module:

addition.py

```
def add(a, b):
    return a + b
```

The subtraction.py module:

subtraction.py

```
def subtract(a, b):
    return a - b
```

The __init__.py file:

```
from .addition import add
from .subtraction import subtract
```

To use the mymath package in your code:

Using the mymath package

```
import mymath

result_add = mymath.add(5, 3)
result_sub = mymath.subtract(5, 3)
print(f"Addition: {result_add}, Subtraction: {result_sub}")
```

The output would be:

```
Addition: 8, Subtraction: 2
```

This example illustrates the creation, organization, and usage of a custom Python package, providing a clear understanding of the concepts discussed.

324

9.10 Creating and Importing Packages

In Python, a package is a directory containing a collection of modules. Packages enable a hierarchical structuring of the module namespace using dot notation. For instance, a module named A.B indicates that module B is a submodule in package A.

Creating a Package

- Create a directory that will represent the package.

- Within this directory, create an __init__.py file.

- Add module files (i.e., Python scripts) to this directory.

The __init__.py file can be empty or can contain package initialization code. It is required to make Python treat the directory as a package.

Suppose we want to create a package named mypackage with two modules: module1.py and module2.py. The file structure would be:

```
mypackage/
    __init__.py
    module1.py
    module2.py
```

Example Implementation

Consider the following example where module1.py and module2.py contain simple functions.

```python
# File: mypackage/module1.py
def func1():
    return "Function 1 from Module 1"
```

```python
# File: mypackage/module2.py
def func2():
    return "Function 2 from Module 2"
```

An empty __init__.py file:

```python
# File: mypackage/__init__.py
```

Importing a Package

Once the package is created, it can be imported just like any other module. The syntax for importing a package and its modules is as follows:

```python
import mypackage.module1
import mypackage.module2
```

```
print(mypackage.module1.func1())
print(mypackage.module2.func2())
```

This will output:

```
Function 1 from Module 1
Function 2 from Module 2
```

Using from and import Statements

Python allows for more granular control over what is imported from a package. You can import specific attributes or functions from submodules:

```
from mypackage.module1 import func1
from mypackage.module2 import func2

print(func1())
print(func2())
```

This produces the same output but avoids referencing the module names further in the code.

Namespace Packages

Namespace packages allow you to split a single package across multiple directories. This is useful for large-scale applications where different teams manage different parts of the package. Python's PEP 420 allows for implicit namespace packages by omitting the __init__.py file.

Create multiple directories with the following structure:

```
pkg_part1/
    namespace_a/
        module_a1.py
pkg_part2/
    namespace_a/
        module_a2.py
```

Ensure both pkg_part1 and pkg_part2 directories are in sys.path. This will enable importing modules from the namespace package namespace_a:

```
import namespace_a.module_a1
import namespace_a.module_a2
```

Namespace packages simplify package management by enabling a modular distribution of package components.

Relative Imports

For intra-package references, relative imports can be used to import a module relative to the current module's path. For example, inside

326

module1.py, to import function func2 from module2.py, you can write:

```
# File: mypackage/module1.py
from .module2 import func2

def func1():
    other_func_result = func2()
    return f"Func1 calling func2: {other_func_result}"
```

Creating and importing packages in Python enhances code organization, modularization, and reusability. By understanding the directory structure, __init__.py requirements, namespace packages, and import techniques, developers can structure complex applications effectively.

9.11 Namespace Packages

Namespace packages are a feature in Python that allows for the distribution of a single logical package across multiple directories. They offer a critical advantage for large projects where different portions of the project need to be managed, maintained, or distributed independently. The concept of namespace packages was introduced in PEP 420 and became available starting with Python 3.3.

A namespace package is a composite package whose sub-packages and modules can be spread across multiple, distinct locations in the filesystem. Unlike regular packages, namespace packages do not contain an __init__.py file. This absence signals to the Python interpreter that the directory represents a namespace package.

Namespace packages are especially useful in the following scenarios:

- **Large Projects**: When a large application or library needs to be segmented into smaller, manageable parts that can be developed, versioned, and distributed independently.

- **Third-Party Plugins**: When third-party plugins or extensions need to be developed for an existing package framework without modifying the original package structure.

- **Modular Distribution**: When different parts of a package are maintained by different teams or need to be deployed in different environments.

To create a namespace package, simply omit the __init__.py file in the directories that should be treated as namespace packages.

Creating a namespace package

```
# Directory structure for package 'foo'
# foo/
#   bar/
#     module_bar.py
#   baz/
#     module_baz.py
# Note: No __init__.py files present

# foo/bar/module_bar.py
def bar_function():
    return "This is Bar"

# foo/baz/module_baz.py
def baz_function():
    return "This is Baz"
```

In this example, both bar and baz are sub-packages of the namespace package foo.

Importing from namespace packages is straightforward and follows the same syntax as regular packages.

Importing from a namespace package

```
# Importing functions from the namespace package
from foo.bar import module_bar
from foo.baz import module_baz

print(module_bar.bar_function())
print(module_baz.baz_function())
```

```
This is Bar
This is Baz
```

Namespace packages can coexist with regular packages. However, care must be taken to avoid conflicts and ensure that the regular package's __init__.py does not interfere with the namespace packages.

Consider the following directory structure:

Coexistence of namespace and regular packages

```
# foo/
#   __init__.py # Regular package
#   bar/
#     module_bar.py
#   baz/
#   module_baz.py

# foo/qux/ # Namespace package
#   alpha.py
#   beta.py
```

Python's `pkgutil` and `importlib` modules provide various utilities to work with namespace packages.

Listing modules within a namespace package

```
import pkgutil

# Listing all modules within a namespace package 'foo'
package = 'foo'
for module in pkgutil.iter_modules([package]):
    print(module.name)
```

```
bar
baz
qux
```

Furthermore, the `importlib` module can be used to dynamically import sub-packages or modules.

Dynamically importing modules from a namespace package

```
import importlib

module_bar = importlib.import_module('foo.bar.module_bar')
module_baz = importlib.import_module('foo.baz.module_baz')

print(module_bar.bar_function())
print(module_baz.baz_function())
```

```
This is Bar
This is Baz
```

Namespace packages provide a robust and flexible way to organize large and modular Python projects. By leveraging Python's filesystem structure and import mechanisms, namespace packages facilitate better distribution, maintainability, and the incorporation of third-party extensions. Developers should consider namespace packages in scenarios involving large-scale applications or when designing modular, pluggable architectures.

In the next section, we will discuss the importance and utilization of the __init__.py file in defining regular packages and the implications of its presence or absence.

9.12 __init__.py

The __init__.py file is essential for the structure and functionality of Python packages. This section delves into the purpose and intricacies of __init__.py, alongside practical implementation scenarios to enhance understanding.

Purpose of _ init__.py

The __init__.py file serves several crucial roles:

- It indicates to the Python interpreter that the directory should be treated as a package.

- It can execute initialization code for the package or set the __all__ attribute.

- It allows for the definition of the package's namespace.

Without the presence of an __init__.py file, a directory, even if structured otherwise like a package, cannot be identified as one by the Python interpreter. This file is mandatory for older Python versions (before Python 3.3) but still widely used for explicitly managing package initializations.

Creating an __init__.py File

Creating an __init__.py file is straightforward. Here is a basic example:

```
# content of mypackage/__init__.py

# Initialize the package
print("Initializing mypackage")

# Define what is included in the package's namespace
__all__ = ["module1", "module2"]
```

This example demonstrates a couple of key points:

1. **Initialization Code**: Any code within the __init__.py file will be executed when the package is imported.

2. **__all__ Attribute**: Lists the modules that should be imported when from mypackage import * is used.

Namespace Definition and Organization

By defining the __all__ attribute, the __init__.py file plays a vital role in controlling the namespace of the package. This control is beneficial for organizing the public interface of the package. Here is a more structured approach:

```
# content of mypackage/__init__.py

from .module1 import function1, Class1
```

330

```
from .module2 import function2, Class2

__all__ = ["function1", "Class1", "function2", "Class2"]
```

In this example:

- Relative imports are used to include specific components from submodules.

- __all__ now includes the explicitly imported functions and classes.

Practical Examples

Consider a more comprehensive package structure with an __init__.py file.

```
mypackage/
    __init__.py
    module1.py
    module2.py
```

The __init__.py file could be used to simplify access to certain functionalities directly from the package:

```
# content of mypackage/module1.py
def function1():
    return "Function 1"

class Class1:
    def __init__(self):
        self.name = "Class1"

# content of mypackage/module2.py
def function2():
    return "Function 2"

class Class2:
    def __init__(self):
        self.name = "Class2"

# content of mypackage/__init__.py
from .module1 import function1, Class1
from .module2 import function2, Class2

__all__ = ["function1", "Class1", "function2", "Class2"]
```

With this setup, the package can be used as follows:

```
# In a separate Python script or interactive session
from mypackage import *

print(function1()) # Output: Function 1
print(function2()) # Output: Function 2
```

This approach simplifies the user's experience by allowing direct access to function1, Class1, function2, and Class2 directly from the package.

Advanced Usage: Dynamic Imports and Conditional Initializations

Complex modules may require more sophisticated setup within the __init__.py file, such as dynamic imports or conditional initializations.

```python
# content of mypackage/__init__.py
import os

if os.getenv('DEBUG_MODE') == 'true':
    from .debugmodule import DebugClass as MainClass
else:
    from .normalmodule import NormalClass as MainClass

__all__ = ["MainClass"]
```

In this scenario, the specific class implementation imported into the namespace depends on the environment variable DEBUG_MODE. This technique is useful for toggling between different configurations or environments.

The __init__.py file remains an integral part of Python's package system, enabling the grouping of related modules, control of namespaces, and dynamic configuration setups. Proper utilization of __init__.py enhances package organization and maintains clarity and usability for end users. Familiarity with its capabilities ensures robust and well-crafted Python packages.

9.13   Distributing Modules and Packages

Distributing Python modules and packages is essential to sharing your code with the broader community or deploying it in production environments. The process involves several well-defined steps, from packaging your code to publishing it on repositories like the Python Package Index (PyPI). This section provides an in-depth discussion on the tools and methodologies for effectively distributing Python modules and packages.

Setting Up Your Package

To distribute a Python package, it is necessary to structure it correctly. A well-structured package should include essential files such as setup.py, documentation, and any additional metadata.

The setup.py File

The setup.py file is the cornerstone of any Python package. It contains metadata about the package and instructions for installation. A typical setup.py file might look like this:

A typical setup.py file

```
from setuptools import setup, find_packages

setup(
    name='mypackage',
    version='0.1.0',
    author='Author Name',
    author_email='author@example.com',
    description='A brief description of the package',
    long_description=open('README.md').read(),
    long_description_content_type='text/markdown',
    url='https://github.com/author/mypackage',
    packages=find_packages(),
    classifiers=[
        'Programming Language :: Python :: 3',
        'License :: OSI Approved :: MIT License',
        'Operating System :: OS Independent',
    ],
    python_requires='>=3.6',
    install_requires=[
        'requests',
        'numpy',
    ],
)
```

In the above example, setuptools is utilized, which is the standard library for packaging Python projects. The fields such as name, version, and author provide basic information about your package. The install_requires list specifies the dependencies required by the package.

Creating a Distribution Archive

Once your setup.py is configured, the next step is to create a distribution archive. This can be either a source distribution or a built distribution.

Source Distribution

A source distribution (sdist) contains the files required to run the package. It is created using the following command:

Creating a source distribution

```
python setup.py sdist
```

This command generates a tarball within the dist directory. For example, it might create a file named mypackage-0.1.0.tar.gz.

Built Distribution

A built distribution (wheel) is a precompiled package. It is created using the following command:

Creating a built distribution using wheel

```
python setup.py bdist_wheel
```

The bdist_wheel command produces a file with the .whl extension, such as mypackage-0.1.0-py3-none-any.whl, also located in the dist directory.

Uploading to PyPI

Once your distribution archives are ready, they can be uploaded to PyPI. PyPI is the principal repository for Python packages, facilitating distribution and installation.

Installing twine

Uploading packages to PyPI is performed using twine. First, ensure twine is installed:

Installing twine

```
pip install twine
```

Uploading the Package

With twine installed, the next step is to upload your package:

Uploading package to PyPI

```
twine upload dist/*
```

This command uploads all distribution archives in the dist directory to PyPI. You will be prompted to enter your PyPI credentials.

Publishing on TestPyPI

Before releasing a package on the official PyPI, it is prudent to test the release process on TestPyPI, a separate instance of PyPI for testing.

Uploading to TestPyPI

To upload your package to TestPyPI, use the following command:

Uploading package to TestPyPI

```
twine upload --repository-url https://test.pypi.org/legacy/ dist/*
```

This command uses the --repository-url flag to specify the TestPyPI

URL. After uploading, you can install your package from TestPyPI using `pip`:

Installing from TestPyPI

```
pip install --index-url https://test.pypi.org/simple/ mypackage
```

Maintaining Your Package

Maintenance is crucial for the long-term success of your package. Regular updates and addressing user issues help in building credibility and trust.

Versioning

Follow semantic versioning to manage changes and updates to your package. Semantic versioning uses a `MAJOR.MINOR.PATCH` format.

Changelog

Maintain a changelog to document improvements and bug fixes. This helps users understand the changes in each release.

Responding to Issues

Engage with the user community and respond to issues raised on platforms such as GitHub. Provide timely fixes and improvements to enhance user satisfaction.

Distributing modules and packages is a meticulous yet vital aspect of Python development. By adhering to best practices for packaging, creating distribution archives, and managing releases, developers can effectively share their work with a global audience. Ensuring proper maintenance and user engagement further augments the package's reliability and usability across diverse applications.

Chapter 10

Standard Libraries and Third-Party Modules

This chapter explores Python's standard libraries and popular third-party modules. It covers essential modules such as os, sys, re, json, and urllib, demonstrating their key functionalities. The chapter also highlights modules for mathematical operations, data structures, and date/time handling, including math, cmath, and datetime. Additionally, it introduces important third-party modules like NumPy, pandas, and matplotlib, and explains how to find, install, and manage these modules using pip, along with creating virtual environments using venv.

10.1   Introduction to Standard Libraries

Python's standard library is a collection of modules and packages included with every Python installation. These modules provide standardized solutions for many programming tasks, such as file I/O, system calls, data serialization, and much more. Utilizing the standard library allows developers to implement solutions without the need for third-party dependencies, thereby simplifying the development and deployment process.

The standard library is extensive and well-documented, making it a powerful tool for developers. This section delves into some of the most commonly used modules in Python's standard library, highlighting their functionalities and providing examples to demonstrate their usage.

The os Module and System Functions

The os module provides a way of using operating system-dependent functionality like reading or writing to the file system. This module offers a portable way of interacting with the underlying operating system.

Listing directories with the os module

```
import os

# List all files and directories in the current directory
entries = os.listdir('.')
for entry in entries:
    print(entry)
```

In this example, os.listdir is used to retrieve the list of entries in the current directory. The os module also provides functions for creating and removing directories, fetching their contents, moving files, and obtaining system information.

The sys Module and System Arguments

The sys module provides access to some variables used or maintained by the interpreter and to functions that interact strongly with the interpreter. For instance, it is commonly used to manipulate the Python runtime environment.

Accessing command-line arguments with the sys module

```
import sys

# Print all command-line arguments
for arg in sys.argv:
    print(arg)
```

Here, sys.argv represents the list of command-line arguments passed to the script, with the first element being the script name itself.

The re Module and Regular Expressions

The re module provides support for regular expressions, enabling complex string matching and manipulation tasks. Regular expressions are powerful tools for tasks such as validating input, searching within text, and transforming text patterns.

Using regular expressions with the re module

```
import re

# Check if the string starts with 'Hello'
pattern = re.compile(r'^Hello')
result = pattern.match('Hello, World!')

if result:
    print("Match found!")
else:
    print("No match.")
```

The re.compile function compiles a regular expression pattern into a regular expression object, which can be used for matching using match, search, findall, and other methods.

The json and xml Modules

The json module provides an easy way to encode and decode data in JSON format, facilitating work with web services or APIs that exchange JSON data.

Encoding and decoding JSON with the json module

```
import json

# Encode a Python object into JSON
data = {"name": "John", "age": 30}
json_data = json.dumps(data)
print(json_data)

# Decode JSON back into a Python object
decoded_data = json.loads(json_data)
print(decoded_data)
```

Similarly, the xml.etree.ElementTree module offers methods for parsing and creating XML documents. Here is an example of creating a simple XML document:

Creating an XML document with the xml module

```
import xml.etree.ElementTree as ET

# Create the root element
root = ET.Element("root")
# Add a subelement
child = ET.SubElement(root, "child")
child.text = "This is a child element"

# Convert to string
xml_data = ET.tostring(root, encoding='unicode')
print(xml_data)
```

The urllib and requests Modules for HTTP Requests

The urllib module is a collection of modules for working with URLs

339

and HTTP. Although `urllib` supports many functionalities, the third-party module `requests` is often preferred for making HTTP requests due to its simplicity and user-friendly API.

Making HTTP requests with the requests module

```
import requests

response = requests.get('https://api.example.com/data')
if response.status_code == 200:
    print(response.json())
```

The `math` and `cmath` Modules for Mathematical Functions

The `math` module provides access to mathematical functions for floating-point arithmetic, while the `cmath` module deals with complex numbers.

Using mathematical functions from the math module

```
import math

# Calculate the square root
result = math.sqrt(16)
print(result)
```

The `collections` Module for Specialized Data Structures

The `collections` module implements specialized container datatypes providing alternatives to Python's general-purpose built-in containers like dictionaries, lists, and tuples.

Using the defaultdict from the collections module

```
from collections import defaultdict

# Create a defaultdict with default value type as int
default_dict = defaultdict(int)
default_dict['key1'] += 1
print(default_dict['key1'])
```

Working with Dates and Times: `datetime` Module

The `datetime` module supplies classes for manipulating dates and times.

Getting current date and time using the datetime module

```
import datetime

# Get current date and time
now = datetime.datetime.now()
print(now)
```

The `threading` and `multiprocessing` Modules

The `threading` and `multiprocessing` modules allow for concurrent execution of code.

Using threading to create a new thread

```python
import threading

def print_hello():
    print("Hello from the thread!")

# Create a new thread
thread = threading.Thread(target=print_hello)
thread.start()
thread.join()
```

The `multiprocessing` module facilitates process-based parallelism.

Using multiprocessing to create a new process

```python
import multiprocessing

def print_hello():
    print("Hello from the process!")

# Create a new process
process = multiprocessing.Process(target=print_hello)
process.start()
process.join()
```

By leveraging these modules, developers can handle a wide range of tasks efficiently, from file manipulation and system operations to network communications and mathematical computations.

10.2 The `os` Module and System Functions

The `os` module in Python provides a way of using operating system-dependent functionality. This module offers a comprehensive interface for interacting with the underlying operating system, making it an invaluable tool for tasks that require manipulation of the file system, execution of shell commands, process management, and querying of system information.

File and Directory Manipulation

The `os` module excels in its ability to work with file and directory operations. Key functions include creating directories, changing the working directory, and listing directory contents.

Creating Directories

341

The os.makedirs function can create a directory recursively:

```
import os

# Create a nested directory structure
os.makedirs('path/to/desired/directory', exist_ok=True)
```

The exist_ok parameter prevents an error if the directory already exists.

Changing the Working Directory

The os.chdir function changes the current working directory:

```
# Change to a different directory
os.chdir('/path/to/new/directory')
```

After calling os.chdir, all relative file operations will refer to the new directory.

Listing Directory Contents

To list the contents of a directory, use os.listdir:

```
# List all files and directories in the current directory
contents = os.listdir('.')
print(contents)
```

```
['file1.txt', 'file2.txt', 'directory1', 'directory2']
```

For a more comprehensive directory traversal, os.walk can be utilized:

```
# Walk through the directory tree
for dirpath, dirnames, filenames in os.walk('.'):
    print('Directory:', dirpath)
    print('Subdirectories:', dirnames)
    print('Files:', filenames)
```

Environment Variables

Environment variables are a set of dynamic values that can affect the behavior of running processes on an operating system. The os module provides methods to access, modify, and manage these variables.

Accessing Environment Variables

Use os.environ to access environment variables:

```
# Get the value of an environment variable
path = os.environ.get('PATH')
print(path)
```

Setting Environment Variables

To set a new environment variable, assign a value to the appropriate key in os.environ:

```
# Set a new environment variable
os.environ['NEW_VAR'] = 'value'
print(os.environ['NEW_VAR'])
```

Executing System Commands

The os.system function can execute a command in the subshell. However, it does not capture output, making it less useful for complex tasks.

```
# Execute a system command
os.system('echo "Hello, World!"')
```

For more intricate command executions, including capturing output, the subprocess module is recommended over os.system.

Process Management

Process management functions allow the creation and simplification of process operations.

Forking Processes

On Unix platforms, os.fork is used to fork processes:

```
# Fork a process
pid = os.fork()

if pid == 0:
    # This is the child process
    print("Child process")
else:
    # This is the parent process
    print("Parent process")
```

Process Identification

The os module contains functions to retrieve and manipulate process IDs.

```
# Get the current process ID
pid = os.getpid()
print(f'Current process ID: {pid}')

# Get the parent process ID
ppid = os.getppid()
print(f'Parent process ID: {ppid}')
```

Error Handling

The os module raises OSError exceptions when operations fail. These exceptions should be appropriately handled to ensure robust code.

```
try:
    os.mkdir('existing_directory')
```

```
except OSError as e:
    print(f"Error: {e.strerror}")
```

Proper exception handling allows for graceful degradation of the program when encountering unexpected situations. Understanding and leveraging these capabilities can lead to more efficient and effective Python applications, especially in scripts and automation tools. Whether managing files and directories, interacting with environment variables, executing system commands, or handling processes, the os module provides the necessary functions to accomplish these tasks seamlessly.

10.3   The sys Module and System Arguments

The sys module provides access to essential variables used or maintained by the Python interpreter and interacts strongly with the interpreter itself. It is pivotal for handling command-line arguments, managing the runtime environment, and performing various system-specific tasks.

Accessing Command-Line Arguments

Command-line arguments are parameters provided to a script or program during its invocation from a terminal or command prompt. These arguments are accessed using the sys.argv list, where each element represents a command-line parameter passed to the script.

Accessing Command-Line Arguments Using sys.argv

```
import sys

# Display the command-line arguments
print("Command-line arguments:", sys.argv)

# The first argument is always the script name
script_name = sys.argv[0]
print("Script name:", script_name)

# Subsequent arguments are the additional parameters passed
if len(sys.argv) > 1:
    for i, arg in enumerate(sys.argv[1:], start=1):
        print(f"Argument {i}:", arg)
else:
    print("No additional arguments were provided.")
```

```
$ python script.py arg1 arg2 arg3
Command-line arguments: ['script.py', 'arg1', 'arg2', 'arg3']
Script name: script.py
Argument 1: arg1
Argument 2: arg2
Argument 3: arg3
```

sys.exit() Function

The sys.exit() function terminates a Python script. It optionally takes an integer argument that is returned to the calling process as the exit status. The default value is None, translating to an exit status of zero (indicating no errors).

Using sys.exit() to Terminate a Script

```python
import sys

def main():
    print("This is the main function.")
    # Exit the script with a status code of 0
    sys.exit(0)

if __name__ == "__main__":
    main()
    # This line will not be executed since the script will exit in the main()
        function
    print("This will not be printed.")
```

Managing Standard Input, Output, and Error

The sys module allows redirection and manipulation of standard input, output, and error streams using sys.stdin, sys.stdout, and sys.stderr, respectively.

Redirecting Standard Output

Standard output (sys.stdout) can be redirected to a file or any writable object.

Redirecting sys.stdout to a File

```python
import sys

# Open a file to write
with open('output.txt', 'w') as f:
    # Save the current stdout
    original_stdout = sys.stdout
    try:
        # Redirect stdout to the file
        sys.stdout = f
        print("This will be written to the file, not to the console.")
    finally:
        # Restore the original stdout
        sys.stdout = original_stdout

print("This will be printed on the console.")
```

345

```
$ cat output.txt
This will be written to the file, not to the console.
```

Handling Standard Error

Similarly, standard error (`sys.stderr`) can be redirected. This is useful for logging errors while keeping standard output clean.

Redirecting `sys.stderr`

```python
import sys

# Redirect stderr to a file
with open('error.log', 'w') as f:
    original_stderr = sys.stderr
    try:
        sys.stderr = f
        raise ValueError("This error message will be written to the error log.")
    except ValueError as e:
        print(f"Error: {e}", file=sys.stderr)
    finally:
        sys.stderr = original_stderr

print("This will be printed on the console.")
```

```
$ cat error.log
Error: This error message will be written to the error log.
```

Inspecting the Python Runtime Environment

The sys module contains several attributes providing information about the Python runtime environment.

sys.version

The `sys.version` attribute returns a string containing the version number of the Python interpreter, along with additional information about the build.

Inspecting `sys.version`

```python
import sys

print("Python version:")
print(sys.version)
```

```
Python version:
3.8.10 (default, May 19 2021, 18:05:58)
[GCC 7.5.0]
```

sys.path

The `sys.path` attribute is a list of strings that specifies the search path for modules. This list is initialized from the environment variable PYTHONPATH, plus an installation-dependent default.

Inspecting and Modifying `sys.path`

346

```
import sys

# Display the module search path
print("Current module search path:")
for path in sys.path:
    print(path)

# Append a new path to sys.path
sys.path.append('/path/to/my/module')
```

```
Current module search path:
/usr/lib/python3.8
/usr/lib/python3.8/lib-dynload
...
/path/to/my/module
```

sys.platform

The sys.platform attribute provides a string that identifies the platform on which the interpreter is running.

Inspecting sys.platform

```
import sys

print("Running on platform:", sys.platform)
```

```
Running on platform: linux
```

The sys module is integral for interacting with the Python runtime environment and performing system-level operations. By leveraging sys.argv, users can access command-line arguments, and through sys.exit(), they can manage program termination. Additionally, standard input/output/error redirection can be efficiently handled using sys.stdin, sys.stdout, and sys.stderr. Moreover, attributes such as sys.version, sys.path, and sys.platform offer valuable insights into the interpreter's configuration and environment, making the sys module a cornerstone for robust and dynamic Python applications.

10.4   The re Module and Regular Expressions

In Python, the re module provides support for working with regular expressions, which are powerful tools for matching patterns in text. Regular expressions can be used for a variety of text-processing tasks, such as searching, replacing, and parsing strings. This section delves into the core functionalities offered by the re module and illustrates their use through practical examples.

347

Basic Pattern Matching

The fundamental function for pattern matching in the `re` module is `re.match`. This function attempts to match a pattern at the beginning of a string.

```
import re

pattern = r'\d+' # Matches one or more digits
string = "123abc"
match = re.match(pattern, string)

if match:
    print("Match found:", match.group())
else:
    print("No match found")
```

The output of the above code will be:

```
Match found: 123
```

The `group` method of the match object returns the part of the string that matched the pattern.

Searching for Patterns

To search for a pattern anywhere in a string, the `re.search` function is used. Unlike `re.match`, `re.search` does not require the pattern to match at the beginning of the string.

```
import re

pattern = r'\d+' # Matches one or more digits
string = "abc123xyz"
match = re.search(pattern, string)

if match:
    print("Search found:", match.group())
else:
    print("No match found")
```

The output will be:

```
Search found: 123
```

Finding All Occurrences

The `re.findall` function returns all non-overlapping matches of a pattern in a string, as a list of strings.

```
import re

pattern = r'\d+' # Matches one or more digits
string = "abc123xyz789"
matches = re.findall(pattern, string)

print("All matches:", matches)
```

348

This code will produce the following output:

```
All matches: ['123', '789']
```

Replacing Patterns

The re.sub function is used to replace occurrences of a pattern with a replacement string.

```
import re

pattern = r'\d+' # Matches one or more digits
string = "abc123xyz789"
new_string = re.sub(pattern, '#', string)

print("Replaced string:", new_string)
```

The output of this example will be:

```
Replaced string: abc#xyz#
```

Splitting Strings

The re.split function splits a string by the occurrences of a pattern, returning a list of substrings.

```
import re

pattern = r'\d+' # Matches one or more digits
string = "abc123xyz789"
split_list = re.split(pattern, string)

print("Split list:", split_list)
```

The output will be:

```
Split list: ['abc', 'xyz', '']
```

Compiling Regular Expressions

For repeated use of the same pattern, it is efficient to compile it into a regular expression object using re.compile. This object can then be used to perform pattern matching independently.

```
import re

pattern = re.compile(r'\d+') # Pre-compiled regular expression
string = "abc123xyz789"
matches = pattern.findall(string)

print("All matches with compiled pattern:", matches)
```

The output of this code snippet will be:

```
All matches with compiled pattern: ['123', '789']
```

Example: Email Validation

As a practical example, consider the task of validating an email address using a regular expression pattern.

```
import re

email_pattern = r'^[a-zA-Z0-9_.+-]+@[a-zA-Z0-9-]+\.[a-zA-Z0-9-.]+$'

def is_valid_email(email):
    return re.match(email_pattern, email) is not None

email_list = ["user@example.com", "user.name@domain.co", "invalid-email@", "
    name@domain"]
valid_emails = [email for email in email_list if is_valid_email(email)]

print("Valid emails:", valid_emails)
```

The output of this example will be:

```
Valid emails: ['user@example.com', 'user.name@domain.co']
```

This regular expression pattern covers basic email address formats, although more complex validations may be necessary for specific requirements.

Mastering the re module can significantly enhance your ability to perform sophisticated text processing tasks effectively.

10.5   The json and xml Modules

This section delves into the functionalities provided by the json and xml modules in Python, which are pivotal for data interchange and manipulation. Both modules enable developers to process textual data formats that are widely adopted across various systems and applications.

The json Module

The json module provides an efficient way to parse JSON (JavaScript Object Notation) data in Python. JSON is a lightweight data-interchange format that is easy for humans to read and write, and easy for machines to parse and generate. Below, we detail the primary functions available in the json module.

- json.loads and json.load

  json.loads parses a JSON string into a Python dictionary.

Parsing JSON from a string

```
import json

json_str = '{"name": "Alice", "age": 30, "city": "New York"}'
data = json.loads(json_str)
print(data)
```

```
{'name': 'Alice', 'age': 30, 'city': 'New York'}
```

json.load reads JSON data from a file object.

Reading JSON from a file

```
with open('data.json', 'r') as file:
    data = json.load(file)
print(data)
```

- json.dumps and json.dump

  json.dumps serializes a Python object into a JSON formatted string.

Serializing Python object to JSON string

```
import json

data = {"name": "Alice", "age": 30, "city": "New York"}
json_str = json.dumps(data)
print(json_str)
```

```
{"name": "Alice", "age": 30, "city": "New York"}
```

json.dump writes a Python object as a JSON string to a file.

Writing JSON to a file

```
data = {"name": "Alice", "age": 30, "city": "New York"}

with open('data.json', 'w') as file:
    json.dump(data, file)
```

- Customization Options

  The json module allows customization for pretty-printing and formatting.

Pretty-printing JSON

```
json_str = json.dumps(data, indent=4, separators=(",", ": "))
print(json_str)
```

```
{
    "name": "Alice",
    "age": 30,
    "city": "New York"
}
```

351

The xml Module

The xml module provides classes and functions for parsing and creating XML (eXtensible Markup Language) documents. XML is a markup language that defines a set of rules for encoding documents in a format that is both human-readable and machine-readable.

- Parsing XML with `ElementTree`

  `ElementTree` is a commonly used class from the `xml.etree.ElementTree` module. It provides methods for parsing XML from strings or files, and for creating new XML documents.

  Parsing XML from a string using ElementTree

  ```python
  import xml.etree.ElementTree as ET

  xml_str = '''<data>
      <person>
          <name>Alice</name>
          <age>30</age>
          <city>New York</city>
      </person>
  </data>'''
  root = ET.fromstring(xml_str)
  for person in root.findall('person'):
      name = person.find('name').text
      age = person.find('age').text
      city = person.find('city').text
      print(f'Name: {name}, Age: {age}, City: {city}')
  ```

  ```
  Name: Alice, Age: 30, City: New York
  ```

- Creating XML with `ElementTree`

  Creating an XML document and writing it to a file.

  Creating and writing XML to a file

  ```python
  import xml.etree.ElementTree as ET

  data = ET.Element('data')
  person = ET.SubElement(data, 'person')
  name = ET.SubElement(person, 'name')
  name.text = 'Alice'
  age = ET.SubElement(person, 'age')
  age.text = '30'
  city = ET.SubElement(person, 'city')
  city.text = 'New York'

  tree = ET.ElementTree(data)
  with open('data.xml', 'wb') as file:
      tree.write(file)
  ```

352

- Modifying XML

  To modify existing XML, one can simply locate the elements and adjust their properties.

  ### Modifying XML

  ```python
  tree = ET.parse('data.xml')
  root = tree.getroot()

  for person in root.findall('person'):
      age = person.find('age')
      age.text = str(int(age.text) + 1) # Increment age by 1

  tree.write('data.xml')
  ```

  ```xml
  <data>
      <person>
          <name>Alice</name>
          <age>31</age>
          <city>New York</city>
      </person>
  </data>
  ```

- Efficient XML Parsing with `minidom`

  The `xml.dom.minidom` provides a minimal implementation of the Document Object Model interface. It can be used for both parsing and creating XML.

  ### Parsing XML with minidom

  ```python
  from xml.dom.minidom import parseString

  xml_str = '''<data>
      <person>
          <name>Alice</name>
          <age>30</age>
          <city>New York</city>
      </person>
  </data>'''
  dom = parseString(xml_str)
  person = dom.getElementsByTagName("person")[0]
  name = person.getElementsByTagName("name")[0].firstChild.data
  age = person.getElementsByTagName("age")[0].firstChild.data
  city = person.getElementsByTagName("city")[0].firstChild.data
  print(f'Name: {name}, Age: {age}, City: {city}')
  ```

  ```
  Name: Alice, Age: 30, City: New York
  ```

  ### Creating XML with minidom

  ```python
  from xml.dom.minidom import Document

  doc = Document()

  data = doc.createElement('data')
  doc.appendChild(data)
  ```

```
person = doc.createElement('person')
data.appendChild(person)

name = doc.createElement('name')
name.appendChild(doc.createTextNode('Alice'))
person.appendChild(name)

age = doc.createElement('age')
age.appendChild(doc.createTextNode('30'))
person.appendChild(age)

city = doc.createElement('city')
city.appendChild(doc.createTextNode('New York'))
person.appendChild(city)

with open('data_minidom.xml', 'w') as file:
    file.write(doc.toprettyxml())
```

The json and xml modules in Python offer robust support for parsing, manipulating, and generating data in JSON and XML formats, respectively. These modules are essential tools for developers working with web services, configuration files, or any data interchange tasks where structured text formats are utilized.

10.6 The urllib and requests Modules for HTTP Requests

In Python, the urllib and requests modules are essential tools for making HTTP requests. These libraries facilitate interaction with web resources by enabling the execution of HTTP requests directly from within Python scripts. This section provides a comprehensive overview of both modules and demonstrates their core functionalities through precise code examples.

Using urllib for HTTP Requests

The urllib module is part of Python's standard library, ensuring its availability without the need for external installation. It provides functionalities to work with URLs and perform typical HTTP operations, such as sending GET and POST requests.

Retrieving Web Content with urllib

The urllib.request submodule is commonly used for making HTTP requests. Below is an example of how to fetch web content using urllib.

Fetching Web Content with `urllib`

```
import urllib.request

url = 'http://example.com'
response = urllib.request.urlopen(url)

# Read and decode the response content
content = response.read().decode('utf-8')
print(content)
```

The `urlopen` method sends a GET request to the specified URL and returns an HTTPResponse object. The response content can be read using the read method and must be decoded accordingly.

Submitting Data with `urllib`

To send data via a POST request, the following code creates a dictionary of form data, encodes it, and utilizes the `urlopen` method.

Sending Data with `urllib`

```
import urllib.request
import urllib.parse

url = 'http://example.com/post'
data = {'key1': 'value1', 'key2': 'value2'}
data = urllib.parse.urlencode(data).encode('ascii')

response = urllib.request.urlopen(url, data)
content = response.read().decode('utf-8')
print(content)
```

This example demonstrates how to encode data using the `urllib.parse.urlencode` method before sending it with the `urlopen` method.

Handling HTTP Headers with `urllib`

Headers can be managed by creating a `Request` object and adding the desired headers.

Handling HTTP Headers with `urllib`

```
import urllib.request

url = 'http://example.com'
headers = {'User-Agent': 'Mozilla/5.0'}
request = urllib.request.Request(url, headers=headers)

response = urllib.request.urlopen(request)
content = response.read().decode('utf-8')
print(content)
```

Using the `Request` object allows for greater control over the HTTP request, including the addition of custom headers.

Using requests for HTTP Requests

The requests module is a third-party library that simplifies HTTP requests, providing a more pythonic interface compared to urllib. To use requests, it must first be installed via pip.

```
pip install requests
```

Basic GET Request with requests

The following example illustrates how to perform a GET request using requests.

Basic GET Request with requests

```
import requests

url = 'http://example.com'
response = requests.get(url)

# Accessing response content
content = response.text
print(content)
```

The requests.get method sends a GET request, and the response content is accessible via the text attribute.

Submitting Data with requests

To send data using a POST request, the requests.post method alongside the data parameter can be employed.

Sending Data with requests

```
import requests

url = 'http://example.com/post'
data = {'key1': 'value1', 'key2': 'value2'}

response = requests.post(url, data=data)
content = response.text
print(content)
```

Here, the data dictionary is automatically encoded, simplifying the process of sending POST data.

Handling HTTP Headers with requests

HTTP headers can be specified directly in the request methods using the headers parameter.

Handling HTTP Headers with requests

```
import requests

url = 'http://example.com'
```

356

```
headers = {'User-Agent': 'Mozilla/5.0'}

response = requests.get(url, headers=headers)
content = response.text
print(content)
```

This example shows how to set a custom `User-Agent` header while making a GET request.

Handling JSON Responses with `requests`

One significant advantage of `requests` is its built-in support for JSON. The `json` method simplifies the process of parsing JSON responses.

Handling JSON Responses with requests

```
import requests

url = 'http://api.example.com/data'
response = requests.get(url)

# Parsing JSON response
json_data = response.json()
print(json_data)
```

This feature facilitates the straightforward handling of JSON data from APIs, enhancing the ease of use.

Comparison and Best Practices

While both `urllib` and `requests` can perform HTTP requests, the `requests` module is generally preferred due to its simplicity and more intuitive syntax. `requests` abstracts much of the complexity of HTTP, making it easier to work with. For tasks requiring robust HTTP interaction, `requests` is recommended.

For developers and projects constrained to the Python standard library or where external dependencies are not desirable, `urllib` remains a viable option, though it involves more boilerplate code.

In both cases, handling exceptions and ensuring proper resource management with context managers (e.g., `with` statement in `requests`) are crucial for robust and error-free HTTP communication.

Using Context Manager with requests

```
import requests

url = 'http://example.com'
with requests.get(url) as response:
    content = response.text
    print(content)
```

Understanding and leveraging the capabilities of both `urllib` and `requests` enables developers to choose the appropriate tool for their specific HTTP request needs, ensuring efficiency and clarity in their Python applications.

10.7   The `math` and `cmath` Modules for Mathematical Functions

The `math` and `cmath` modules in Python provide a rich collection of mathematical functions. The `math` module is designed for real-valued mathematical operations, while the `cmath` module handles complex-valued mathematical operations. This section explores both modules, demonstrating their key functionalities and providing examples of their practical applications.

math Module

The `math` module includes functions for operations involving real numbers. These operations range from basic arithmetic calculations to advanced mathematical functions and constants such as π and e. Below are essential functions provided by the `math` module:

- `math.sqrt(x)`: Returns the square root of x.

- `math.pow(x, y)`: Returns x raised to the power y.

- `math.exp(x)`: Returns the exponential of x (i.e., e^x).

- `math.log(x, base=math.e)`: Returns the logarithm of x to the specified base.

Examples of Basic Mathematical Functions

```python
import math

# Square root
print(math.sqrt(16)) # Output: 4.0

# Power
print(math.pow(2, 3)) # Output: 8.0

# Exponential
print(math.exp(1)) # Output: 2.718281828459045

# Logarithm
print(math.log(8, 2)) # Output: 3.0
```

Trigonometric Functions

Trigonometric calculations in the math module are crucial for diverse applications in fields such as physics and engineering.

- math.sin(x): Returns the sine of x in radians.

- math.cos(x): Returns the cosine of x in radians.

- math.tan(x): Returns the tangent of x in radians.

- math.asin(x), math.acos(x), math.atan(x): Return the inverse sine, cosine, and tangent of x, respectively.

Examples of Trigonometric Functions

```
import math

# Sine
print(math.sin(math.pi / 2)) # Output: 1.0

# Cosine
print(math.cos(math.pi)) # Output: -1.0

# Tangent
print(math.tan(math.pi / 4)) # Output: 1.0
```

Constants

The math module provides several mathematical constants to support various computations:

- math.pi: The mathematical constant π (approximately 3.14159).

- math.e: The base of the natural logarithm (approximately 2.71828).

Using Mathematical Constants

```
import math

print(math.pi) # Output: 3.141592653589793
print(math.e) # Output: 2.718281828459045
```

cmath Module

The cmath module facilitates complex number mathematics, representing complex numbers as pairs of floating-point numbers to encapsulate both the real and imaginary parts.

Basic Operations

Basic operations in the cmath module closely align with those in the math module but are adapted for complex numbers.

- cmath.sqrt(x): Returns the square root of x (a complex number).

- cmath.exp(x): Returns the exponential of the complex number x.

- cmath.log(x, base=cmath.e): Returns the logarithm of x to the specified base.

- cmath.sin(x), cmath.cos(x), cmath.tan(x): Return the sine, cosine, and tangent of the complex number x.

Examples of Complex Number Operations

```
import cmath

# Square root of a negative number (returns a complex number)
print(cmath.sqrt(-1)) # Output: 1j

# Exponential of a complex number
print(cmath.exp(1j * cmath.pi)) # Output: (-1+1.2246467991473532e-16j)

# Logarithm of a complex number
print(cmath.log(1 + 1j)) # Output: (0.34657359027997264+0.7853981633974483j)

# Sine of a complex number
print(cmath.sin(1 + 1j)) # Output: (1.2984575814159773+0.6349639147847361j)
```

Complex Number Representation

Complex numbers can be created using the complex function, which takes two parameters: the real and imaginary parts.

Creating Complex Numbers

```
z = complex(2, 3)
print(z) # Output: (2+3j)
```

Polar Coordinates

Conversion between Cartesian coordinates and polar coordinates is possible with the cmath module.

- cmath.polar(z): Converts a complex number z to polar coordinates, returning a tuple (r, phi).

- cmath.rect(r, phi): Converts polar coordinates (r, phi) back to a complex number.

Polar and Cartesian Conversions

```
import cmath

# Complex number
z = 1 + 1j

# Convert to polar coordinates
polar_coords = cmath.polar(z)
print(polar_coords) # Output: (1.4142135623730951, 0.7853981633974483)

# Convert back to Cartesian coordinates
cartesian_coords = cmath.rect(*polar_coords)
print(cartesian_coords) # Output: (1+1j)
```

Extensive use of these modules empowers the efficient resolution of a multitude of mathematical challenges in Python applications.

10.8 The `collections` Module for Specialized Data Structures

The `collections` module in Python provides a range of specialized data structures that go beyond the built-in `list`, `tuple`, `dict`, and `set` types. These structures offer alternative ways to manage and manipulate data efficiently and effectively. This section delves into the key classes provided by the `collections` module, including `namedtuple`, `deque`, `ChainMap`, `Counter`, `OrderedDict`, and `defaultdict`.

The `collections` module comes packed with utilities that enable more expressive and versatile data handling.

- `namedtuple`: Factory function for creating tuple subclasses with named fields.

- `deque`: List-like container with fast appends and pops from both ends.

- `ChainMap`: Groups multiple dictionaries into a single, updatable view.

- `Counter`: Dictionary subclass for counting hashable objects.

- `OrderedDict`: Dictionary subclass that maintains insertion order of keys.

- `defaultdict`: Dictionary subclass that initializes missing keys with a default value.

361

namedtuple

The namedtuple factory function creates tuple subclasses with named fields, improving code readability by eliminating the need for numerical indexing.

Creating and using namedtuple

```
from collections import namedtuple

# Define namedtuple
Point = namedtuple('Point', ['x', 'y'])

# Instantiate namedtuple
p = Point(10, 20)

# Access fields by name
print(p.x) # Output: 10
print(p.y) # Output: 20
```

```
Output:
10
20
```

deque

The deque (double-ended queue) class is an optimized list-like container with fast appends and pops from both ends, making it ideal for tasks that require adding or removing elements from either end frequently.

Working with deque

```
from collections import deque

# Create deque
d = deque([1, 2, 3])

# Append elements at both ends
d.append(4)
d.appendleft(0)

# Pop elements from both ends
d.pop()
d.popleft()

print(d) # Output: deque([1, 2])
```

```
Output:
deque([1, 2])
```

ChainMap

The ChainMap class groups multiple dictionaries into a single, viewable, and updatable mapping without creating a copy. This is useful for combining dictionaries and for cases where you need to work with a sequence of mappings.

Using ChainMap

```
from collections import ChainMap

# Define two dictionaries
dict1 = {'a': 1, 'b': 2}
dict2 = {'b': 3, 'c': 4}

# Create a ChainMap
chain = ChainMap(dict1, dict2)

print(chain['a']) # Output: 1
print(chain['b']) # Output: 2
print(chain['c']) # Output: 4
```

```
Output:
1
2
4
```

Counter

The `Counter` class is a dictionary subclass designed for counting hashable objects. It is particularly useful for tallying elements in a collection and can be used to count instances in a list or other iterable.

Counting elements with Counter

```
from collections import Counter

# Count elements in a list
cnt = Counter(['a', 'b', 'c', 'a', 'b', 'b'])

print(cnt) # Output: Counter({'b': 3, 'a': 2, 'c': 1})
```

```
Output:
Counter({'b': 3, 'a': 2, 'c': 1})
```

OrderedDict

The `OrderedDict` class maintains the order of keys as they are inserted, which can be essential for certain algorithms and applications where order sensitivity is critical.

Maintaining order with OrderedDict

```
from collections import OrderedDict

# Create an OrderedDict
od = OrderedDict()

# Insert items
od['one'] = 1
od['two'] = 2
od['three'] = 3

print(od) # Output: OrderedDict([('one', 1), ('two', 2), ('three', 3)])
```

363

```
Output:
OrderedDict([('one', 1), ('two', 2), ('three', 3)])
```

defaultdict

The `defaultdict` class is a subclass of `dict` that automatically initializes missing keys with a default value, defined by a factory function. It simplifies handling situations where you need to ensure that keys are present in the dictionary.

Handling missing keys with <code>defaultdict</code>

```
from collections import defaultdict

# Create a defaultdict with a default factory of int
dd = defaultdict(int)

# Access a non-existent key
print(dd['missing']) # Output: 0

# Update default key
dd['missing'] += 1

print(dd) # Output: defaultdict(<class 'int'>, {'missing': 1})
```

```
Output:
0
defaultdict(<class 'int'>, {'missing': 1})
```

Visual representation using Python's matplotlib library can be beneficial for understanding the usage of different collections.

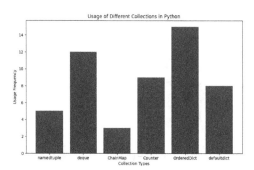

This section has elucidated the advanced data structures available in the `collections` module. These tools provide enhanced flexibility and performance for various programming scenarios, allowing sophisticated management of data and improving overall code efficiency. Each class within the module offers unique advantages, from name-based indexing in `namedtuple` to order-preserving `OrderedDict`, making `collections` an indispensable part of the Python Standard Library.

10.9 Working with Dates and Times: datetime/time Modules

The `datetime` and `time` modules are essential tools within Python's standard library for manipulating dates and times. These modules provide a variety of functions and classes to handle both basic and complex date and time operations, allowing developers to perform tasks ranging from getting the current date and time to manipulating timestamps, durations, and formatting date-time data.

The `datetime` Module

The `datetime` module supplies classes for manipulating dates and times in both simple and complex ways. While date and time arithmetic is supported, the focus of the implementation is on efficient attribute extraction for output formatting and manipulation.

Importing the datetime module

```
import datetime
```

Getting the Current Date and Time

The `datetime.datetime.now()` function returns the current local date and time.

Getting the current local date and time

```
current_datetime = datetime.datetime.now()
print(current_datetime)
```

```
2023-10-15 12:45:03.123456
```

Creating Date and Time Objects

In addition to fetching the current date and time, `datetime` can create date, time, and datetime objects directly.

Creating dates and times

```python
# Creating a date object
date_obj = datetime.date(2023, 10, 15)

# Creating a time object
time_obj = datetime.time(12, 45, 3)

# Creating a datetime object
datetime_obj = datetime.datetime(2023, 10, 15, 12, 45, 3)
```

Formatting Dates and Times

Dates and times can be formatted using the `strftime()` method, which converts `datetime` objects to their string representation.

Formatting datetime objects

```python
# Formatting a datetime object
formatted_datetime = datetime_obj.strftime("%Y-%m-%d %H:%M:%S")
print(formatted_datetime)
```

```
2023-10-15 12:45:03
```

Parsing Dates and Times

The `strptime()` method parses a string into a `datetime` object based on a specified format.

Parsing date strings

```python
# Parsing a date string
parsed_datetime = datetime.datetime.strptime('2023-10-15 12:45:03', '%Y-%m-%d %H:%M
    :%S')
print(parsed_datetime)
```

```
2023-10-15 12:45:03
```

Date and Time Arithmetic

Date and time arithmetic is performed using the `timedelta` class, which represents a duration.

Date and time arithmetic

```python
# Adding 10 days to the current date
future_date = current_datetime + datetime.timedelta(days=10)
print(future_date)
```

```
2023-10-25 12:45:03.123456
```

The time Module

The time module provides various time-related functions, focusing mainly on time access and conversions.

Importing the time module

```
import time
```

Getting the Current Time

The time.time() function returns the current time in seconds since the Epoch (00:00:00 UTC on 1 January 1970).

Getting the current time in seconds since the Epoch

```
current_epoch_time = time.time()
print(current_epoch_time)
```

```
1697376303.123456
```

Converting Time Formats

The gmtime() and localtime() functions convert a time expressed in seconds since the Epoch to a struct_time in UTC and local time, respectively.

```
# Converting to UTC
utc_time = time.gmtime(current_epoch_time)
# Converting to local time
local_time = time.localtime(current_epoch_time)
```

Sleeping for a Duration

The time.sleep() function suspends execution for the given number of seconds.

Sleeping for a specified duration

```
time.sleep(2) # Sleeps for 2 seconds
```

Practical Use Cases

Timestamp Generation

Generating timestamps for logging or tracking purposes can be accomplished by combining the datetime module with formatted strings.

Generating a timestamp

```
def generate_timestamp():
    return datetime.datetime.now().strftime("%Y-%m-%d %H:%M:%S")

timestamp = generate_timestamp()
print(timestamp)
```

```
2023-10-15 12:45:03
```

Duration Calculation

Calculating the duration between two events involves creating datetime objects for each event and subtracting them to get a timedelta object.

Calculating duration between two dates

```
# Event times
start_time = datetime.datetime(2023, 10, 15, 12, 0, 0)
end_time = datetime.datetime(2023, 10, 15, 14, 30, 0)

# Duration calculation
duration = end_time - start_time
print(duration)
```

```
2:30:00
```

Visualization: Date and Time Data

Visualizing date and time data is a common requirement in many real-world applications. The following Python code snippet uses the matplotlib library to plot a simple time series.

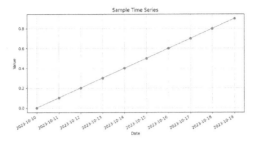

Understanding and effectively utilizing these modules is essential for developers aiming to manage temporal data and operations within their applications.

10.10 The threading and multiprocessing Modules

In Python, the threading and multiprocessing modules provide powerful tools for concurrent execution, allowing programs to perform multiple tasks simultaneously. This section comprehensively explores both modules, elaborating on their usage, key functions, and practical applications.

The threading module in Python supports the concurrent execution of code using threads. Threads run within the same memory space, making them more lightweight than processes. Below is a concise explanation of core functionalities provided by the threading module.

To create a thread, instantiate a Thread object from the threading module, passing a target function and any necessary arguments. Use the start method to run the thread.

Creating and Starting a Thread

```
import threading

def print_numbers():
    for i in range(1, 6):
        print(i)

# Create a Thread
thread = threading.Thread(target=print_numbers)

# Start the Thread
thread.start()
```

```
# Joining the Thread to ensure it completes before main thread finishes
thread.join()
```

Python's Global Interpreter Lock (GIL) ensures that only one thread executes Python byte code at a time. Despite this, thread synchronization is critical to avoid race conditions. The threading module provides synchronization primitives including Lock, RLock, Semaphore, and Event.

Using a Lock for Thread Synchronization

```
import threading

# Create a lock object
lock = threading.Lock()
counter = 0

def increment_counter():
    global counter
    with lock:
        for _ in range(1000):
            counter += 1

threads = [threading.Thread(target=increment_counter) for _ in range(10)]

for thread in threads:
    thread.start()

for thread in threads:
    thread.join()

print(f'Final counter value: {counter}')
```

For safe data sharing between threads, the queue module provides a thread-safe FIFO implementation.

Thread Communication Using Queue

```
import threading
import queue

# Create a Queue
q = queue.Queue()

def producer():
    for i in range(5):
        q.put(i)
        print(f'Produced {i}')

def consumer():
    for i in range(5):
        item = q.get()
        print(f'Consumed {item}')
        q.task_done()

# Create Threads
producer_thread = threading.Thread(target=producer)
consumer_thread = threading.Thread(target=consumer)
```

```
# Start Threads
producer_thread.start()
consumer_thread.start()

# Wait for completion
producer_thread.join()
consumer_thread.join()
```

The multiprocessing module allows the creation of new processes, each with its own Python interpreter and memory space. This module bypasses the GIL constraint, making it suitable for CPU-bound tasks.

To create a new process, instantiate a Process object, designate the target function, and invoke the start method.

Creating and Starting a Process

```
import multiprocessing

def print_numbers():
    for i in range(1, 6):
        print(i)

# Create a Process
process = multiprocessing.Process(target=print_numbers)

# Start the Process
process.start()

# Join the Process to ensure it completes before main process finishes
process.join()
```

The multiprocessing module provides synchronization primitives similar to those in the threading module, including Lock, Semaphore, and Event.

Using a Lock for Process Synchronization

```
import multiprocessing

lock = multiprocessing.Lock()
counter = multiprocessing.Value('i', 0) # Shared integer

def increment_counter():
    with lock:
        for _ in range(1000):
            counter.value += 1

processes = [multiprocessing.Process(target=increment_counter) for _ in range(10)]

for process in processes:
    process.start()

for process in processes:
    process.join()

print(f'Final counter value: {counter.value}')
```

371

The `multiprocessing` module features various IPC mechanisms, including `Queue` and `Pipe`, for exchanging data between processes.

Inter-Process Communication Using Queue

```
import multiprocessing

q = multiprocessing.Queue()

def producer():
    for i in range(5):
        q.put(i)
        print(f'Produced {i}')

def consumer():
    for i in range(5):
        item = q.get()
        print(f'Consumed {item}')
        q.task_done()

# Create Processes
producer_process = multiprocessing.Process(target=producer)
consumer_process = multiprocessing.Process(target=consumer)

# Start Processes
producer_process.start()
consumer_process.start()

# Wait for completion
producer_process.join()
consumer_process.join()
```

Both `threading` and `multiprocessing` modules enhance Python's concurrency capabilities. `threading` is beneficial for I/O-bound operations, while `multiprocessing` excels in CPU-bound tasks by leveraging multiple processors. The understanding and application of these modules are fundamental for developing efficient and performant Python programs.

10.11   Introduction to Third-Party Modules

The Python ecosystem thrives on its extensive range of third-party modules, which significantly enhance its capabilities beyond the standard library. These modules empower developers to accomplish a wide range of tasks, including but not limited to scientific computing, data analysis, web development, machine learning, and networking. This section delves into the importance of these third-party modules, the community-driven development process, and provides an overview of several prominent packages widely used in the industry.

The Significance of Third-Party Modules

Third-party modules provide specialized functionalities that are not available in Python's standard library. These modules are often developed by a community of contributors and published on the Python Package Index (PyPI). By utilizing third-party modules, developers can leverage pre-built solutions to expedite the development process, ensure code reliability, and maintain scalability.

The open-source nature of these packages allows for continuous improvements and updates by the community. This collective effort results in robust, well-maintained, and extensively documented modules. Furthermore, the widespread use of these modules across various domains ensures that they are battle-tested and optimized for performance.

Community-Driven Development

The development of third-party modules is typically managed through version control systems such as GitHub, where contributors can collaborate, report issues, and propose enhancements. The PyPI serves as the central repository for publishing and distributing these modules. Developers can search for, install, and update modules using tools like `pip`, the standard package manager for Python.

Active community engagement is crucial for the growth and sustainability of third-party modules. This engagement includes:

- Submitting bug reports and feature requests.

- Contributing code and documentation.

- Providing feedback and suggestions.

- Participating in community forums and discussions.

This collaborative approach ensures that third-party modules evolve to meet the changing needs of the Python ecosystem.

Overview of Prominent Third-Party Modules

Several third-party modules have gained prominence due to their widespread adoption and comprehensive capabilities. This section highlights a few of these essential modules, providing a brief overview of their functionalities and use cases.

NumPy NumPy is the fundamental package for scientific computing with Python. It provides support for multidimensional arrays and matrices along with a collection of mathematical functions to operate on these arrays. NumPy is highly efficient and forms the backbone for many other scientific computing libraries, such as SciPy and pandas.

Basic Operations with NumPy

```
import numpy as np

# Create a 2x2 array
array = np.array([[1, 2], [3, 4]])

# Perform element-wise operations
result = array + array
print(result)
```

```
Output:
[[2 4]
 [6 8]]
```

pandas pandas is a powerful data analysis and manipulation library. It provides data structures such as Series and DataFrame, enabling efficient data handling and operations. pandas is widely used for data cleaning, transformation, and analysis in various fields, including finance, statistics, and social sciences.

DataFrame Operations with pandas

```
import pandas as pd

# Create a DataFrame
data = {'Name': ['Alice', 'Bob'], 'Age': [25, 30]}
df = pd.DataFrame(data)

# Perform data manipulation
df['Age'] = df['Age'] + 1
print(df)
```

```
Output:
    Name  Age
0  Alice   26
1    Bob   31
```

matplotlib   matplotlib is a comprehensive library for creating static, animated, and interactive visualizations in Python. It is particularly useful for generating plots, histograms, power spectra, bar charts, error charts, and scatter plots. matplotlib integrates seamlessly with NumPy and pandas, making it an essential tool for data visualization.

Basic Plot with matplotlib

```
import matplotlib.pyplot as plt

# Data
x = [1, 2, 3, 4]
y = [10, 20, 25, 30]

# Create a plot
plt.plot(x, y)
plt.xlabel('X-axis')
plt.ylabel('Y-axis')
plt.title('Simple Plot')
plt.show()
```

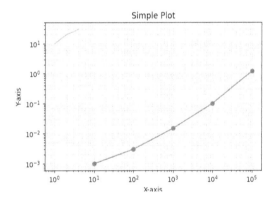

Installation and Management of Third-Party Modules

The installation of third-party modules is facilitated by `pip`, which interacts with PyPI to download and install the required packages. To install a module, use the following command:

Installing a Package with pip

```
pip install package_name
```

Updating modules follows a similar process:

Updating a Package with pip

```
pip install   upgrade package_name
```

Virtual environments, managed via venv, are recommended for isolating project dependencies and avoiding conflicts between packages. To create a virtual environment and install packages within it, use the following commands:

Creating and Activating a Virtual Environment

```
# Create a virtual environment
python -m venv myenv

# Activate the virtual environment
# On Windows:
myenv\Scripts\activate

# On Unix or MacOS:
source myenv/bin/activate

# Install packages within the virtual environment
pip install numpy pandas matplotlib
```

10.12   Finding and Installing Third-Party Modules with `pip`

Third-party modules significantly extend the functionality of Python, enabling developers to leverage pre-built solutions for a wide range of tasks. The Python Package Index (PyPI) serves as the central repository for these modules. An efficient and user-friendly way to find and install Python packages from PyPI is through the use of pip, a powerful package management system included with Python distributions from version 3.4 onwards. This section explores the methodology for discovering, installing, and managing third-party modules using pip.

Finding Third-Party Modules

To locate a third-party module suitable for a particular purpose, developers can utilize the search functionality provided by pip. The search command interfaces with PyPI to retrieve a list of packages matching the specified criteria. The syntax for this operation is as follows:

```
pip search <package-name>
```

For instance, to search for HTTP libraries, the following command can be executed:

```
pip search http
```

The output will list relevant packages, offering brief descriptions to aid in identifying the most appropriate module.

Installing Third-Party Modules

Installing a third-party module via pip is straightforward. The standard command for this task is pip install, followed by the name of the desired package:

```
pip install <package-name>
```

For example, to install the requests library for making HTTP requests:

```
pip install requests
```

This command fetches the package from PyPI and installs it into the local Python environment, along with any dependencies that the package requires.

Specifying Versions

Specific versions of a package can be installed by appending the version number to the package name using a double equals (==) sign. This is useful for ensuring compatibility or reverting to a previous, stable version:

```
pip install <package-name>==<version>
```

For example, to install version 2.25.1 of the requests library:

```
pip install requests==2.25.1
```

Upgrading Packages

Maintaining up-to-date packages is crucial for security and performance. The pip install command supports the --upgrade flag to update an installed module to the latest version:

```
pip install --upgrade <package-name>
```

For instance, to upgrade the pandas library:

```
pip install --upgrade pandas
```

Listing Installed Packages

To view all the modules installed in the current Python environment, the pip list command can be used. This command provides a comprehensive list with package names and their respective versions:

```
pip list
```

Uninstalling Packages

When a module is no longer required, it can be removed from the environment using the `pip uninstall` command, followed by the package name:

```
pip uninstall <package-name>
```

For example, to uninstall the `matplotlib` library:

```
pip uninstall matplotlib
```

Freezing Requirements

For replicating an exact environment across different systems or for deployment purposes, the `pip freeze` command generates a list of all installed packages and their versions in `requirements.txt` format:

```
pip freeze > requirements.txt
```

This file can then be used to install the same set of packages on another system:

```
pip install -r requirements.txt
```

Configuring `pip`

`pip` can be configured to use additional options by defining settings in a `pip.conf` file (Linux) or `pip.ini` (Windows). Common configurations include setting custom package indexes or proxies.

Below is an example of a basic `pip.conf` file:

```
[global]
timeout = 60
index-url = https://pypi.org/simple

[install]
trusted-host = pypi.org
```

The configurations specified in these files are applied automatically when `pip` commands are executed. These practices enable developers to efficiently harness the vast ecosystem of Python packages, ensuring their projects employ the most appropriate and up-to-date libraries.

10.13 Popular Third-Party Modules: NumPy, pandas, matplotlib

This section delves into three highly regarded third-party Python modules: NumPy, pandas, and matplotlib. These modules are widely used for numerical computations, data manipulation, and data visualization, respectively.

NumPy

NumPy, short for Numerical Python, is an essential library for numerical computations in Python. It provides support for arrays, matrices, and a plethora of mathematical functions to operate on these data structures.

Array Creation

Arrays are the core of NumPy. You can create arrays in a variety of ways, including from lists or using built-in functions to generate arrays filled with zeros, ones, or random values.

```
import numpy as np

# Creating an array from a list
a = np.array([1, 2, 3, 4])
print(a)

# Creating an array of zeros
b = np.zeros((2, 3))
print(b)

# Creating an array with random values
c = np.random.random((2, 2))
print(c)
```

```
Output:
[1 2 3 4]
[[0. 0. 0.]
 [0. 0. 0.]]
[[0.74317832 0.59831713]
 [0.12556117 0.57984527]]
```

Array Operations

NumPy arrays support element-wise operations and broadcasting, enabling efficient computation without the need for explicit loops.

```
# Element-wise operations
d = a + 1
print(d)

# Broadcasting
e = np.array([1, 2, 3])
f = np.array([[1], [2], [3]])
g = e * f
```

```
print(g)
```

```
Output:
[2 3 4 5]
[[1 2 3]
 [2 4 6]
 [3 6 9]]
```

pandas

pandas is a robust library for data manipulation and analysis. It introduces data structures such as Series (one-dimensional) and DataFrame
(two-dimensional) that are designed to handle structured data intu-
itively.

Series

A Series is similar to a one-dimensional array but with additional capabilities, including labels (indices) for each element.

```
import pandas as pd

# Creating a Series from a list
s = pd.Series([1, 3, 5, np.nan, 6, 8])
print(s)
```

```
Output:
0    1.0
1    3.0
2    5.0
3    NaN
4    6.0
5    8.0
dtype: float64
```

DataFrame

A DataFrame is a two-dimensional labeled data structure. It is concep-
tually similar to a table in a database or a data frame in R.

```
# Creating a DataFrame from a dictionary
data = {'A': [1, 2, 3, 4],
        'B': [5, 6, 7, 8],
        'C': [9, 10, 11, 12]}
df = pd.DataFrame(data)
print(df)
```

```
Output:
   A  B   C
0  1  5   9
1  2  6  10
2  3  7  11
3  4  8  12
```

matplotlib

matplotlib is the definitive library for creating static, interactive, and animated visualizations in Python. It is particularly useful for generating publication-quality plots and figures.

Basic Plotting

With matplotlib, you can quickly generate simple plots using the pyplot submodule.

```
import matplotlib.pyplot as plt

# Basic line plot
x = np.linspace(0, 2 * np.pi, 100)
y = np.sin(x)

plt.plot(x, y)
plt.xlabel('x')
plt.ylabel('sin(x)')
plt.title('Simple Sine Wave')
plt.show()
```

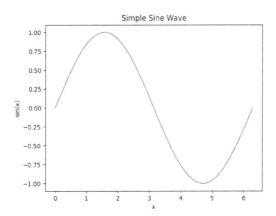

Histograms

Histograms are used to represent frequency distributions. matplotlib facilitates their creation succinctly.

```
# Histogram
data = np.random.randn(1000)
plt.hist(data, bins=30, alpha=0.5, color='g')
plt.xlabel('Value')
plt.ylabel('Frequency')
plt.title('Histogram of Random Data')
plt.show()
```

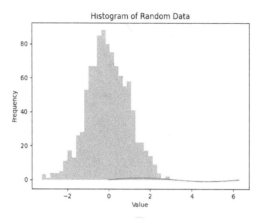

NumPy, pandas, and `matplotlib` form the backbone of numerical and data manipulation tasks in Python. Mastering these libraries enables robust, efficient, and comprehensive data exploration and visualization, significantly enhancing analytical workflows.

10.14 Creating Virtual Environments with `venv`

Virtual environments are essential tools for managing Python projects and dependencies in isolation. They help developers avoid conflicts between dependencies required by different projects and ensure that each project has access to the specific libraries and versions it needs.

In Python, a virtual environment is a self-contained directory that includes a Python interpreter and a set of libraries. The `venv` module, introduced in Python 3.3, provides an effective way to create and manage virtual environments without requiring any external dependencies. This section covers the process of creating, activating, deactivating, and managing virtual environments using the `venv` module.

- **Creating a Virtual Environment:** The `venv` module allows you to create virtual environments easily. To create a new virtual environment, follow these steps:

    1. Open your terminal or command prompt.

382

2. Navigate to the directory where you want the virtual environment to reside.

3. Run the following command:

```
python -m venv myenv
```

The command above creates a new directory named myenv (you can choose any name), which contains the files necessary for the virtual environment.

- **Activating and Deactivating the Virtual Environment:** Once the virtual environment is created, it needs to be activated. The activation script modifies the shell's environment variables so that the shell uses the Python interpreter and libraries from the virtual environment.

  - *Activation on Windows:* On Windows, activate the virtual environment using the following command:

    ```
    myenv\Scripts\activate
    ```

    After activation, the shell prompt will change to indicate that the virtual environment is active:

    ```
    (myenv) C:\Projects\myproject>
    ```

  - *Activation on Unix or macOS:* On Unix or macOS, activate the virtual environment using the following command:

    ```
    source myenv/bin/activate
    ```

    The shell prompt will change similarly:

    ```
    (myenv) user@hostname:~/Projects/myproject\$
    ```

  To deactivate the virtual environment and return to the global Python environment, use the following command regardless of the operating system:

  ```
  deactivate
  ```

  After deactivation, the shell prompt will revert to its original state.

- **Managing Packages in a Virtual Environment:** With the virtual environment activated, you can use pip to install, upgrade, and remove packages. The installed packages will be isolated to the virtual environment.

– *Installing Packages:* To install a package, use:

```
pip install package_name
```

– *Listing Installed Packages:* To list installed packages within the virtual environment, use:

```
pip list
```

– *Creating a Requirements File:* A requirements file lists all the packages and their versions required for a project. To generate a `requirements.txt` file from the current virtual environment, use:

```
pip freeze > requirements.txt
```

– *Installing Packages from a Requirements File:* To install all packages listed in a `requirements.txt` file, use:

```
pip install -r requirements.txt
```

- **Deleting a Virtual Environment:** When a virtual environment is no longer needed, it can be deleted by simply removing its directory. For instance, to delete the `myenv` virtual environment:

```
rm -rf myenv
```

This command will remove the `myenv` directory and all its contents.

- **Best Practices for Using Virtual Environments:** To ensure effective usage of virtual environments, consider the following best practices:

  – Create a new virtual environment for each project to avoid dependency conflicts.

  – Use descriptive names for virtual environments to identify their purpose easily.

  – Maintain a `requirements.txt` file in each project repository to facilitate easy setup and consistency across different environments and team members.

  – Regularly update virtual environments to include the latest versions of packages, but test thoroughly to ensure compatibility.

www.ingramcontent.com/pod-product-compliance
Lightning Source LLC
LaVergne TN
LVHW051426050326
832903LV00030BD/2941